D1714780

Women and the Politics of Self-Representation in Seventeenth-Century France

Women and the Politics of Self-Representation in Seventeenth-Century France

Patricia Francis Cholakian

DELAWARE

Newark: University of Delaware Press
London: Associated University Presses

Associated University Presses
440 Forsgate Drive
Cranbury, NJ 08512

Associated University Presses
16 Barter Street
London WC1A 2AH, England

Associated University Presses
P.O. Box 338, Port Credit
Mississauga, Ontario
Canada L5G 4L8

The paper used in this publication meets the requirements of the American National Standard for Permanence of Paper for Printed Library Materials Z39.48-1984.

Library of Congress Cataloging-in-Publication Data

Cholakian, Patricia Francis.
 Women and the politics of self-representation in seventeenth-century France / Patricia Francis Cholakian.
  p.   cm.
 Includes bibliographical references and index.
 ISBN 0-87413-735-7
 1. French prose literature—Women authors—History and criticism. 2. French prose literature—17th century—History and criticism. 3. Women authors, French—17th century—Biography—History and criticism. 4. Autobiography—Women authors. 5. Self-presentation—France—History—17th century. I. Title: Women and the politics of self-representation in 17th century France. II. Title.

PQ149 .C48 2000
848'.40809492'082—dc21
                                                                    00-029910

Pour Anna

Un bouquet de houx vert et de bruyère en fleur

Contents

Preface

For many years as I passed through the library stacks my gaze was arrested by an antique set of leather-bound tomes—Petitot's *Collection des mémoires relatifs à l'histoire de France*. They had obviously not been opened for ages. Their spines were dry and cracked, and a thick layer of dust lay over them. From time to time I would pause to read the authors' names, and one would always catch my eye: Montpensier, the famous "Grande Mademoiselle" whom I had seen referred to so many times in books about seventeenth-century France. More than once I was tempted to pry out these volumes and take them home, but I always decided not to in the end, for they were large and heavy, and I knew full well that I would never read them. One day, however, I noticed Steegmuller's *La Grande Mademoiselle* on a nearby shelf, and since it was relatively short I decided to take it out instead, on the assumption that I would learn from it more than enough about these famous memoirs and their author. Such was not the case. It was indeed a good read and the subject was fascinating, but far from putting an end to my curiosity, it only increased it. Also there was something about it that disturbed me. If it was not exactly condescending, it nonetheless seemed to suggest that everything connected with La Grande Mademoiselle bordered on being a joke. Had she really been nothing more than a narcissistic old maid, alternately afflicted with *folie de grandeur* and libidinal desire? Was it really her own fault that she never married? And why in the world had she wanted to marry Lauzun? In the end, I found I had so many questions that I could only do what I had resisted doing for so long—I took down the dusty volumes to find out what the memoirist had said for herself. I dipped into Petitot's edition looking for answers to my questions and found myself immersed in her story. Nor could I stop there, for as I soon learned, Petitot had not published the autograph version of Montpensier's memoirs, but a copy made by secretaries, who had taken considerable liberties with what she had originally written. I was obliged, therefore, to procure a copy

9

of Chéruel's edition of the autograph manuscript. There I discovered that the passage in which she explained her decision to marry Lauzun had been completely rewritten by the copyist. That settled it; I had to see the manuscripts for myself. I went to the Bibliothèque Nationale on the rue de Richelieu, the very edifice in which her archenemy, Cardinal Mazarin, had once dwelt. I spent several weeks in the frigid manuscript room pouring over the autograph manuscript as well as the other copies of her memoirs in the Bibliothèque's collection. I published two articles on Montpensier. I began to read other early women's memoirs and what had been written about them. And once again I was annoyed by the superficial manner in which they were treated and intrigued by the questions that had not been asked or answered. That is how I came to write this book.

It is not meant to be an exhaustive review of early women's memoirs, or even of those written in the seventeenth century. It does not, for instance, deal with the texts of Madame de Motteville, Madame de Lafayette, or Madame de Caylus, who wrote primarily as biographers. It is intended instead as a discussion of issues that I see as central to women's autobiographical writing of that period. My overarching question has been, "How do these writers represent themselves *as women?*"

One of my aims has been to bridge the gap between early modern scholarship and feminist theory. Although feminists argue that both gender and sexuality are historically constructed, they frequently do not use early women's works to document how femininity was produced in a past more remote than the nineteenth century. Nor do they venture often into lands where English was not spoken. As Laurie Finke has written, "If Western feminism, as many argue, has excluded and silenced women of non-Western races and cultures, it has also ironically excluded much of its own history before the eighteenth century" (1993, 2). A case in point is Denise Riley's attempt to answer the question "Does a sex have a history?" (1988, 1). She analyzes works ranging from Plato to Merleau-Ponty, but mentions only a handful of early women writers. More than half of her analysis is devoted to women who lived after the French Revolution; and most of her arguments are based on secondary sources like Peter Dronke's *Women Writers of the Middle Ages* and Ian Maclean's *Renaissance Notion of Woman.* Such an approach hardly exhausts the history of "a sex." Nor does it explain such intriguing assertions as "The slow loss of the sexually democratic soul was the threat to late seventeenth-century forms of feminism in particular" (18).

The split between feminist theory and scholarship on early modern European women has weakened both. Perhaps due to this perceived lack of interest, those who work on women's literary history have often stayed within their own narrowly defined fields and given little thought to the larger issues raised by feminist theory. Yet pre-Enlightenment self-representations of women provide valuable documentation on how gender, selfhood, and sexuality were actually constructed in the past. They are also case studies in the representation of victimization, internalized oppression, and strategies of resistance. And as such, they have much to teach about the problem of how women's writing can either recirculate domination or subvert dominant ideologies.

In this study, I examine the works of six writers: five women and a male-to-female transvestite. The choice was not easy. There were several other authors that could have been included if I had had more time and space; and by the same token I could arguably have excluded some of those I did choose.

Marguerite de Valois, for instance, belongs more to the sixteenth than to the seventeenth century, for although some scholars believe that her memoirs were written about 1600, internal evidence suggests that they were composed in 1594. Hers are the first full-length woman's memoirs in the French language. When they were published in 1628, they were an instant success and were widely read throughout the seventeenth century. Pellisson considered them to be a masterpiece, and Mademoiselle de Montpensier was inspired by them to embark on her project. Concentrating on the intellectual, political, and spiritual dimensions of the author's existence, they expand the emerging genre of historical memoirs to explore the personal facets of a princess's life. It seemed to me, therefore, that they had to be part of my study, even if, strictly speaking, they did not qualify as seventeenth-century memoirs.

There was, of course, never any question about including Montpensier's memoirs. They are the centerpiece of feminine self-representation in the ancien régime. Begun in midcentury and composed in three installments, they cover a span of fifty years and have always been recognized as an unparalleled source of information on life under the Sun King. They are also one of the most complete chronicles of a woman's life ever written. Following in the footsteps of Valois, Montpensier enlarged the subgenre of women's court memoirs by portraying life as it was lived behind the scenes; and like her predecessor, she placed her thoughts and feelings at the center of her narrative, representing herself first and foremost as a royal woman who deserved to play a larger role in history than she did.

The next two texts pursue a somewhat different agenda. They do not deal with court politics as such. Neither Hortense nor Marie Mancini was concerned with carving out a niche in history or even with documenting historical events she may have witnessed. They wrote exclusively of their private lives, concentrating on the problems they encountered when they left their husbands and attempted to live independently. In fact, their reputations as notorious adventuresses have caused scholars like Démoris to read their texts more as first-person novels than as memoirs. What is more, they daringly departed from tradition and published their books in their own lifetimes. I thought that they should be in this study not only because, like Valois and Montpensier, they grew up at court but because even after they married, their lives were controlled to a large extent by the monarch and those who carried out his will. Furthermore, they too recorded their struggle against the repressive customs designed to contain unruly females; and even more important, they refused to represent themselves as the sexually obsessed creatures invented by rumor and legend.

From a generic point of view, *La Vie de Madame Guyon,* the last woman's text I chose, is the most divergent, for it belongs to spiritual autobiography, a genre that emerged from a completely different discursive tradition than memoirs. Unlike the other writers, its author lived in the provinces and had only the most tenuous connection to court society. I thought it was important to study it for several reasons, however. For one thing, unlike historical memoirs, which constituted an essentially masculine genre, spiritual autobiography had been written by women since the Middle Ages and had many female practitioners in seventeenth-century France. It therefore seemed to me that a study of how women represented themselves in this period needed to include at least one example from this group. But there were other reasons why I felt Guyon fitted into my overall plan. Her frank revelations about her girlhood, her family relationships, and her marriage make her narrative one of the most personal and self-revealing ones of the century, a facet of her *Vie* that has not received much attention from scholars, who have concentrated primarily on her religious views. Furthermore, although she wrote as a spiritual autobiographer rather than as a secular memoirist, she developed the topos of feminine autonomy that runs through the other women's texts. And finally, she too wrote to defend herself from attacks that were essentially political in nature and that tried to reduce her life to its sexual dimension.

I decided to devote the last chapter to the two sets of memoirs written by the transvestite abbé de Choisy. This was obviously a controversial move, but I believe that it is justified. For one thing Choisy, like Valois, Montpensier, and the Mancinis, grew up at court and was subject as they were (and, for that matter, Guyon was) to the long arm of the monarch. In addition, Choisy's memoirs, like theirs, confirm the fact that women's confinement to the private sphere was used to reduce the threat of the feminine to the established order. Revealing the political origins of his cross-dressing,

Choisy shows how gender identity was constructed and controlled under the Bourbons, and how self-representation could contest the gender stereotypes of masculine and feminine that sustained the king. However, they also reveal the difference between the lives of real women, no matter how privileged, and the fantasies of a feminized male. Dressed as a woman, Choisy still enjoyed the prerogatives of masculinity that were denied to the women of his day. His texts thus bring into sharper relief the women's self-representations that I discuss here.

Despite their dissimilarities, all of these autobiographical writings employ self-representation to resist the repressive ideology of gender that was deployed under the Bourbon kings. Moreover, and this was not a frivolous consideration, they are all obtainable in modern editions, a fact that made it much easier for me to study them in depth and that I hope will encourage my readers to do likewise.

Each chapter is preceded by a biographical sketch of the writer's life and a publication history that sums up what is known about the means of production, revisions, and variants. The latter is particularly important because, as I discovered in my early reading of Montpensier, it is not always easy to decide what constitutes authenticity in these works. Aristocrats, who considered themselves above the mundane task of preparing a fair copy, frequently entrusted their work to men of letters who not only corrected their spelling and grammar but made substantial stylistic changes, and even added or deleted entire passages. Editors also corrected, paraphrased, and expurgated with a free hand. Nor, as Marie Mancini learned to her cost, were publishers above printing pirated, apocryphal, and unauthorized editions to bring in quick profits.

These practices make it particularly difficult to establish the authenticity of women's texts, for scholars have always been quick to assume that women's books were really written by men. This has been the case with Hortense Mancini, whose memoirs are sometimes attributed to Saint-Réal. In several other cases, masculine rewritings have been assumed to be more authentic than the originals. Thus versions in which men of letters imposed what Susan Schibanoff has called "the latinate veneer of objectivity, detachment, and authority" (1983, 483) have consistently been reprinted, whereas the originals have been unavailable except in rare book collections. Down to the middle of the nineteenth century, the scribal copy of Montpensier's memoirs supplanted her autograph manuscript. Until 1998, all the published editions of Marie Mancini's memoirs reproduced Sébastien Brémond's rewriting of her *La Vérité dans son jour*. And to this day, the authenticated Oxford manuscript of Guyon's *Vie* has never been published without the cuts made in it by the editor. The necessity of distinguishing

the woman writer's voice from that of her male correctors is crucial, however, to the central concern of this study—how these writers represented
themselves. Accordingly, I have not only devoted a section of each chapter
to it but have shown how it is germane to the analyses themselves.

I have given all citations in English, and all translations are my own,
unless otherwise indicated. The analyses are arranged chronologically according to dates of composition, although in the cases of Montpensier and
Guyon there is some overlapping due to the extended time involved in
writing and revision. Substantially different versions of the chapters on
Valois, Montpensier, Hortense Mancini, and Choisy have appeared in journals and anthologies. This study was made possible in part by grants from
the Dean's Office of Hamilton College and the Kirkland Endowment.

Two people deserve special thanks for helping me see it through to
completion. One is my husband, Rouben C. Cholakian, who has been my
lifelong companion and guide. The other is my friend and one-woman sup-
port-group, Nancy Sorkin Rabinowitz. Both of them have read innumerable versions of every chapter, offered sage advice, and tendered unflag-
ging encouragement over the many years it took to complete this project.
In addition, I am indebted to Peter J. Rabinowitz for his loyalty and aid. I
am grateful to Cathleen Bauschatz for her advice and friendship, to Donna
Kuizinga for her perceptive reading and invaluable suggestions, and to my
women colleagues in the Faculty for Women's Concerns of Hamilton College, especially Bonnie Krueger, Cheryl Morgan, and Martine Guyot-
Bender, for their support. Finally, I want to express my gratitude to the
staff of Hamilton College's Burke Library for their unfailing helpfulness in
all the phases of this work.

*   *   *

The author gratefully acknolwedges permission to use material from the
following essays:

"A House of Her Own: Marginality and Dissidence in the *Mémoires* of La Grande
Mademoiselle," published in *Prose Studies,* 1986, vol. 3, no. 3, pp. 3–21 by Frank
Cass Publishers, London.

"Sex, Lies, and Autobiography: Hortense Mancini's Memoires." Copyright © 1990.
From *Women Writers in Pre-Revolutionary France.* Edited by Colette H. Winn and
Donna Kuizinga, pp. 17–30. Reproduced with permission of Taylor & Francis,
Inc./Garland Publishing, http://www. taylorandfrancis.com.

Women and the Politics
of Self-Representation
in Seventeenth-Century France

1

Introduction: The Woman in the Mirror

THE PROBLEMATICS OF SELFHOOD

At the end of the sixteenth century, Marguerite de Valois wrote to her friend Brantôme that she did not recognize herself in the flattering portrait he had drawn of her in his *Dames illustres*.[1] It made her feel, she said, like a woman whose mirrors had been covered for so long after her husband's death that when she accidentally caught sight of herself in someone else's mirror, she did not know who she was. By insisting on the difference between how she saw herself and how she was portrayed in Brantôme's essay, Valois's letter goes to the heart of the autobiographical act.[2] It also marks a turning point in the history of women's writing—the moment when a woman explicitly rejected a man's representation of her and insisted on representing herself. The letter to Brantôme was accompanied by her memoirs, the first autobiography by a woman in the French language.[3]

Prior to this, literary images of women had been drawn for the most part by men, who wrote about them as they believed, or wanted, or feared them to be. They described them as virtuous and good, like the Virgin Mary, or wicked and evil, like Eve. Sometimes they represented them with sexual appetites and an unlimited talent for leading men astray; at other times they placed them on a pedestal as chaste goddesses who should be worshiped on bended knee. These contradictory views of the feminine other inspired the "quarrel about women," the literary debate about the nature of women that began in the Middle Ages and continued into the seventeenth century, with each side cataloguing the virtues or vices of women to support their contentions.[4] Although Caroline Bynum believes that medieval women did not necessarily internalize these literary representations of women, but saw themselves first and foremost as *human* beings created in God's image (1987, 296), the fact remains that until the sixteenth century few secular French women actually wrote about the feminine experience from their own perspective.

19

What is more, the antiwoman faction maligned women so viciously that when they did write about the female experience, they were forced to expend most of their energy refuting their vilifiers. Thus Christine de Pizan's "Epistre au dieu d'Amours" (1399) is a reply to Jean de Meung's attacks in the *Roman de la rose;* and Marguerite de Navarre's *Heptameron* counters the fictions perpetrated by the misogynist fabliaux and novellas.

There had, of course, been French women writers up to this point. In the twelfth century, there was Marie de France, although nothing is known about her beyond her signature. And at the end of the fourteenth century, there was Christine de Pizan, a learned widow who lived by her pen and produced an impressive oeuvre. The sixteenth century saw a dramatic rise in female authorship: in addition to Marguerite de Navarre, there were Jeanne Flore, Hélisenne de Crenne, Louise Labé, Pernette du Guillet, and the dames des Roches, to name only the most prominent. There is little evidence, however, that their writings had any serious impact on traditional literary representations of women, or on the way women viewed themselves. Certainly it had occurred to none of them to write a book devoted solely to the story of her life.

Given the pervasiveness of masculine representations of women, how did women view themselves when they began to write self-narratives? According to Nussbaum, they inevitably mimicked male definitions of themselves: "[T]heir self-fashionings were bound up in cultural definitions of gender," she writes, "those assumed, prescribed, and embedded in their consciousness" (1988, 154). That being the case, how did they free their self-reflections from the masculine gaze that had heretofore defined, validated, and reified them? How did they answer the question, "Who am I?"

Twenty-five years ago, the answer to these questions would have been relatively simple. In those days, the recovery of women's literary history seemed a very straightforward project. At the beginning of the twenty-first century, however, it is not at all clear how to approach the self-narratives of women who lived in a time, place, and class so different from ours. My title itself reflects theoretical concerns that were largely ignored a generation ago. The very concept of "selfhood" is more and more problematic, largely because of the influence of postmodern thinkers like Lacan and Foucault, who reject a metaphysics of substance and hold that the self is an illusion produced by discourse.[5] Lacan defines the self as a fictitious image, like what is seen in a looking glass. Foucault argues that it is an illusion constituted by the dominant discourses of a particular time and place: "Self is a reflexive pronoun . . . but it also conveys the notion of identity. The latter meaning shifts the question from 'What is this self?' to 'What is the plateau on which I shall find my identity?'" (1988, 25). Coherence and continuity are no longer seen to inhere in personhood, but rather, as Butler puts it, in "socially instituted and maintained norms of intelligibility" (1990, 17). Created through language, the self is defined as subjectivity. It comes into being by use of the first-person pronoun, which shifts from speaker to speaker, but *has no reality of its own.*[6]

Such ways of thinking about selfhood make the discussion of self-representation in seventeenth-century France far more vexed than it would once have been. Who or what is being represented in these texts? What kind of identity is constructed in them? The "modern" concept of self, it has been argued, did not come into being until the Enlightenment, when it was born from the revolutionary politics of individualism, defined by Irving Howe as "A claim for space, voice, identity. A claim that man is not the property of kings, lords, or states. A claim for the privilege of opinion, the freedom to refuse definitions imposed from without" (1992, 253). Prior to the eighteenth century, or at least until Descartes, it is said, the individualized sense of self that claimed the right to self-determination did not exist. In that time identification with family or lineage, and the duties implied in that identification, nullified all sense of personal identity or the rights implied in such a concept. In other words, one had no sense of oneself as separate from the group into which one had been born.

I am not entirely convinced, however, that this was as true for early modern women as it supposedly was for their masculine counterparts. For one thing, as I have pondered Howe's androcentric rhetoric, I have discerned in it an unintentional description of the very texts I am studying here. All of these writers seem to be claiming "space, voice, identity" as well as "the privilege of opinion, the freedom to refuse definitions imposed from without." Indeed, it seems to me that they are profoundly involved with the *politics* of self. And this is significant, because in Howe's essay, he, like many others, links such political claims to the creation of a "new," "modern" way of representing the self that is now called "autobiography."[7]

I believe that for the writers discussed here, gender, and more precisely femininity, created tensions between the individual and the social structures that moved them in the direction of the "modern" self and "real" autobiography. As I read these texts in which the struggle for identity was played out within the private spaces of feminine lives, it seems to me that an acute awareness of victimization both explains and individualizes them; and that in giving voice to that awareness, these writers took an important step toward the discourse of "selfhood." And this was so precisely because their claims were not directed against a political entity (the state), but against the very structure from which early modern man supposedly derived his identity (the patriarchal family).

In order to show more specifically why I believe this was so, I want to review briefly how identity was constructed under the ancien régime. For the male aristocrat, puberty conferred the right to enter into the adult world of war and politics and to fulfill the responsibilities to which he had been born. Courtship and marriage were often footnotes to the public life of a *grand seigneur.* A woman, on the other hand, was defined after puberty in terms of her sexual and procreative functions and excluded from other areas of life. Her public role, if any, was determined by her husband's status. In the rare cases in which a woman exercised direct political power, she did so on the basis of marital or maternal status, not on the basis of her own rank or abilities. Marriage, which marked women with a new name and title, cut them off from what they had been before. For women of intelligence and ambition, this led to what we would call today a crisis of identity. Recognizing their lack of political power and their alienation from the public arena, noblewomen had to come to terms with who they were and why. The sense of self emerges in their texts in their awareness of the gap between the person they wanted to be and the prescribed role imposed on them by their gender.

* * *

The problematization of the self is only one hurdle in coming to terms with the implications of postmodern theory for this study. Although it has been half a century since Simone de Beauvoir penned the words "One is not born a woman; one becomes one," in this decade her feminist axiom has been pushed to its logical extreme. Rejecting the age-old assumption that women are necessarily defined as those born with female genitalia, many now maintain that it is not biology but social, psychological, and cultural conditioning that determines gendered behavior; and some even go so far as to question whether it is possible to speak of women as a category, or of a female self. These perceptions intersect with the increased visibility of cross-dressing and transsexualism, which have demonstrated how the boundaries that separate men from women can be blurred, and have suggested that "women" can be created at will by men who have learned to be *feminine,* according to whatever that may entail in a specific context.

As a consequence, the once commonly accepted notion that there are two genders, determined by two biological sexes, has been seriously eroded. What gender is a male who considers himself/herself to be a woman, or a female who considers herself/himself to be a man? The word *female* has been increasingly restricted to the biological components of a woman's body; and surgical and hormonal procedures have left even that usage open to question. The word *feminine* on the other hand has been stretched to connote not just certain stereotypical traits (frivolousness, narcissism, passivity, nurturance, etc.) but all the outward and visible signs that make a woman seem a woman in the eyes of her society. The theoretical implications of pursuing the constructivist theory of gender to its logical limits are far-reaching. Agreeing with Foucault that the concept of sexuality is in fact a socially-imposed "technology," De Lauretis asserts that gender "is not so bound up with sexual difference" as it is with a "technology of sex" (1987, 2). This concept, she maintains, suggests a way of viewing gender both as representation and self-representation: "the product of various social technologies, such as cinema, and of institutionalized discourses, epistemologies, and critical practices, as well as practices of daily life" (2). Butler, one of the most widely discussed constructivists, claims that when gender is theorized as radically independent of sex, it becomes necessary to admit that *man* and *masculine* might just as easily signify a female body, and *woman* and *feminine* a male one (1990, 6).[8] Queer theory has gone even further, contending that sexuality is as important as gender in determining identity.[9]

The de-essentialization of womanhood has also had political ramifications. Theorists like Denise Riley have insisted that since femininity is determined by culture rather than by birth, women cannot be lumped together in a single, unified, and universal category, independent of race, class, ethnicity, sexual preference, and historical moment. As a result, feminism's original assumption that women are united by patriarchal oppression is now open to question.[10] Attention has been focused on differences between women, rather than on the differences between women and men. Women are no longer identified as "women," but categorized in terms of the positions they occupy in the social spectrum; and a far greater priority has been placed on studying women of color, ethnic minorities, working-class and third-world women, and lesbians.

These changes in the way feminists theorize about women have had important effects on this study. The most conspicuous is my decision to include the memoirs of a man who misrepresented himself as a woman by cross-dressing. But there are many others. For instance, I use the words "woman" and "women," to designate those who think of themselves and are thought of by others as women. I use the word "feminine" to refer to their gender, by which I mean the learned behavior, seeming evidence of secondary sex characteristics, and dress codes used to assign gender to women. The word "female" refers to inborn biological characteristics, as opposed to gender signifiers that can be constructed. I have also tried to avoid generalizing about "woman" or "women." I regard gender and sexuality in these texts as historically constructed both by the ideology of the time and place *and* by the writers themselves, to the extent that by the act of self-representation they resist and subvert received ideas.

In addition, I have looked carefully at the significance of class in these texts. Dewald states that the nobility constituted about 1 percent of the total French population and that "the wealthiest and most articulate nobles, those most closely attached to Paris and the royal court, those most intent on giving written form to their experiences and concerns" represented an even smaller percentage (1993, 1). This fact is often mentioned in passing, but it is seldom pursued. To leave the matter there, however, says both too much and too little about the issue of class. On one hand, it draws attention to the fact that women writers benefited from class privilege in the ancien régime, but, on the other, it overlooks the fact that their male counterparts were just as privileged and had to overcome far fewer obstacles than they. What needs to be done, therefore, is to explore the intersections of class and gender in these early noblewomen's texts.

TEXT AND CONTEXT

Class is more than a sign of privilege. It is the key to specific and particular constructions of femininity. In some ways, the very concept of gender was reserved to the upper classes under the ancien régime. The attributes of femininity were conflated with the idea of being "ladylike," thus making gender identity an indicator of social status. This is demonstrated dramatically by the fact that chambermen often helped French ladies with their toilettes, showing that from the aristocratic point of view, a servant did not have to be taken seriously as a man.[11]

What is more, gender ideology for upper-class French women was to all intents and purposes a form of racism. In the twentieth century, race is associated with color and geographical origin, but in the seventeenth century it denoted "blood."[12] The social dominance of the great families was supported by the belief that merit was not acquired by conditioning or education but transmitted at birth, via the family bloodline. This meant that the inferior status of the lower classes was genetically predetermined and, as Ronzeaud points out, ruled out any possibility of improving on one's birth through education or personal experience (1988, 356). The aristocratic order rested on property and political rights passed down from father to son. "Nobles could view their behavior and their political powers as reflections of the world's natural order," writes Dewald; "they could view individual qualities and choices as reflections of the family's qualities and needs. To see links between the biological and the social inspired intellectual and moral assurance" (1993, 2).

Wealth and power, as well as the moral and intellectual self-assurance of the upper classes, were transmitted through the male line. The quintessence of this concept was the Salic law, which at the end of the sixteenth century had placed the Bourbon dynasty on the throne and disinherited Marguerite, the last of the Valois. Under its tenets, women were reduced to passive transmitters of royal blood, which they legitimated by their chastity. In addition, according to Schalk, in the seventeenth century nobility became even more closely linked to birth than it had been in the Middle Ages and Renaissance, when it had been validated to some extent by military prowess. Schalk suggests that the absolute monarchy encouraged this emphasis on heredity because it helped to maintain order over unruly noblemen who resorted too frequently to the sword.[13]

It follows that women's autonomy diminished as they became pawns in the battle to retain rank or gain ascendancy. And those women who resisted being used as objects of exchange would have been viewed as a threat to the system. In 1556, Henri II had issued an edict making it illegal to contract a marriage without parental consent. From then on, the legal position of women, and especially their right to choose a mate, had declined.[14] According to Collins, this decline was a direct response to "the threat women posed to the existing patriarchal economic and social systems" (1989, 467); and, he adds, the mercantile bourgeoisie and the masculine nobility were united in the effort to assure "continued male dominance of public society by using the state to restrict women's legal rights" (470).

In other words, the texts studied here were *produced* within in a milieu whose ideology of gender was not only class-specific but inextricably linked to an economy that used women to obtain money or social position. If they were allowed to enjoy some of the benefits of their noble status, they were nonetheless a means to an end for those in power. In some ways, consequently, they had less autonomy than women of the lower and lower-middle classes, who often worked or engaged in trade and achieved thereby a certain amount of economic independence. Of course, working women also encountered hostility and prejudice in the exercise of their functions, especially if they stepped out of traditional roles; and then as now, they earned far less than did their male counterparts (Gibson 1989, 112–13).[15] Nevertheless, because of the upper class's obsession with birth and blood, the lives of these women were controlled to an extraordinary degree by patriarchal power. This power is in evidence throughout these self-narratives, so much so that without understanding the laws and customs under which they lived, one cannot fully comprehend the significance of certain episodes.

The rules and rituals of female conduct were enforced by the paterfamilias. Legally a girl could not be married before the age of twelve, but contracts were often signed earlier, the two spouses being separated until the wife reached puberty. Richelieu's niece was married at thirteen to the Grand Condé, and was made to wear wobbly high heels so that she would appear taller at the ceremony. Hortense Mancini was fifteen when her uncle, Cardinal Mazarin, awarded her and his fortune to the man who later wanted to pull his daughters' teeth to safeguard their chastity. Sometimes children were affianced at birth. Nor was it rare to celebrate marriages in which the bride and groom barely knew each other. Guyon's father made her sign her marriage contract without telling her what it was. At forty-four Perrault married a girl of eighteen after a single interview. A Mademoiselle de Mayrian, aged fifteen, met her fiancé for the first time while still in a convent school— three days before their marriage (Piettre 1974, 227).

Fathers and husbands had legal control of wives' and children's property, and could enjoy the revenue it produced. This right could be forfeited only in cases of profligacy, when a wife could sue for separation of goods, but not for civil divorce. Women could not go to court without their husband's permission, except in cases of marital cruelty. The law permitted men to discipline wives and children either by physical punishment or by consigning them to correctional institutions. Unmarried women were considered minors until they were twenty-five, and then they remained under the tutelage of their closest male relative. Even rich heiresses could not claim autonomy or control their destinies. Only widows enjoyed any real freedom from masculine control, for they were their children's guardians and could dispose of their husband's property as they saw fit.[16] The patriarchal-monarchical structures controlling women were supported by church and state, kinship systems, and communal units, all of which exerted moral and social pressure to reinforce women's compliance. "When we are born, we are not only slaves of our parents, who dispose of us as they see fit," bemoans Tullie in Scudéry's *Clélie*, "but we are [slaves] of custom and propriety, because as soon as we are capable of reasoning and discernment, we are told that we must submit ourselves to convention."[17]

Ideology and discourse caused women to internalize attitudes towards femininity that were essential to the racist and classist concerns of the French upper classes. One of these was the doctrine of the "good woman"—the chaste, obedient, long-suffering wife. Women's "virtue" was evaluated almost entirely on the basis of sexual conduct. This meant that unlike men, who were praised for glorious words and deeds, women were judged on *what they did not do.* As Hortense Mancini put it in her memoirs, "a woman's honor lies in not getting herself talked about" (1965, 32). And by the same token, women were nearly always discredited on the basis of licentious behavior, real or supposed. The result was that silence reigned about many aspects of women's lives, either in the belief that they held little worthy of writing about, or that if they were noteworthy, it was for the wrong reasons, and the less said about it, the better.

The doctrine of the "good woman" relied to a large extent on literary representations. Virtuous women like Lucretia and Griselda were held up to women as examples, and women were taught to shudder at the names of those who strayed from the straight and narrow. Gournay's early novel *Le Proumenoir* dramatizes how women were taught to fear that the story of their misconduct would be repeated to generations of dutiful daughters: "Shall it be said," cries the contrite heroine who has eloped with her lover, "that forevermore mothers will use my horrible example to instruct their daughters to avoid evil?"[18]

Producing texts that placed themselves at the center of their own narrative was a radical gesture for women who had been taught to remain silent and avoid getting themselves talked about. Furthermore, it must be understood that the very act of writing a work of any magnitude posed practical problems for them. None of these women writers had received much formal education. By the end of the sixteenth century, noblemen's sons were attending Jesuit *collèges,* which made them, as Brockliss says, "heirs to the intellectual achievements of two thousand years of European history" (1987, 7). Choisy, despite his predilection for wearing feminine garb, attended both a prestigious *collège* and, as a future priest, the university. Bussy-Rabutin writes that he was enrolled in the Jesuit school in Autun at nine, and then in the celebrated Collège de Clermont after the family moved to Paris. "At twelve I was such a good humanist," he brags, "that when I was thirteen, I was judged strong enough to proceed directly to philosophy, without doing rhetoric" (1857, 5–6). While the minds of upper-class men were being formed on classical lines, upper-class women were prevented, solely on the basis of their gender, from receiving more than the rudiments of book learning. "One may say what one will of the great books of the world," Madeleine de Scudéry wrote to Bussy-Rabutin, "one must have seen other [books] to profit from it, and I regret every day that I was taught nothing."[19] Few were as fortunate as Madame de Sévigné and Madame de Lafayette, who were instructed by Ménage, or the future Madame de Maintenon, who was tutored by the chevalier de Méré. More often, women who pursued cultural and intellectual improvement did so on their own initiative and had to overcome many obstacles. Marie de Gournay learned

Greek and Latin by comparing texts in the original with French translations. Valois and Montpensier turned to books during periods of exile and
imprisonment, having read almost nothing until then.

Young ladies were either kept at home with their mothers or enrolled
for brief periods in convent schools. What they learned there was designed
primarily to preserve them from idleness and temptation. The first priority
was to acquaint them with church doctrine and to instill in them moral
virtues.[20] The rest of the curriculum was devoted to genteel accomplishments like music and handiwork. There was no effort to train their minds;
and the study of literary works was banned (C. Dulong 1969, 23). The
general consensus was that women had no intellectual aptitude anyway,
and should not be taught subjects for which they had no use.[21] There was
also concern that the study of history and literature might lead young women
astray by exposing them to immoral examples. Throughout the century,
education for women was linked to sexual misconduct, and the prowoman
faction was forced to counter this prejudice by arguing that it was ignorance and not learning that made women susceptible to vice. As Gournay
remarked tartly, "The common man says that in order to be chaste a women
should not be clever. . . . But on the contrary, she should become as cun-
ning as possible so that if every man is wicked enough to want to deceive
her, no man will be clever enough to do so" (1985, 41 r° and v°).[22] "Lacking an appropriate institutional and professional position," writes Moriarity,
"those women who did become learned inevitably appeared as marginal:
as prodigies or freaks, depending on one's point of view" (1988, 39). Even
if most men did not share Arnolphe's conviction in Molière's L'Ecole des
femmes that educated women were more likely to cuckold their husbands,
learning was generally perceived as unfeminine. Madame de Maintenon
instructed the teachers at Saint-Cyr, the school she founded for poor gentle-
women, that they should avoid inculcating too precise notions of spelling,
lest their pupils appear pedantic (Gibson 1989, 273 n. 141).

As a result, many women never learned to spell correctly or write legibly. Mademoiselle de Montpensier's handwriting was so atrocious and
her orthography so inaccurate that her father forbade her to send him letters in her own hand. Saint-Evremond was often obliged to assist Hortense
Mancini with her correspondence, due to her shaky knowledge of grammar and spelling, for which he gallantly excused her on the ground that
such things were beneath her dignity (1927, 2:227). This inability to write
correctly had a considerable effect on the production of women's memoirs,
for their manuscripts often had to be recopied or even written out for them
by men, who did not hesitate to alter the style or even the content of their
texts as they saw fit.

Nor were women writers taken seriously in the literary world. Although Marie de Gournay presided in her home over linguistic discussions that would later be pursued by the Académie Française, she was not made a member when Richelieu officially established that august body in 1634. Ironically, the transvestite abbé de Choisy was elected to the Académie in 1687 and became its secretary.

SIGNS OF RESISTANCE

Beneath the seemingly secure hegemony of patriarchal/aristocratic values lay cultural tensions and anxieties, however. The so-called classical age was not a time of monolithic stability but a transitional period during which the old orders were being challenged and replaced.[23] Social historians have pointed out that the growth of capitalism and the rise of industry placed considerable stress on the class structure. "The process by which the forming bourgeoisie developed a new mode of production and a new ideological mode from the old is what characterizes social relations in France at this time," writes Harth (1983, 22). And Dewald argues that these economic changes produced splits not merely between the aristocracy and the bourgeoisie but between those French nobles who "participated enthusiastically in many of the most innovative currents in early modern culture" and those who supported "the confident ideology of dynastic continuity" (1993, 2). What has *not* always been acknowledged, however, is the extent to which changing attitudes toward women's place in society were also a cause of social unrest.

In a hierarchical society structured by lineage, the female was a threat to the established order because of her biological capacity to pass the father's name along to illegitimate offspring. As a consequence, the absolute monarchy was under considerable pressure to impose order and unity through the containment of the feminine. Greenberg calls attention to the fact that both Richelieu and Louis XIV warned "of the troublesome, chaotic consequences of allowing women any influence in the politics of the realm" (1992, 5). Particularly telling is this passage from the memoirs of Louis XIV, who wrote to instruct his son in the duties of kingship:

No sooner do you give a woman freedom to speak on important matters, than it is impossible that she will not cause us to weaken. The tenderness we have for them, which makes us appreciate their worst reasons, causes us to fall insensibly into their way of thinking; and their natural weakness, which often causes them to prefer frivolous interests over more solid considerations, nearly always makes them choose the wrong side. (1978, 259)

This warning was not just an expression of the king's subconscious fears, for he knew all too well of what he spoke. The women of his entourage were not given to holding their tongues; and the intervention he feared was not imaginary. He had been surrounded from childhood by strong-minded women who insisted on speaking their minds: his mother, Anne d'Autriche; his sweetheart, Marie Mancini; his mistress, Madame de Montespan; his morganatic wife, Madame de Maintenon; and last but not least, his sharp-tongued cousin, La Grande Mademoiselle, who had turned the cannons of the Bastille on his troops.

As Lévi-Strauss so astutely admitted, even in a man's world a woman is still a person, and therefore a generator of signs (1969, 496). Under the Bourbon kings, women's place in upper-class society was highly contested, and women frequently and vociferously challenged the ideology that enforced their inferior status. Women's writings, of which these self-narratives constitute an important part, were among the most important signs of resistance to the laws and customs reviewed above. As Joan Kelly argued, "feminism" can be traced back at least to the fourteenth-century, when Christine de Pizan imagined a city-state organized and run by women (1984, 5). In the sixteenth century, Marguerite de Navarre's *Heptameron* attacked the double standard of sexual conduct that conflated honor with chastity for women, but not for men. By the end of the Renaissance, women's dissident voices were no longer isolated phenomena. They formed a chorus.

Women were becoming more and more aware of themselves *as women.* If, as Bynum argues, medieval women saw themselves first and foremost as members of humanity as it was incarnated by Christ, by the seventeenth century this was no longer the case. They were beginning to view traditional attitudes toward women with impatience. In her 1595 preface to Montaigne's *Essais,* Gournay describes the mocking smiles, jokes, and shrugs that greeted women when they attempted to offer an opinion on a serious subject: "Happy are you, Reader," she exclaims, "if you do not belong to a sex to which is denied all goods . . . in order to offer it, as sole virtue and blessing, the right to be ignorant and to suffer" (1989, 27).[24] Valois reacted in the same vein to a derogatory essay by Loryot: "I cannot tolerate the scorn you display for my sex, wanting it to be honored by mankind for its infirmity and weakness; you will pardon me if I say that infirmity and weakness do not engender honor but scorn and pity. And that it is more than apparent that women should be honored by men for their excellence" (Valois 1999, 269–70).[25]

These protofeminists contended that women were at least equal, if not superior, to men. They argued with increasing vehemence that they should be given greater autonomy and have the right to be educated. During Anne

D'Autriche's regency, there was renewed interest in the question of whether women were fit to reign, and a new crop of prowoman writings appeared, among them Du Bosc's *Femme héroïque* and Le Moyne's *Gallerie des femmes fortes*. Later Poulain de la Barre argued for the education of women in *De l'Égalité des deux sexes*.

Prowoman militancy carried over into pictorial representation during the thirties and forties. Noblewomen had themselves painted wearing helmets, armor, shields, and swords.[26] They also participated vigorously in equestrian sports and hunting. Many of these *femmes cavaliers* became the Amazons who galloped on horseback across France during the Fronde—commanding troops, inciting citizens to combat, capturing cities, ordering attacks on the royal army. "For nearly six years," writes DeJean, "they dominated French political life in heroic style, forcing a suspension of the ancien régime's normal hierarchy of authority. They threw their world upside down, made the early years of Louis XIV's majority the equivalent of Bakhtin's carnivalized world, and thereby won by conquest a territory where women could live as men when they chose to. For a brief time, women in effect governed France on major occasions, and those who negotiated with them, from princes to parliamentarians, recognized their authority as legitimate" (1991, 38). The memoirs of the duchesse de Nemours, Madame de la Guette, and Mademoiselle de Montpensier all record this unprecedented moment when women exercised military and political power. At the end of the Fronde, the *femme cavalier* gave way to the *femme docteur* and the *précieuse:* women endowed with a desire for learning and a determination to develop such feminine faculties as *finesse, pénétration,* and *vivacité d'esprit* (Maclean 1977, 268–69). And as Harth shows in *Cartesian Women,* some women also displayed interest in science and philosophy, attracted especially by the writings of Descartes and the possibility of debating propositions like "The soul does not have a sex."[27]

During the first part of the century, women were already winning greater liberty and social prominence in the assemblies or salons known as *alcôves* or *ruelles,* so called because guests were seated in the spaces around the hostess's bed.[28] As an alternative to the raucous reunions of old comrades-in-arms that passed for court society under Henri IV, noblewomen began to receive select groups of cultivated people in their homes. "The salon emerged in the first half of the seventeenth century as a new, exclusive space for the nurturing of elite culture," writes Goldsmith. "While most of the habitués of both court and salon preferred to pass freely between both places, the social milieu of the salon was increasingly viewed as the more hospitable environment for perfect sociability" (1988, 6–7).

Madame de Rambouillet's *chambre bleue* is often credited with being the first and most famous of the *ruelles*. In point of fact, this seventeenth-century institution was a descendent of the predilection for refined social intercourse that had been introduced by the first Marguerite de Navarre under François I and had become the hallmark of the Valois dynasty.[29] Its practice, which Marguerite de Navarre described in the framework of her *Heptaméron,* had been handed down through the women of the line; and her grand-niece, Marguerite de Valois, had managed even in desolate Usson to surround herself with poets, musicians, and philosophers. After Valois's return to Paris in 1605, she invited artists and writers to elegant gatherings that were tacit reminders of what court life would have been had she, and not her ex-husband, acceded to the throne. At these assemblies, Valois was called "Vénus Uranie" and presided over discussions on subjects proposed by her, practices later adopted by the *précieuses.*

After her death, the art of conversation was fostered in more private and intimate settings. The salon of Madame des Loges was the scene of heated discussions on language and literature. In her more humble quarters, Gournay also received the intelligentsia and participated in debates about poetry and linguistic change. Certainly the marquise de Rambouillet, known as "la divine Arthénice," was the most famous salon hostess. Under her guidance, elegant language replaced the earthy gasconisms of Henri's court, and vulgar pastimes gave way to moral and psychological analyses of love.[30] After the Fronde, the salon movement shifted to the rue de Beauce, where the novelist Madeleine de Scudéry, known as Sapho, presided over her celebrated *samedis.*

Literature played a crucial role in salon culture. Poets and dramatists were encouraged to read from their works in progress, improvise gallant lyrics, and collaborate on literary projects. From the days of Marguerite de Valois, polite society had been both inspired and influenced by the writings of Honoré d'Urfé. His pastoral novel *L'Astrée,* which recounted interminable love affairs between shepherds and shepherdesses, revived themes of courtly love that still had intense appeal for romance-starved women condemned to loveless marriages. The gentlemen who frequented the *chambre bleue* were expected to treat its ladies like the heroines of fiction, deferring all hope of physical satisfaction. Madame de Rambouillet's daughter Julie imposed a fifteen-year courtship on her suitor Montausier; she finally agreed to marry him as she was approaching forty, and then only because she was pressed to do so by both the queen and the prime minister. The *Guirlande de Julie,* a collection of verses in her honor composed by salon members and luxuriously bound by Montausier stands as a monument to the romantic sensibilities of this milieu. Likewise, the famous *Carte de Tendre* in Scudéry's *Clélie* delicately maps the lover's journey.

All the autobiographers studied here were in one way or another involved in the salon movement. Montpensier frequented the gatherings at both Rambouillet's and Scudéry's, and during her exile in Saint-Fargeau, she re-created the pastimes they had made fashionable.[31] It was she who edited and published a collection of verbal *portraits,* thus preserving in writing one of *préciosité*'s most popular pastimes.[32] These *portraits,* in which ladies and gentlemen attempted to recapture their own and their friends' physical and characterological traits, were, of course, highly sophisticated exercises in self-fashioning. Choisy's mother, known as "Célie," belonged to Montpensier's circle and is portrayed in the collection. The social gatherings that her cross-dressed son describes in his memoirs consciously reproduce the atmosphere of the *alcôves* she frequented. Marie Mancini was eulogized by Somaize in his *Dictionnaire des précieuses* under the rubric "Maximiliane." He called her the "perle des précieuses." During her exile in England, her sister Hortense presided over a London salon on the French model, to which she invited distinguished thinkers and writers from both England and France. Even Jeanne Guyon, with her pious, provincial upbringing, was encouraged to acquire the conversational skills prized by *précieuse* society and attended provincial assemblies that emulated the Parisian *alcôves.*

Who constituted the enclave of "precious women" has continued to be the subject of debate. As Stanton states, "The only reality that can be claimed for the précieuse is her representation in a body of mid-seventeenth-century texts which are designed to chastise her pervasive faults. She exists only through the prism of comic degradation" (1981, 113). What is certain is that a feminocentric social movement with a literary, intellectual, and prowoman agenda was instigated and directed by upper-class women in the seventeenth century.[33]

Dubbed "the Jansenists of love" and mocked as squeamish prudes by satirists like Molière,[34] the women known as *précieuses* or *femmes savantes* were the standard-bearers of resistance to women's oppression. Claude Dulong goes so far as to contend that although they belonged to the aristocracy, their influence eventually extended to all women: "It is a well-known and unforgettable fact that in the large cities, hardly 40% of Frenchwomen were capable of signing their name. But it is in the salons that the minority of this minority became an elite; and without this elite, would the mass of others even have been conscious of its lacks and learned to formulate its demands? From whence, in this society made by and for men, could change come, if not from the women themselves?" (1974, 125–26).

By imposing on their suitors long periods of celibacy disguised as obedience to courtly ideals, these latter-day followers of the "belle dame sans mercy" sought relief from the loveless marriages and perilous pregnancies imposed on them in their milieu. In the *ruelles,* women who had been forced to marry men they hardly knew could engage in platonic flirtations without being suspected of adultery, a crime carrying with it the threat of perpetual reclusion. Unmarried women like Julie de Rambouillet could postpone and perhaps avoid the dangers of child-bearing. To see this behavior as prudish is to ignore the fact that the mortality rate was far higher for women of childbearing age (twenty to thirty-five) than it was for men in the same age bracket (C. Dulong 1974, 84). And here their class imposed a particularly heavy burden on noblewomen. Whereas parish registers show that the majority of seventeenth-century Frenchwomen did not marry until the age of twenty-five, noblewomen were usually married soon after puberty, thus increasing by ten years or so the period of time when they could bear children.[35] In addition, the custom of handing their babies over to wet nurses reduced the amount of time between pregnancies.

Madame de Sévigné reflected the thinking of many noblewomen when she wrote to her daughter, "Poor Madame de Béthune is pregnant again. I feel so sorry for her. . . . It is feared that the princesse d'Harcourt is pregnant too" (1972–78, 1:241). "Mme de Soubise is pregnant; she complains about it to her mother, but to no avail" (1:252). Sévigné also pleaded with her son-in-law to exercise abstinence: "Do you think I gave her to you so that you could kill her, destroy her health, her beauty, her youth?" (1:365). Likewise Marie Mancini insisted her husband cease sexual relations because of her conviction that she would not survive another pregnancy.

In *La Prétieuse,* the abbé de Pure reports the passionate outburst of a certain Eulalie: "She complains," he writes,

> of a youth that is too fecund and too abundant, which has made her a mother, and which exposes her every year to a new burden, to a visible peril, to an important responsibility, to indescribable suffering and a thousand unpleasant consequences. However, one must submit to them and suffer them without saying a word. The thought of duty takes precedence over all others and reproaches you for all the moments of indifference that you may feel. A refusal is a crime; pain, mortification, coldness, and that elevation of an honest person above the material and the brutality of a husband are crimes of state under the tyrannical yoke of marriage. (1938, 1:285)

The institution of marriage itself came under severe fire from the *précieuses.* De Pure describes women denouncing the abuses of marriage, defending divorce, demanding punishment for masculine infidelity, advocating marriages contracted for a year at a time, and claiming the right to terminate conjugal relations, or even the marriage itself, after the birth of the first child. Although it is not certain whether de Pure was sympathizing with these women or mocking them, *La Prétieuse* documents women's growing dissatisfaction with traditional roles.[36]

Tullie in Scudéry's *Clélie* gives voice to these sentiments. Scudéry herself refused to marry and accepted the "friendship" of her admirer Pellisson only after she had subjected him to a series of trials roughly equivalent to the stations of her *Carte de Tendre*. Another interesting example of antimarriage sentiment is an epistolary exchange between Madame de Motteville and Mademoiselle de Montpensier, in which the latter imagines a utopian community where all the inhabitants would be unmarried, because, she says, "it is marriage that has given men their superiority, and what has made us known as the weaker sex is the dependence to which we have been subjugated, often against our will, for reasons of family, and of which we have been the victims" (Montpensier 1806, 5–6). Motteville, *who had been married at eighteen to a man of eighty,* wrote back that she considered the idea of such a utopia impractical, but that she herself had no desire whatsoever to be married.

The *précieuses* also advocated what seemed on the surface a less drastic way of improving women's lot within marriage. Inspired by popular romantic fiction, they encouraged the idea that *inclination,* that is to say, an attraction based on manners, looks, and personal merit, was a better foundation for marriage than lineage. Such a point of view represented an insidious threat to the established order, for it was fundamentally incompatible with the aristocratic view of marriage. Lougee's study of the effects of salon culture on marriage patterns provides statistical evidence that women who frequented salons frequently married outside their social bracket, thus causing long-lasting modifications in the social structure. Lougee argues that opposition to the *précieuses* and the public role they exercised in the salons was related to fear of the way the old rules governing social stratification were being eroded. The salons "propagated a vision of an expanded aristocracy open to those who acquired any of numerous forms of prominence," she writes; "they celebrated ennoblement, arguing the superiority of acquired nobility over inherited nobility, and with this social vision praised women as a social force which promoted the integration of new individuals into the elite" (1976, 41). It is also worthy of note that their insistence on education contained within it the seeds of opposition to a class system in which merit was linked to aristocratic birth rather than to personal attainments. "Salons acted as a kind of social laboratory, where nobles and non-nobles alike proposed to discover new definitions of what it meant to be 'naturally' superior," writes Goldsmith (1988, 8–9).

In other words, *préciosité* not only worked against the exploitation of women within marriage; it subverted the aristocratic order that arranged marriages on the basis of lineage. Its counterideology was instrumental in breaking down old barriers between the classes by advocating marriage based on merit rather than on blood. It even went so far as to defend misalliances between rich commoners and impoverished aristocrats, especially if they were based on romantic love. So great was the impact of these ideas that at one point even the young Louis XIV was nearly persuaded to ignore his royal duty and marry the totally unsuitable Marie Mancini. Likewise, Montpensier made the radical decision to marry Lauzun on the basis of his admirable qualities, and in spite of his social inferiority.

Thus consciousness raised by the protofeminist conversations of the *ruelles* activated opposition to the institutions that deprived women of autonomy. Women learned to think thoughts not connected to their domestic roles, and to question their traditional function in society. These assemblies also functioned as centers of education for women. They not only imparted a model of social conduct based on verbal skills, they instilled analytical habits of thought and stimulated the practice of reading and writing. This in turn created a demand for writing by, for, and about women. The Amazonian women who had dreamed of military power during the Fronde turned, during Louis XIV's reign, to writing as a form of social and political expression; and memoirs were ideally suited to their agenda. DeJean has shown how the novels of seventeenth-century Frenchwomen grew out of the politics of salon culture.[37] But just as important, and in some ways more so, was the production of woman-authored autobiography.

POLITICS AND POETICS: THEORIES OF THE AUTOBIOGRAPHICAL

Self-representation became widespread in the Renaissance as personal accomplishments acquired significance and recognition. Gusdorf gives various explanations as to why at this particular moment people were inspired to write their life stories: the birth of historical consciousness, belief in progress and individual responsibility, increased social mobility due to the breakdown of the old feudal structures, a new sense of human intellectual capacities due to scientific discoveries, the humanist secularization of thought, and greater faith in the power of the human mind and its capacity for reason, as well as renewed interest in classical models of life-writing like Plutarch's *Lives*. Discussing these explanations of the rise of autobiography, Sidonie Smith cautions, however, that literary historians like Gusdorf have been speaking of a new concept of *man,* which construes the autobiographical subject as always male and delineates autobiography as "public narratives men write for each other as they lay claim to an immortal place within the phallic order" (S. Smith 1987, 26). Smith goes on to argue that, by contrast, early women's "life script" imposed silence on them. As a result, early modern women, "suspended between culturally constructed categories of male and female selfhood," created texts that slipped between "ideology and subjectivity . . . conformity and resistance" (41).

French women's lives certainly did not follow the scenarios that dominated early life-writing in their country, nor did their texts observe the rules that defined it. Indeed, French secular autobiography emerged from particularly masculinist concerns.[38] Descended from Caesar's commentaries on the Gallic Wars and the medieval court chronicles of Joinville, Villehardouin, Froissart, and Commynes, they concentrated on the military, diplomatic, and political accomplishments of the *noblesse d'épée*.[39] "When I went out into the world," writes Bussy-Rabutin, "my first and greatest desire was to become an *honnête homme* and to attain great honors in war. To this end, I tried as much as I possibly could to frequent *honnêtes gens;* and when my father enrolled me in the army, I wrote down my campaigns in order to retain what had happened in them" (1857, 3). If personal recollections were included, they were generally limited to eyewitness accounts of historical events. The self-reflections of the essayist Montaigne, who took himself as the subject of his work, meditating on his personal strengths and weaknesses and revealing intimate details of his existence, were seen by his contemporaries as useless, childish, and vain.[40] According to Lejeune, it was widely believed, even in the nineteenth century, that autobiography, with its emphasis on the personal, was not suited to the French temperament (1971, 15). He cites the *Grand Dictionnaire universel* of 1866, where one reads, "Very few French memoirs merit the name of *autobiography*. It is more an English and American genre. In France, no matter how high an opinion one has of oneself when one transmits one's personal memories to posterity, one always tends to write more about the lives of others than about one's own."

As Fumaroli states, these early *mémoires* were produced almost exclusively by the aristocracy (1979, 27). Their authors were intent on providing what they saw as truthful versions of what they had done and eyewitness accounts of the events they had lived through. Underlying this project, however, was their resentment that as members of the feudal aristocracy, they had been cheated of their rightful place in an increasingly centralized monarchy administered by bourgeois civil servants. Many of them, like Monluc, had seen their services go unrewarded, or had been unjustly punished. Writing memoirs became a means of setting the record straight and defending traditional feudal values against social change.[41] They also used them to justify themselves to posterity, especially their descendants, drawing parallels between their actions and those of past heroes.[42] This tendency toward nostalgia for a bygone era reached its apogee in the memoirs of Saint-Simon, who chronicled the progressive dilution of the royal line by Louis XIV's illegitimate offspring.

For such men, the question of lineage was of prime importance.[43] They were obsessed with family and the desire to transmit its values and virtues from generation to generation. Many of them addressed their texts to (male) progeny, whom they sought to inspire by their example. "Memoirs play first and foremost the role of transmitting the paternal model," writes Hennequin, "of encouraging imitation of the father's or grandfather's virtues. In the feudal context of the beginning of the century, it is even the virtues and values of the entire line that must be transmitted" (1979, 89–90).[44] Bertière expresses much the same idea: "Memoirs appear to be at the same time a monument erected on the domestic altar to remind descendents of their ancestor's virtues and an account book, in the original sense of the word, to which are consigned the rights of the clan to the sovereign's honors and favors" (1977, 21).

As Marin shows, implicit in such endeavors was a subversive critique of royal power. This is dramatically illustrated in Pellisson's "Project for the History of Louis XIV," in which the author specifically excluded journals and memoirs as source material for an official history of the reign. Pellisson wrote, "History overlooks many circumstances that journals and Memoirs report. . . . But in compensation, when it is a question of the Master and of an informative example of his value, firmness, and great sense, of which our King has given us a thousand, history lifts and makes the most of many little things about actions and principal persons that journals and Memoirs are accustomed to neglect. History puts all the great things it encounters in a better light through a nobler and more composed style, which encloses a lot in a little space with no wasted words" (qted. in Marin 1988, 40–41).[45]

Pellisson's project was submitted to Colbert around 1670, and won his approval. Boileau and Racine, who also served as Louis XIV's official historiographers, continued to follow the principles he had laid down. Memoirs were thus excluded from the official history, according to Marin, because by their very nature they undermined the myth of the king as the universal subject from whom all history emanates. Texts written in the first person "imply, by definition, a reference to a subject who writes *his* history —the history of what has happened *to him* and that of which he has been spectator, witness, or actor," writes Marin (1988, 47). In other words, by their use of the narrative "I," memoirs refuted the ideology of the absolute monarch and suggested the possibility of a narrative of events differing from, or even contradicting, the official version.[46]

If, however, men's memoirs threatened the myth of the absolute monarch's infallibility by calling into question his status as the universal subject, the destabilizing power of women's memoirs was even greater; for they called into question not only the foundations of the monarchy but the phallocentric ideology ratified in both history *and* men's memoirs. In a symbolic sense, moreover, they threatened the king's hegemony by contesting the silencing of women implicit in the Salic law.

The subversive implications of these memoirs has been largely ignored, however, because they are seldom included in discussions of the genre. Their relative obscurity corroborates Sidonie Smith's assertion that "the contributions of women to the genre have traditionally been perceived as forms of contamination, illegitimacies, threats to the purity of the canon of autobiography itself; and their works, defined as anomalous, are set aside in separate chapters, at ends of chapters" (1987, 43). The canonical definition of early French memoirs is based on the life-writings of men who viewed digressions into private life as lapses for which the author should apologize to his reader.[47] Self-narratives that did not adhere to this view of life-writing were excluded from the canon and their importance dismissed.

Nonetheless, early Frenchwomen's self-narratives made significant contributions to the development of autobiography and comprise a considerable corpus. Prior to the memoirs of Valois, there had been several shorter works: Anne de Beaujeu's *Les Enseignements d'Anne de France à sa fille Suzanne de Bourbon* (1504), Louise de Savoie's *Journal* (1522), and Jeanne d'Albret's, *Mémoires et poésies* (1572). Nor was Valois the only woman of her time to write about herself. In the memoirs devoted largely to her husband's career, the Huguenot Madame de Mornay provided a hair-raising record of her escape during the St. Bartholomew's massacres. Marie de Gournay offered a brief verse account of her life in her *Copie de la Vie de la Demoiselle de Gournay*.[48] She also recounted her battle to gain recognition as a writer in her "Apologie pour celle qui escrit,"[49] and described her association with Montaigne in her 1595 preface to his *Essais*.

The seventeenth-century corpus of women's memoirs is not limited to those studied here. The Fronde inspired not only the memoirs of Mlle. de Montpensier but those of Madame de la Guette and the duchesse de Nemours. Not only Marie Mancini, Louis XIV's first love, but Louise de la Vallière, his mistress, wrote about their lives. Women memoirists who devoted themselves to writing royal women's biographies—Madame de Motteville, Madame de Lafayette, and Madame de Caylus—wove their own stories into their texts. And women were also, of course, prolific contributors to the subgenre of spiritual autobiography.

Scholars of seventeenth-century autobiography often minimize the importance of women's memoirs, however, because the masculine proto-type has dominated attempts to define the genre. Retz, considered its great-est practitioner, wrote about himself as a public figure. He did not engage in introspection. In consequence, scholars like Bertière dismiss early women's autobiographical writing because in them the private individual "indiscreetly invades the narration and in telling about herself forgets to tell about history." He sees this as a "quite feminine weakness," citing Mar-guerite de Valois and La Grande Mademoiselle as examples. "Only those works whose accounts are heavily weighted toward history seem to us to merit truly the name of memoirs," he concludes (1977, 403). Bertière's insistence that memoirs should concentrate on public and historical con-cerns is typical of definitions that trivialize feminine contributions to the genre.

On the other hand, theorists of autobiography like Lejeune tend to situ-ate its origin in the eighteenth century and to hold up Rousseau as its ideal practitioner. "Autobiography appeared in the second half of the eighteenth century," Lejeune writes, "at the same time in most of the countries in Europe" (1971, 63). Although he does caution against attributing its inven-tion solely to Rousseau, he maintains that it was Rousseau who "realized in a single stroke nearly all the virtualities. He wrote in the *Confessions* not only the first of the autobiographies, historically, since the *Confessions* were composed between 1762 and 1770, but probably the most daring of those written in relation to the civilization of the period" (65).[50]

Only a few scholars have discerned in seventeenth-century women's life-writing the determination to go beyond the generic limits of memoirs and explore a new form of self-representation. At the end of his essay situ-ating memoirs at the "crossroads" of history, autobiography, and the novel, Fumaroli speaks briefly of the importance of two variant genres—the spiri-tual confession and what he calls "worldly memoirs." Démoris assimilates women's memoirs to the novel, but in so doing calls into question their veracity. Hipp also relates them to the novel, suggesting that they are better understood by observing them "de l'intérieur" than by attempting to im-pose on them a lexicographical definition (1976, 23). Only Beasley has seen their political and historical implications and argued that they revise and enlarge the masculinist concept of history in order to show that par-ticular events lay behind it.[51]

In fact, the very existence of personal and private matters in women's memoirs constitutes a political statement on behalf of those whose lives were deemed unimportant to history. This is what a critic like Voltaire failed to comprehend when he dismissed Montpensier's memoirs as the writings of "a woman preoccupied with herself" rather than of a "princess who witnessed important events" (1957, 1189). In this view, she does not provide the "right" kind of information, because the life of a "princess" can be of no importance in and of itself. Yet the text he branded as inferior was in fact the meticulously documented record of the political marginalization of a member of the royal family because of her gender.

Voltaire and his followers judge women's memoirs on the basis of what Watson calls the "*bios* component." "*Bios,*" writes Watson, "is not synonymous with identity, but signals the significance of a life within authorized traditions of representing lives in Western culture. The delineation of actions signifying greatness in Plutarch's *Lives,* for example, indicates the monumental public stature of 'the great'" (1993, 58). It is this concept of life-writing, she argues, that has caused the autobiographical canon to be limited to those who are "white, male, and highly literate—and to the metaphysical aspiration of that culture itself, whose achievement was to produce a universalizing, transcendent subject memorialized by life writing in metaphors of stasis and permanence" (59). Watson's critical perspective is shared by many theorists working today in the field of women's autobiography.[52] Earlier in this chapter, I reflected on how theoretical debates about selfhood and gender have shaped this study. I shall end it by suggesting how these self-narratives relate to current discussions about what constitutes autobiography, and especially what constitutes the difference of the texts I study here.

The spectacular growth of autobiographical theory has caused one recent anthologist to claim that autobiography now occupies the position held during the time of high New Criticism by the poem (Folkenflik 1993, 11). I shall not attempt to review in depth the huge and ever-growing mass of theorizing about a genre that seems to defy all attempts to define it.[53] Such summaries are already plentiful. As Watson says, "It has become a critical topos to begin discussions of the theory of autobiography by rehearsing the changing positions assumed by critics over the last three decades" (1993, 57). I will simply make a few points that are germane to this analysis.

The postmodern debates about selfhood and gender have profoundly modified critical attitudes toward women's autobiography. Early attempts to found a poetics on the basis of women's difference have largely been abandoned. The argument that women's self-narratives display some recognizable difference—a greater sense of connectedness, or a less individualistic sense of self—have not only proved impossible to verify, they have now been called into question because of their essentialist stereotyping.[54]

On the other hand, increased attention has been paid to autobiographies that reject conventional approaches and forms, especially those by women who are not heterosexual, white, Western European, or middle class. Leigh Gilmore, Françoise Lionnet, Sidonie Smith, Trinh T. Minh-ha, and Julia Watson, to mention some prominent examples, have used postcolonialist critiques of Eurocentric culture to show how the self-narratives of such women resist and subvert canonical ideas about what constitutes a life that is worth narrating and what constitutes an acceptable model for telling a life story. They view autobiography as a genre constantly reinventing itself by resisting the boundaries imposed on it by established discourses. The focus of the discussion has therefore shifted away from defining what women's autobiography is to concentrate on the political implications of women's autobiographical acts. As Gilmore argues, "[T]he incoherence in the category can be used to further a feminist theory of autobiographical production" (1994, 13). "Autobiographics"—a term Gilmore uses to denote the writing of autobiography—"avoids the terminal questions of genre and close delimitation and offers a way, instead, to ask: Where is the autobiographical? What constitutes its representation?" (13).

On the surface, the writers analyzed by Gilmore et al. have nothing in common with those I am studying. But these theorists' refusal to define autobiography narrowly according to a generic formula makes it possible to see more clearly what these early French autobiographers accomplished. By demonstrating how autobiographical writing validates the life stories of the disenfranchised, these theorists suggest that certain self-narratives have a common basis across time, space, and social class, by dint of their marginal and subversive relationship to the dominant discourses of their milieu.

Like the minority and third-world women analyzed by postmodern feminists, the autobiographers I study here did not conform to the prevailing rules of life-writing. They challenged the presupposition that the only life worth recording was that of a "great man." Furthermore, they portrayed themselves as *they* saw themselves, and as they wanted to be seen, tacitly countering the stereotypical representations that reduced the feminine to sexual and procreative functions. Refusing to perform only as signs in a social structure that perpetuated itself through the exchange of women, they fashioned self-narratives that staked the claim to identity on their own terms. This is why I think it is important that feminist critics give these texts the same attention they are giving to the writings of marginalized women, rather than ignoring them as canonical critics have done for so long.

THE PERSONAL AND THE POLITICAL

These autobiographical writings departed from the preoccupations and norms of masculine memoirs, improvising new scenarios that filled in the gaps between women's lives and the narrow preoccupations of the genre. This was due in large part to the way men and women lived in upper-class France. Aside from a brief interlude during the Fronde, women (and those like Choisy who embraced a feminine lifestyle) were barred from engaging directly in politics.[55] As Marguerite de Valois discovered, even when a woman wanted to write about her role in public events, her marginalization forced her to write as an outsider or to concentrate on the personal aspects of court life.

Yet these writers chose to write about lives that did not conform to accepted ideas of what made a life worth writing about. And this, I believe was largely due to the growing sense of feminine identity and prowoman attitudes that emerged from the salon movement. The qualities of mind and the topics of conversation cultivated in the *ruelles* inspired women to reflect on their lives. What is more, the *précieuses'* predilection for romantic fiction inspired them to see their lives as narratives, to identify the turning points of their existence, and to explore and analyze their emotions. The passionate encounters and happy endings they found in novels made them rebel against sacrificing their health, their ambitions, and their personal desires to the demands of their fathers and husbands. The gap between their sense of themselves as heroines and their inferior status in the family impelled them to explain and justify themselves, in the hope that their readers would perceive their merits. In writing about their lives, they were not only coming to terms with who they were, they were refusing to submit silently to the constraints that femininity imposed on them.

These texts record how the conflict between the patriarchal code and the protofeminist attitudes propagated in the *ruelles* was played out in individual lives. And it is here, I believe, that the sense of self-worth instilled in women by the salon movement intersected with the ideology of class that identified them as members of the privileged aristocracy. Confronting the disparity between what their birth should have entitled them to, and what, in fact, it deprived them of, they were no longer willing to be consigned to silence and invisibility. Contemplating the constraints imposed on them by womanhood, they were aroused to recount their struggle to fashion identities that resisted the feminine stereotypes of their class.

Accordingly, they situated the roots of personhood in the experiences of childhood (a phase of existence that men memoirists almost never described). They delved into their relationships with parents and siblings, the physical and psychological changes of adolescence, and the pivotal significance of marriage. Abandoning the pursuit of history that characterized masculine memoirs, they turned from the public sector to the private, creating a new kind of life-writing—in which the author's self is differentiated from the expectations of society and in which she represents herself as *she* sees herself, and not as *others* see her.

2

Marguerite de Valois

In the Library of Congress online catalog, Marguerite de Valois is not listed under her family name—Valois. One can only find her by looking up "Marguerite, Queen, consort of Henri IV, King of France." Thus, in our time as in hers, her identity is absorbed in a man's. In order to identify her, one must name the kings who were her male relatives: François I, her grandfather; Henri II, her father; François II, Charles IX, and Henri III, her brothers; and Henri IV de Navarre, king of France, the husband who eventually divorced her. She was also, however, the grand-niece of that other Marguerite de Navarre, the author of the *Heptaméron*, and the daughter of that formidable queen-regent, Catherine de Médicis.

The sixth of seven children, Valois was born in 1553. In 1559, her father's death following a tournament caused her mother to be named regent for her brothers, first François II and then Charles IX. Valois's marriage to her cousin Henri de Navarre, the leader of the Protestant faction, set off a violent reaction among the ultra Catholics headed by the Guise family and resulted in the St. Bartholomew's Day massacres (23–24 August 1572), during which Protestants were slaughtered all over France. When her third brother, Henri III, came to the throne, her fortunes took a decided turn for the worse. He accused her of both political disloyalty and sexual promiscuity. After her husband's escape to his kingdom in Gascony, he held her a virtual prisoner at court, refusing for many months to allow her to go to Navarre. Once established in the southwest as queen of Navarre, however, she found life pleasant, despite her inability to give birth to an heir, her occasional clashes with Protestants, and Henri's infidelities. However, at the end of 1582, when his affair with one of her ladies-in-waiting resulted in a stillborn child, she decided to return to the French court. It is at this point that her memoirs break off.

In August 1583, her brother Henri III banished her from court and had her arrested for lewd behavior at Palaiseau, where he tried to force her servants to testify against her. Although he later retracted his charges for lack of evidence, Marguerite found herself alone and friendless in the middle of a war-torn country. Attempts at a reconciliation with her husband failed. They were followed by a period of rootlessness and unsuccessful efforts to support the Catholic cause. She was driven to retreat to the fortress-castle of Usson, where her husband forced her to remain for twenty years. It was during these years of solitude that she wrote her memoirs.

When Henri III died without a legitimate heir in 1589, her husband, Henri de Navarre, was named king, despite the fact that his patrilinear claim to the throne was extremely tenuous. To reunite a kingdom torn asunder by religious strife, he abjured Protestantism; and then, since an heir was essential to ensure political stability and firmly establish the Bourbon line, he petitioned Rome to annul his marriage to Marguerite, on the grounds of consanguinity and nonconsent. After lengthy negotiations, she agreed, provided she be allowed to keep the title of queen of Navarre. The divorce became final in 1599. Henri married Marie de Médicis, who gave birth to two sons—the future Louis XIII and Gaston d'Orléans, who would later father another celebrated woman memoirist, Mademoiselle de Montpensier.

Valois was allowed to return to Paris in 1605. There her home became a meeting place for the cultivated and refined people of the city and set the stage for the salon movement. Among its celebrated habitués were the poets of the new age: Malherbe, Maynard, and Régnier, as well as Honoré d'Urfé, who portrayed her as Galathée in L'Astrée. Marie de Gournay, another distinguished protégée, was placed in charge of purchasing books for her library.

Valois's liberality was legendary. She spent money and gave gifts in the manner of the grands seigneurs from whom she was descended. When Henri IV reproached her for her profligacy, she is supposed to have laughed and said that she was only carrying on the family tradition. She remained on good terms with Henri and the other members of the royal family until he was assassinated in 1610. In the troubled period that followed, Valois, who was very popular, threw her support to Marie de Médicis, thereby saving the regency and assuring the reign of her godson, Louis XIII. She died in 1615. It was rumored that she owed 200,000 écus at her death, a debt that the queen repaid in her honor.

The facts I have just set down willfully skirt the legend of "La Reine Margot" that is usually served up as Valois's biography. This legend portrays her as one of the most promiscuous nymphomaniacs in French history, a woman whose sexual escapades began in adolescence and continued unabated until well after menopause. As Babelon puts it, "[L]a Reine Margot lives in the eyes of posterity as the incarnation, the paragon of the most deliberate kind of lewdness, and is never spoken of without a smirk" (1965, 238). Scholars have usually accepted this legend at face value. Cazaux does not hesitate to begin his introduction to her memoirs with the words, "A pretty woman, an assiduous practitioner of love . . ." (1971, 9). However, in an exhaustive and meticulously documented study of the question, Viennot has shown that her reputation is based not on historical fact but on her enemies' efforts to defame her. Then as now, the factions who wanted to discredit her knew that the quickest and surest way to disgrace a woman was to spread rumors of her sexual escapades. These stories were subsequently perpetuated and enlarged upon by the ignorance, misogyny, and prurient sensationalism of historians and biographers.

Valois's conflicts with her brother Henri III partially explain how her name came to be synonymous with feminine debauchery. In her memoirs, she depicts him as obsessed by her sexuality and eager to prove her wantonness. As an ardent Catholic married to the Protestant chief she was an obvious target for vilification by both religious factions. Later, of course, her debauchery was used to justify Henri's decision to divorce her. *La Ruelle mal assorti,* an erotic dialogue falsely attributed to Valois, also reinforced her reputation as a shameless and depraved woman.[1] The most notable attack on her during her lifetime was the *Divorce satyrique* (1607), which Viennot calls "the most violent text ever written against Marguerite" (1992, 88). It is usually attributed to Agrippa d'Aubigné, but his authorship has not been established with certainty.[2] The *Divorce* has Henri denouncing his wife's "lubricity" and reading out an endless list of her lovers, including a horde of nameless cooks and servants, with whom she supposedly satisfied her unbridled sexual needs.[3]

According to Viennot, the campaign to malign her was continued by Richelieu, who wanted to discredit those who had backed his enemy Marie de Médicis. In 1630, following the Journée des Dupes, he exiled the Queen Mother and ordered his historiographers to calumniate Valois. The most vituperative of these was Scipion Dupleix, who had once been her friend and ally, and whose betrayal elicited protests from Matthieu de Morgues, Sully, and Bassompierre.[4] Tallemant des Réaux (1960, 59–62) added fuel to the fire with his story of the famous petticoat where she supposedly kept the embalmed hearts of her lovers. He also went out of his way to make her appear grotesque, asserting that she became bald and so fat that she could not get through a doorway.

Viennot claims that many other lurid details concerning "La Reine

Margot" actually were fabricated in nineteenth-century novels: Mérimée's *Chronique du roi Charles IX*, Stendhal's *Le Rouge et le noir,* Hérold's *Le Pré aux clercs,* and of course, Dumas's *La Reine Margot.* Although Viennot concedes that Valois undoubtedly had several lovers, including the dashing Bussy and Champvallon, she asserts that she was never the insatiable nymphomaniac portrayed in these novels. On the contrary, she contends, Valois was a committed Neoplatonist, who advocated idealized friendships with members of the opposite sex.[5] Such "courtly" or "platonic" love affairs were a common feature of Renaissance court life; and it was customary for a lady to have one or more "servitors," even if she was married. The memoirs allude to this custom several times: when Marguerite tells how her father asked her to choose a "servitor" from among her playmates; when she quotes her mother's remark that in *her* day women were free to enter into friendships without being suspected of immorality; and when she describes the pleasures of life at the court of Nérac. Notwithstanding Viennot's efforts to rehabilitate Marguerite de Valois, yet another link in the legend of "La Reine Margot" has recently been forged. Chéreau's film based on Dumas's novel is a tissue of historical inaccuracies that could have been avoided if the scenarist had cast even a cursory glance at her memoirs. The scholarly community has at last begun to reassess her life and writing, however, as was evidenced in 1991, when a colloquium was devoted to her.[6]

PUBLICATION HISTORY: *MÉMOIRES DE MARGUERITE DE VALOIS*

Valois's memoirs were composed in Usson. Although most scholars date them around 1600, Viennot believes they were written in 1594 because of their precise references to Brantôme's *Discours sur la Reyne de France et de Navarre,* which suggest that she began them shortly after he sent her a copy in 1593. Viennot also points to the similarities between their opening statement and a sonnet by Valois, dated December 1593;[7] both attempt to explain her life in terms of "envious fortune." However, she could not have written either text before February 1594 (the date of Henri IV's coronation), since in them she refers to him as king of France.[8]

Unfortunately, the manuscript Valois sent to Brantôme requesting his corrections has been lost, and the text that was eventually published is incomplete. It is not known whether Brantôme ever corrected it. As it now stands, it covers the years 1558 to 1582, telling of her childhood, her marriage, and her marriage's bloody sequel—the St. Bartholomew's Day massacres, the court intrigues spawned by the rivalry between Catholics and

Protestants, her mission to Flanders, her sojourn in Gascony, and the events preceding her estrangement from her husband. Schrenck suggests that she only wrote about the first thirty years of her life because she wanted to avoid having to confess to "truths difficult to assume in the eyes of her readers" (1991, 188).[9] Viennot dismisses this hypothesis and argues that the last part of the memoirs was lost. She points out that the narrative shows no sign of the author's fatigue and that the evident pleasure Marguerite took in writing about her life, combined with her lack of a serious occupation at Usson, would surely have inspired her to complete them: "She still had much to recount, which she would have turned to her advantage" (1993, 191). Furthermore, she contends, the three lacunae in the published text indicate that the manuscript used for the first edition was in poor condition.

Valois's *Mémoires* were published posthumously in 1628. Her first editor extolled them as the French equivalent of Caesar's *Gallic Wars*. They were an instant success, and were republished six times within the next year. They also appeared in English and Italian. Montpensier testifies to their popularity two generations later.[10] In his history of the Académie Française, Pellisson cites Valois's narrative as one of four texts proving the superiority of French over the language of Cicero. He adds that when he was young, he once read them twice in the same night.[11]

In 1971, Mercure de France made Valois's memoirs available to modern readers in its popular series Le Temps Retrouvé, with an introduction by Yves Cazaux. This has now been supplanted by Eliane Viennot's critical edition (1999). My citations refer to the latter, but I have also included the page numbers of Cazaux's edition in brackets.

"I Blame My Sex"

It is sometimes said that women lack the imagination to write about anything but themselves. This would seem to be corroborated by the number of memoirs French women produced during the ancien régime. It does not necessarily follow, however, that an early modern woman found it easy to write about herself. Not only did she have to repudiate the inauthentic representations of women that pervaded European literature, she had no literary models on which to base the story of her life. What one writes is inevitably determined to a large extent by what one has read, but when Marguerite de Valois began her memoirs, no other French women had ever attempted a project of such magnitude, and the men who had written their life stories before her had seen themselves principally as historiographers. They had no interest in private life and concentrated on relating what they had seen of war or politics. Valois's extensive library contained the writings of these early chroniclers, and she was undoubtedly familiar with them.[12] The best known of these were the *Commentaires* of Monluc, an officer for fifty-five years in the royal army, who wrote to refute charges of misappropriating the spoils of war. His text, modeled on Caesar's *Gallic Wars,* was intended for other military officers. A man like Monluc could follow in the footsteps of a classical author who had also written about life on the battlefield. But Valois's life bore little resemblance to either Caesar's or Monluc's. She had no career to vindicate and no advice to offer soldiers. Indeed, if anything, she had to justify her lack of achievement. She had been more a bystander than a participant in the events she had lived through.

Daughter, sister, and wife of kings, she viewed herself nonetheless as superior to other women. After all, she outranked everyone in France except the men of her own family; and had she not been a woman, she would have become king of France. Furthermore, she possessed qualities of mind and spirit that surpassed those of many men. She did not intend, therefore, to be a mere chronicler of what others had said and done. She wanted to place herself at the center of her narrative. To do this, however, she had to represent herself as a member of *mankind,* to effect the shift in identity that Sidonie Smith has called the "transvestism of the soul" (1987, 37).[13]

In the second part of his *discours* on "la reine de Navarre," Brantôme argues that Valois is "a true queen in every detail and worthy of ruling a great kingdom if not an empire" (1991, 133).[14] In addition, he mounts an attack on France's Salic law, contesting its historical basis and maintaining that women were as capable of governing as men. "And since it is right that in Spain, Navarre, England, Scotland, Hungary, Naples, and Sicily daughters reign," he asks, "why is it not right in France also? For what is right is right everywhere and in every place, and the place does not make the law right" (135). Pointing out that women could inherit fiefdoms in France, he asks, "[W]hy are the daughters of dukes in the kingdom more able to govern a duchy or a county, and dispense justice in them, which comes close to the authority of the king, while the daughters of kings cannot govern the kingdom of France?" (136).

However, when it comes to backing up his assertion that Valois is qualified to reign, Brantôme's arguments are less than convincing. He likens her to Cicero, but he does not quote any remarks to prove it; nor does he offer any concrete examples of her statesmanship, tact, or political acumen. Instead, his *discours* constructs her as a precious work of art, richly garbed, covered with jewels, and above all, narcissistically absorbed in enhancing her appearance. He calls her a miracle of God, graced with perfect features, a beautiful body, a superb figure, and the carriage of a goddess. He both objectifies and eroticizes her. Of her bosom he writes, "[N]ever was one seen that was so beautiful and so white, or so fully developed. And she displayed it so freely and openly that most courtiers swooned at the sight of it, even the ladies, and I have seen the ones who were intimate with her ask permission to kiss it rapturously" (127–28).[15] Brantôme represents the queen of Navarre as a construction of the masculine gaze—his, and that of the other men who have been smitten with her beauty: the Polish ambassador, who wants to blind himself on the spot, convinced he will never again see anything so beautiful; the Turkish emissaries, who forget the splendors of the sultan's court when they see her; Don Juan of Austria, who says he would risk eternal damnation for her; and Ronsard, who celebrated her beauty in his poetry.[16]

Valois takes issue forcefully with his remarks about her physical appearance. If she does not praise his flattering portrait of her, she explains, it is because she does not want to be taken for a woman who enjoys flattery even when it is undeserved: "This is a common vice among women . . . I blame my sex in this regard and would not want to be part of it" (1999, 69 [1971, 35]). She disavows her resemblance to his flattering portrait: "[T]he ornamentation of the picture far surpasses the excellence of the figure you wanted to make its subject" (1999, 70 [1971, 35]). On the surface, this may seem nothing more than the coyness of a once-beautiful lady seeking assurance that she is not past her prime. But her demurrals have a serious intent, for they go to the heart of representation. For one thing, Brantôme has failed to record the changes wrought on her by her misfortunes: "If I once had some part of what you attribute to me, the troubles that erased them from my exterior have also erased them from my memory" (1999, 70 [1971, 35]). Autobiography deals with the disparity between present and past, and the extent to which the present has been decided by the past. As Hipp writes, "It is this temporal distancing that in our eyes constitutes the distinctive character of memoirs, for it modifies the image that the subject has of her or his persona. The judgment one makes of one's past determines the architecture of the work by a constant coming and going between the present and the past" (1976, 31). Such distancing is lacking in Brantôme's portrait. He depicts Valois as frozen in time, thereby negating an epistemology that understands identity as the product of past personae, personae that no longer exist. Because Brantôme's *discours* does not take into account the transformations Valois has undergone, it does not represent her as *she* sees herself now: "Looking back at myself in your *discours*, I feel like old Madame de Randan did, when never having looked in her mirror since her husband died, she happened to glimpse her face in someone else's mirror and asked who it was" (1999, 70 [1971, 35]). Thus she sees Brantôme's representation as functioning in direct opposition to what Lacanians call the "mirror stage," the realization of selfhood that occurs when children first catch sight of themselves in a mirror. He undoes Valois's sense of who she is by substituting what *he* sees for the way she sees herself.

Until Valois's time, most representations of women had been written by men, and Brantôme's own prefatory remarks make it clear that his discourses on illustrious women are imbricated in a long line of texts that defined and explained the feminine to a primarily masculine readership. His immediate predecessor in this endeavor was Boccaccio, whom he mentions by name. Boccaccio wrote about women in *De mulieribus claris* (Concerning famous women). However, as Brantôme is probably aware, that text was itself a response to Plutarch's *Mulierum virtutes,* which was in turn a response to Aristotle's depiction of women in the *Poetics,* which saw them "as possessing the cardinal virtues only in a 'mode of subordination'" (Jordan 1987, 25). Brantôme's text differs from Boccaccio's because it does not discuss women of ancient times ("for history books are full of them, and I would only be scribbling on paper for nothing; for enough has been written about them, and even Boccaccio has written a fine book on this subject"); instead he will write about "our own women of France, and those of our time or our fathers', whom we have heard stories about" (1991, 9).

But although he departs from tradition by writing about contemporary women, he resembles Boccaccio in the way he subtly problematizes his eulogistic portrayal of illustrious women. As Jordan has argued, Boccaccio undermines his announced intention to defend women by ironizing his account of their "strength, wit and resourcefulness" (1987, 26). Likewise, Brantôme subverts his arguments against the Salic law by constructing Valois as an object of desire, whose principal function is not to govern men but to arouse their passion. If there is any doubt that this is the subtext of Brantôme's *discours,* it will be dispelled by a quick perusal of the companion volume, *Les Dames galantes*—a scandalous catalog of women's sexual exploits, in which "La Reine de Navarre" is mentioned more than once.[17]

By taking exception to the way Brantôme has depicted her, Valois is rejecting the eroticization of women that ultimately deprives them of power. Her memoirs, the first written by a woman, begin by resisting the representational practice that defines women as narcissists. If Brantôme had really wanted to write the biography of a woman who should have been queen, she implies, he should have contrasted the gifts bestowed on her by "nature" with the unhappy fate she had suffered at the hands of a jealous "fortune": "[Y]ou have taken pleasure in describing the excellence of a beauty, of which no vestige or witness remains outside your writings. If you had done so to represent the contrast between nature and fortune, you could not have chosen a finer subject" (1999, 70 [1971, 36). This interpretation of her destiny in terms of a classical topos functions as yet another strategy to de-feminize the textual persona; it shifts the focus of representation away from the enticements of the female body to resituate it in the neutral/universal territory of moral philosophy.

She then goes on to assert that she, and not Brantôme, is the only one who is truly qualified to undertake such a project: "As regards nature, having been its eye witness, you need no instruction. But as regards fortune, which you can only report second hand, . . . I think that you will be pleased to have the memoirs of the person who knows the most and has the greatest interest in describing the subject" (1999, 70–71 [1971, 36]). Thus Valois prepares the way for her construction of a textual self that will justify Brantôme's contention that she is "truly a queen." She will demonstrate, as he did not, that she is endowed with kinglike virtues and free of the flaws attributed to femininity. He took the unorthodox position that the Salic law was invalid. She will substantiate his arguments, furnishing proof that by "nature" she deserved to reign. This is, therefore, a radically subversive text. It encodes a challenge to Henri IV's reign, and to the Bourbon dynasty he founded.

Her refusal to be flattered by Brantôme's praise of her beauty, her firm declaration of authority, her insistence on the evolution of her identity, her vigorous remapping of theme and narrative—all combine in Valois's opening remarks to counter feminine stereotypes. Writing as a queen in exile, organizing her story around a universal theme that both explains and excuses her destiny, she daringly goes on to imitate not the dusty tomes of Monluc and his ilk, but the text that had set the standard for life-writing since antiquity—Plutarch's *Lives of Great Men*—recasting herself as a "great man" in the classical mold.[18]

It becomes immediately apparent that this is her intention by the way in which she foregrounds two characteristic features of Plutarchan biography: the use of childhood anecdotes to prefigure greatness and the claim that parallels can be drawn between the lives of heroes who have lived in different ages. Imitating Plutarch's emphasis on precocious words and deeds, she includes two anecdotes from her early girlhood and, manifestly referring to the *Lives,* adds that she could offer many more, all "as deserving of being written down" as those of Alexander the Great and Themistocles" (whom she seems to have confused with Alcibiades).[19] The first of these took place shortly before her father's untimely death. She offers it to prove her precocious ability to judge character (1999, 73–74 [1971, 37–38]). It tells how her father once took her on his knees and asked her which of two little boys she would choose to be her "servitor"—the future duc de Guise or the marquis de Beaupréau. She states that although Guise was the handsomer, she chose the marquis because he was a good boy, while the other, she quotes herself as saying, "becomes impatient if he doesn't find a way to hurt someone every day, and always wants to be the master." Then, in case she has not been fully understood, she adds that this was "a certain augury of what we have seen since," reminding her readers that the little boy she disliked because he was mean and bossy turned out to be a traitor.[20]

To the modern reader, however, this episode resonates not only with her ability to judge character but with the ambiguity of her position as a royal woman. On her father's lap she sits where he sits—in the position of authority. But this is also a position with highly erotic connotations. Both his question and the place where she sits underline the fact that her future will be shaped not by political acumen but by sexual liaisons. Intent on demonstrating the parallels between herself and Plutarch's heroes, however, Valois ignores these issues and underlines only the prophetic import of her words. She does not respond to her father's question as a woman but as a seer; nor does she acknowledge that this episode also foretells the role gender and sexuality would play in her destiny. Yet these concerns are nonetheless very present in the episode she describes.

The second anecdote (1999, 74–75 [1971, 38–39]) took place around the time of the Colloque de Poissy (September 1561) when Protestantism briefly "infected" the French court. Her brother, the future Henri III, was a temporary convert and tried to convert her too, throwing her prayer books into the fire and threatening her with a beating. She asserts that she, however, remained steadfast in her Catholic faith. "I replied to such threats, dissolving into tears—since at the age of seven or eight that I was then, I was very sensitive—that he could have me whipped, and that he could kill me if he wanted to; but that I would suffer anything they could do to me rather than see myself damned." This episode, like the other, demonstrates that she possessed the natural gifts of a leader, moral courage and determination; but it also unwittingly suggests a feminine stereotype: a girl at the mercy of a male bully. Despite her fortitude, she is powerless until her mother forces Henri to return to "the true, holy, and ancient religion of our fathers." Furthermore, as she tells the story, Catherine seems far more concerned about her son's errors than about her daughter's valor. Indeed, the anecdote functions more as a preview of her relationships with her mother and brother than as a demonstration of her constancy. Thus although she provides early examples of her leadership abilities, she also reveals her inferior status within the royal family.

The example of Plutarch may also have inspired her to include what modern autobiography theorists would call an epiphany or conversion experience—the discovery of a heretofore unknown aspect of the writer's personality, or the discovery of a goal or mission that gives meaning to existence.[21] Not surprisingly for the daughter of Catherine de Médicis, this rite of passage takes the form of a political initiation (1999, 81–87 [1971, 43–49]). It begins when her brother Henri asks her to become his ally. Telling her that it is time to put away childish pastimes, he informs her that he sees in her the qualities he seeks in an advocate. His proposal causes her to discover a new side of herself. "Such language was totally new to me," she writes, "for until then I had lived without any plan, thinking only of dancing or hunting, not even having the curiosity to dress in such a way as to appear beautiful, because I was not yet old enough to have such ambitions." What is amazing about this passage is the way a proposal that is supposedly non-gendered—to form an alliance with her brother—slips into the domain of gender construction, conflating political immaturity and the lack of sexual awareness (the desire to "appear beautiful"). And yet, the narrator is clearly trying to disavow "feminine" preoccupations here and, as always, to identify herself with a "great man": "I was on the verge of saying, as Moses did when he saw God in the burning bush, 'Who am I?'" The parallel between herself and the founder of occidental monotheism is both ludicrous and pathetic; yet in its very ineptness, it dramatizes the fact that she assimilates this moment to an epiphany. "Nonetheless discovering within myself what I had not thought was there, powers called up by the object of his words, which until then I had not known, . . . coming to myself after my first surprise, these words pleased me, and it seemed to me that in an instant I was transformed, and that I became something more than I had been until then. So much so that I began to have confidence in myself."

Her brother's proposal was in fact an offer she could not refuse. In a milieu where personal relations were the unique path to power, her only hope lay in being on good terms with the heir to the throne and, even more important, the power behind that throne—her mother. This alliance could give her a status so far denied her. When her mother says to her, "It will be a great pleasure to speak to you *as if you were your brother* [emphasis mine]," Valois leaves no doubt as to what these words meant: "All the happiness I had ever known until then was only a shadow compared to this."

This was a threshold that marked her passage from child to adult; but it did not lead her where she wanted to go. Had she been a boy, her discovery of these aspirations would have launched her political career. Since she was a girl, however, it turned out to have just the opposite effect. Henri soon realized that his sister was becoming a young woman and immedi-

ately saw that as a threat to his power. He tells her mother that she is growing beautiful and has attracted the duc de Guise's attention, instructing
Catherine to give her no further information: "[H]e feared that if I should
come to feel affection for him, I would reveal everything she said to him;
that she well knew how ambitious that family was, and how they had always been at odds with ours." The author never draws an explicit connection between her gender and her thwarted ambitions. Instead, she interprets
what happened to her in terms of the grand theme she has chosen to univer-
salize her story: "Young and inexperienced as I was, I was not suspicious
of this prosperity . . . but envious fortune, who cannot bear to see happiness
endure, was preparing for me vexations as great as the pleasure I antici-
pated." Yet it is clearly not "envious fortune" but puberty that put an end to
her political ambitions.

Her reaction to Henri's volte-face underscores what Caroline Heilbrun
has identified as a common thread in women's life stories—their silent
rage.[22] When no one believed her protestations of innocence and her mother
refused to have anything more to do with her, Valois writes, she fell ill and
nearly died.[23] "I, who had been commanded to keep my mouth shut, only
answered his [her brother's] hypocritical questions with sighs, as Burrhus
had Nero, when he was dying of the poison that tyrant had given him."
Only years later, through the act of recording her anger, did she find a way
to break out of this impotent silence.

Valois's coming-of-age story has two phases: First, she discovers something about herself that she didn't know before—the desire and ability to
play a significant role at court. Then she learns that puberty and the concomitant threat of feminine sexuality have made it impossible for her to
fulfill that desire. Although she focuses exclusively on her awakening to a
new kind of selfhood, the subtext of the story is that once she grew up, she
was seen as a stereotypical woman, a person who would put love before
loyalty. It is evident that her status within the royal family was determined
by the fact that she was a female. A heroic future did not lie in store for the
sister of four brothers, all in direct line for the throne. Her mother's lack of
sympathy reflects this, for as a good politician Catherine thought like a
man and knew it was a man's world. What this seemingly Plutarchan anecdote proves, therefore, is that Valois's gender robbed her of the right to
become the person she was meant to be. She does not, however, come to
terms with this fact. Instead she draws yet another parallel between herself
and a Plutarchan hero—Burrhus.

After this account of her failed attempt to gain a foothold in the political arena, it becomes increasingly clear that the Plutarchan model is not
well suited to the story she is telling. If in the first pages she succeeded in

projecting herself as resolute and perceptive, from this point on she seems increasingly ruled by others. In describing the negotiations leading up to her marriage, she assigns to herself the role of dutiful daughter. When Catherine asks if she is willing to marry her cousin Henri de Navarre, she replies that she has no wish or will but hers; she only begs her to remember that she is "strongly Catholic" (1999, 89 [1971, 51]).[24] Ignoring this, Catherine joins her daughter to the Protestant chief.

This marriage effectively put an end to Valois's hope of playing a significant role in history. As a daughter who could not inherit the crown, she had not been taken seriously. As the Catholic wife of a Protestant leader, she became an outsider in both camps. The ambivalence of her position leads to a shift in her self-image that is mirrored in the way she writes about herself at her wedding. In her letter to Brantôme, she took issue with his exaggerated emphasis on her beauty, yet here she expresses the wish that he could describe how she looked on that historic occasion. Indeed, in this passage she reduces herself to the opulently garbed mannequin he eulogized. She emphasizes how she was clothed in "royal garb with the crown and cape of spotted ermine that is worn in front of the body, all shining with the crown jewels and the great blue mantle four yards long carried by three princesses" (1999, 91 [1971, 52]). Her purpose, of course, is to underscore the symbolic significance of these regal trappings, which had conferred on her the title of queen. Yet, it is evident, as it was in Brantôme's *discours,* that this apparel conferred only the illusion of power.

The extent of her marginalization following her marriage becomes immediately apparent in her celebrated account of the St. Bartholemew's massacres. Her report is that of an ignorant, confused bystander, who had no foreknowledge of what was to take place and no power to intervene in the gruesome events she witnessed. She describes her terror and bewilderment as she grew increasingly aware that something ominous was about to happen. Her mother commands her to go to her room lest she reveal their plans to the Protestants; her sister bursts into tears as she leaves, but does not dare to warn her. She goes to bed "absolutely bewildered and terrified, unable to imagine what I had to fear" (1999, 98 [1971, 57]). In the middle of the night, a crowd of her husband's allies enter the bedroom to discuss the assassination of the Protestant leader Coligny. At dawn, her privacy is again invaded by a wounded man pursued by four archers. For a moment, she writes, she didn't know whether she was about to be sexually assaulted or shot. Seeking refuge in her sister's quarters, she is narrowly missed by a halberd, while desperate Huguenots beg her to intercede for them.

In the pages that follow, this seems to be a text in search of a subject. This impression is undoubtedly exacerbated by the sense that the writer does not dare to speak frankly of her relations with her husband, who is now her jailer. But it is also due to her own crisis of identity, her uncertainty about who she is and where she belongs after her marriage. Although she provides fascinating accounts of cloak-and-dagger intrigue in the corridors of the Louvre, the reader is never sure whose side she is on or what her function is in her story. Is she merely a chronicler of palace life or is she a significant participant in the exciting events she describes? Likewise, it is difficult to discern in her actions a coherent and consistent line of conduct. At times she depicts herself as nobly disinterested—as when, for instance, she refuses to divorce her Protestant husband because she suspects that his enemies want to use this as a pretext to kill him. A little later, however, she secretly informs the king that her husband and younger brother François are about to defect to the Huguenots. Then after their arrest, she again switches sides and defends Navarre, composing a strongly worded *Mémoire justificatif* that testifies to her powers of argumentation.[25] Still later she agrees to disguise Henri and François as women and spirit them out of the palace. Yet even as she tells how she aided and abetted the rebels, she asserts her devotion to her brother King Charles IX. The result is a fragmented narrative in which there is no coherent sense of identity. Although she clearly wants to tell about these events as if she had played a principal role, it is evident that she was only peripherally involved. Men were the real actors.

She has no power to decide her own movements and little influence on those around her. At one point, she is locked in her room to prevent her from communicating with her husband and brother, both of whom have managed to escape, the former without even informing her of his departure. After having been given to Henri de Navarre in marriage, Valois becomes in effect a hostage to his return. It is true that in an absolute monarchy, everyone's freedom is severely limited, but while the men she supports are able to command their own destinies, managing spectacular escapes and hatching treasonous plots, such activities never seem to be an option for her. She does not even have the right to join the husband she was forced to marry. She must wait many months before the king gives her permission to meet him in the south of France; and then she must travel in her mother's company. She does not, however, see herself as the victim of gender politics. Instead, she persistently assigns blame to jealous "fortune," refusing to recognize the extent to which for her biology was destiny.

As she continues to insist on a cosmic explanation of her difficulties, there is a constant disparity between what happens to her and the interpretation she attaches to it. What is more, in her eagerness to bestow heroic significance on her life, she transforms the personal into the portentous. A

striking example is her account of her meeting with Henri III after his ac-
cession to the throne. A long peroration on premonitions, including yet
another Plutarchan allusion, this one to Brutus's dream, leads into a digression on how she, like her mother, was endowed with second sight; but the
real point here is that when she came face to face with the new king, she
was seized with violent chills and trembling, hardly an earth-shattering
event. Just as she overdramatizes this meeting, she also inflates the slender
part she played in history. At one point she even alters the chronology of
events to make it appear that her presence was essential to the signing of
the "Paix de Monsieur."[26] She likewise devotes many pages to describing
one of the few occasions on which she was allowed to carry out an official
mission: her trip to Flanders, where she represented her brother François in
his bid for Flemish support.[27]

Despite her initial desire to represent herself as a Plutarchan hero, however, she cannot conceal the facts of her existence. Whereas for a man like
Monluc the private and the public merged in a life of soldiering, for a woman
the public was the peripheral. Valois's high birth *seemed* to make her an
exception to this rule, but in fact for her, as for most noblewomen of her
time, it did not. As Brantôme's *discours* made plain, she was famous not
for her role in history but for her feminine charms. And these had already
given rise to rumors of lascivious conduct. In order to assimilate herself to
a "great man," therefore, she must represent herself as not only ungendered
but unsexual. To those who know nothing of her beyond the scandalous
legend of "La Reine Margot," it comes as a surprise that her memoirs make
almost no mention of her love life. "This most amorous of women [cette
grande amoureuse] is one of most chaste writers of the sixteenth century,"
affirms Mariéjol; "she never wished to express anything but her sentiments,
with so great a sense of decency, and such distance from all that is not
noble, delicate, incorporeal, that in a manner of speaking, she deserves to
be regarded as the first in time of the *précieuses*" (1970, 159).[28] The only
time she ever mentions her conjugal relations with Henri is to report that
when her mother urged her to claim that Henri was "not a man" so as to
annul their marriage, she "begged her to believe that I was not well informed on such matters . . . never having been with any man but him; but
that in any event, since she had given me to him, I preferred to stay with
him" (1999, 100–101 [1971, 59]). She does, however, insist that her brother
Henri III's repeated attempts to catch her in *flagrant délit* were always
unsuccessful. And to make doubly sure that the reader believes her, she
quotes her mother's reaction: "In my day, we spoke freely to everyone, and
all the honest folk . . . were habitually in the bedroom with Madame
Marguerite your aunt, and me; and no one found it strange, as in fact there

was no reason to" (1999, 117–18 [1971, 73]). But although the desire to refute the vicious gossip about her certainly played a part in these assertions, in a larger sense the excising of desire from the record of her life was also a way of erasing the femininity that stood in her way both historically and textually.

For the same reason, she depicts her relationship to her husband as the frank camaraderie of siblings, a representation that also eliminates, of course, any hint of carnality.[29] She wants to come across as disinterested and loyal, motivated only by the male virtue of commitment to duty. She tells of devotedly nursing him through illnesses, some of which, she claims, were brought on by *his* sexual excesses. She insists, however, that his extramarital romances did not upset her, since she was always his trusted confidante: "[H]e had always spoken to me as openly as to a sister," she writes, "well knowing that I was in no way jealous, and desired only his contentment" (1999, 115 [1971, 71]). She is not able to cover over with noble attitudes, however, the fact that she remained all her life in a subservient and precarious position vis-à-vis Henri de Navarre.

Nor can the reader be oblivious to the fact that these claims may not be entirely disinterested, since at the time she wrote, she was hoping that he would relent and allow her to leave Usson. Bauschatz believes that she wrote her memoirs to convince Henri IV of her devotion and loyalty. It is not impossible that she also hoped they would dispose him to leniency. Thus she almost always finds reasons to excuse him, even when the facts she provides show that he treated her badly. For example, when she relates that he once peremptorily dismissed her favorite lady-in-waiting, she excuses him by saying that he was only obeying the king's orders. She also admits that breaking off relations with him after this incident was not a wise move: "I remained so offended by this insult, coming after so many others, that I was unable to resist the just resentment I felt, which robbed me of prudence and abandoned me to trouble" (1999, 123 [1971, 78]). Righteous indignation was a luxury she could not afford. Although Henri escaped from the Louvre without informing her of his departure, when he wrote asking her to keep him informed of happenings at court she complied with alacrity. She asserts that she placed her duty to him above both religious convictions and family ties. Seeking permission to join him in Gascony, she says to the king, "I was not married for pleasure or of my own volition, but by that of King Charles my brother, and of my mother the queen, and his; and since they gave me to him, they could not prevent me from sharing his fortunes" (1999, 139 [1971, 94]). Later when the Huguenots decided to go to war with the Catholics, she again put his interests first. "From the very beginning of the war, seeing that my husband the king

honored me with his friendship, I was bound not to abandon him, and resolved to share his fortunes; not without extreme regret, for I saw that the
causes of this war were such that I could not wish for the victory of either
side" (1999, 202 [1971, 158]).

Yet the very fact that she insists so often on her unfailing dedication to
Henri's best interests underlines the fact of her vulnerability. The young
princess who dreamed of becoming another Moses or Alexander now
equated success with staying in her husband's good graces, dreading not
his infidelity but his displeasure. Just as she feared their estrangement, their
harmonious moments filled her with joy. She looks back with nostalgia on
the years they spent together in his southern kingdom: "[T]his happiness
endured for the space of four or five years when I was in Gascony with
him; spending the greater part of our time there in Nerac, where our court
was so fine and agreeable that we did not envy the one in France" (1999,
199 [1971, 155]).[30] Even when she seems at her most abject, her dependence on Henri is political, not emotional. She wants his friendship because with it she can assume her rightful place as his queen—furthering his
interests, counseling him wisely, and presiding over his court. In fact, the
virtues she attributes to herself as his wife are those more commonly associated with masculinity: unselfishness, high-mindedness, loyalty.[31] It is true
that Valois hardly draws a flattering portrait of the *vert galant*. She writes
that in the early days of their marriage, he conducted himself like a lovesick
puppy, childishly dependent on her for sympathy and advice, easily taken
in by jealous mistresses, and fainting from sexual exhaustion. Of the two
spouses, it is she who emerges as sensible and cool.[32]

This portrayal of herself as dispassionate and unsexual is not unrelated
to another trope she introduces in an effort to counterbalance her political
impotence—stoic resignation to the lot fortune has dealt her. Relating how
reading and meditation taught her to overcome loneliness and boredom
when she was held captive in the Louvre, she writes, "I received these two
benefits from the sadness and loneliness of my first captivity, to take pleasure in study and to give myself to religious devotions, although due to the
vanity and magnificence of my happy fortune, I had never tasted them
previously" (1999, 134 [1971, 90]). When her brother at last allowed her to
leave her room, she declares that she bore him no grudge, "having devoted
my time during my captivity to the pleasures of reading, which I was beginning to enjoy, owing not to fortune but to divine Providence, for it thus
began to provide a good remedy for the troubles that awaited me in the
future" (1999, 133 [1971, 89]).[33]

This philosophical acceptance of adversity contrasts markedly with
the rebellious activism of her husband and her brother François during the

period in question. However, it would be wrong to see it as passive, or as inconsistent with her proud view of herself. As Bauschatz comments, "While reading appears to place women in a passive, submissive relationship to the largely male 'corpus' of literature, writing about that reading and about other forms of intimate experience enabled Valois to achieve control over those areas of her life that were not ruled by her brothers and her husband. Deriving pleasure from reading . . . thus became for Marguerite de Valois a political, although private, act" (1988, 44–45). There can be little doubt that the practices of reading and reflection eventually prompted her to embark on the highly unpassive act of writing her memoirs. And, what is more, her familiarity with what Bauschatz terms the male corpus influenced her to impose the Plutarchan concept of *bios* on her life.

Eager to prove that by "nature" she had possessed the qualities associated with greatness, she tried to represent herself as superior to other women. This in turn caused her to erase her sexuality from her text, a move rendered all the more necessary by the rumors of wantonness that were circulating about her. Yet the very absence of desire underlines its presence. From the moment when she describes how her father took her on his knee, the threat of both gender and sexuality hangs over Valois's story. The woman who represents herself as not a woman in order to represent herself as a hero cannot conceal the fact that her life did not fit into the heroic mold. The disparities, tensions, and paradoxes of these memoirs are, in the last analysis, the sign of her failure to come to terms with who she was. But they are also the sign of her resistance to her marginalization. Even as she recalls the blows dealt her by "envious fortune," she portrays herself as strong-willed, courageous, and nobler than the men around her.

Valois's life did not resemble that of a "great man," but her effort to apply Plutarch's concept of *bios* to her life produced a text that went far beyond the memoirs of earlier times in inscribing an individualized sense of self. Reinventing herself on the classical model led her to reflect on her past, to seek meaning beneath the surface of events, and to clarify how they had shaped her existence. In her determination to represent herself as a great man, therefore, she employed introspective and interpretative strategies that moved life-writing away from the historical chronicle and toward autobiography.

3

Mademoiselle de Montpensier

LIFE

Like Marguerite de Valois, Montpensier's place in the royal family was the source of her identity, while the political benefits of her illustrious lineage were denied her by her gender. Anne Marie Louise d'Orléans, duchesse de Montpensier—Mademoiselle, or "La Grande Mademoiselle" as she was commonly called—was the granddaughter of Henri IV and his second wife, Marie de Médicis, the daughter of Louis XIII's brother, Gaston d'Orleans, and the first cousin of Louis XIV. Louis XIII's inability to produce an heir had caused many to look to Gaston for leadership. Had Mademoiselle been a boy, the sickly, childless king might have been forced to abdicate in his brother's favor, or he might have made Gaston's son his heir and abandoned his halfhearted efforts to beget a son. Thus Montpensier's fate, like that of Valois, was determined by the Salic law.

Mademoiselle's mother, Marie de Bourbon-Montpensier, died a few days after she was born (29 May 1627), leaving her an immense fortune: 400,000 pounds of annual revenue, deriving from the principalities of Dombes and La Roche-sur-Yon, plus the duchies of Montpensier, Châtellerault, and Saint-Fargeau, as well as innumerable marquisats, counties, viscounties, and baronies. Although her fortune and birth seemingly made her the most marriageable woman in France, in actual fact they worked against her "establishment," for her Bourbon relatives were loath to see her vast holdings pass to another French family, let alone to a foreign power. Match after match failed to materialize, and Montpensier found herself scandalously unmarried at twenty-five, the age of legal majority for women.

A new phase of her existence began in 1652 when her father's long career as a conspirator culminated in the Fronde des Princes, in which he and other princes of the blood attempted to wrest control from the prime minister, Cardinal Mazarin. In Holy Week the population of Orléans refused to surrender to the royal army and begged their duke to come to the rescue. Gaston, who had a talent for deserting causes in time of need, asked Montpensier to go in his stead. She accepted with alacrity. There she mounted the walls and triumphantly entered the besieged city, securing it for her father's forces. Later, when Condé's troops were retreating during the battle of the Porte Saint-Antoine, she ordered the canons of the Bastille to fire on the king's army. However, when the Frondeurs' cause was lost and she was obliged to leave Paris, Gaston refused to assist her. She was forced to take refuge in the Burgundian town of Saint Fargeau, where she had inherited a dilapidated castle from her mother.

This enforced retreat led to a period of intellectual growth. She discovered the joys of reading. She undertook the restoration of the château. She did genealogical research on her maternal forebears and consolidated her fortune. She also completed the pseudomemoirs of her ex-friend Madame de Fouquesolles and had them printed secretly in the castle. Encouraged by her overseer, Préfontaine, to take charge of her financial affairs, she became aware that her father had misappropriated large amounts of her fortune and handed over her family's ancestral estate at Champigny to Richelieu in return for a pardon. Still smarting from his rebuffs, she sued him for restoration of what was rightfully hers. A bitter legal battle ensued, during which her father exercised his paternal prerogative and ordered Préfontaine to leave her service. The dispute dragged on for several years, and although she was unable to recover everything he had pilfered from her, she did succeed in having Champigny returned. Only when she had reluctantly made peace with Gaston was she allowed, however, to return to court.

There she was again the object of matrimonial speculations, but again they did not materialize. The king pressured her to marry the king of Portugal, but knowing the latter to be an imbecile with homicidal tendencies, she adamantly refused, for which she was again forced briefly into exile. In 1671, she suddenly decided to take matters into her own hands. Her choice was the courtier Lauzun, and when she had coyly informed him of her intentions, she requested the king's permission to marry him. Louis at first agreed, but was forced to withdraw his permission at the insistence of the royal family and the representatives of foreign governments. She was devastated. Lauzun was eventually imprisoned in Pignerols on the Swiss border; and she spent the next ten years trying to negotiate his release. Louis agreed to free him only when she deeded most of her holdings to the duc du Maine, the king's illegitimate son by Madame de Montespan. There is some evidence that she and Lauzun were married clandestinely after his release, but he soon proved to be both unfaithful and ungrateful for her sacrifices.

Eventually, she became exasperated and ordered him out of her sight. She refused to see him again even on her deathbed. She died of uremic poisoning in 1693. What was left of her fortune she bequeathed to Louis's younger brother, Philippe d'Orléans ("Monsieur"). Before she was finally laid to rest, she managed to create one last scandal. The urn containing her entrails exploded during the wake, causing those present to rush out of the room gasping for air.

PUBLICATION HISTORY:
MÉMOIRES DE MADEMOISELLE DE MONTPENSIER

Mademoiselle de Montpensier was a prolific writer. In addition to her *Mémoires,* which cover nearly a thousand printed pages, she was the author of a pseudomemoir entitled *Histoire de Jeanne Lambert d'Herbigny, marquise de Fouquesolles,* as well as several other works of fiction, many of the *portraits* in the collection that bears her name, and several religious meditations. She composed her memoirs in three installments, each of which was the response to an emotional crisis in which she saw herself as the aggrieved party. Part 1 was begun during her exile in Saint-Fargeau, when she was still smarting from her father's refusal to help her and she had just learned that he had misappropriated her inheritance. Covering the period 1627 to 1659, it tells of her childhood and adolescence, the numerous attempts to arrange her marriage, her dramatic participation in the Fronde, and the years spent in exile. She broke it off in 1660, soon after her return to court and her reconciliation with her father. Part 2 was begun on 18 August 1677. Although she recounts events going back to May 1659, at which part 1 ended (including a fascinating account of the royal wedding in Saint-Jean de Luz), her real objective was to narrate her aborted attempt to marry Lauzun. She probably stopped writing this second installment around 1680, after having chronicled events through April 1676. Part 3 is much shorter and less precise than the other two. It was probably composed in 1688 or 1689 and covers the interval between 1676 and 1686. It tells of her negotiations for Lauzun's release and their subsequent estrangement. She seems to have been stirred to continue her memoirs by her outrage at Lauzun's return to royal favor following his daring rescue of the English queen in 1688.

Describing how she embarked on her project, Montpensier states that she quickly set down most of her experiences before and during the Fronde, handing the manuscript over to Préfontaine, who recopied it as she went along. This was a common practice. Sometimes aristocrats even had entire texts written to order for them, a notable example being her own father, Gaston, whose memoirs were composed in toto by his secretary, Goulas. Préfontaine and his successors had to decipher Montpensier's nearly illegible handwriting and correct her atrocious spelling, but they also made drastic stylistic revisions and even inserted and deleted portions of text. Especially in the later sections of the work, there are significant disparities between the so-called Harlay copy and the autograph manuscript. In parts 2 and 3, the copyists rewrote entire passages in a way that alters their meaning. By the second half of part 2, Chéruel, who edited the autograph manuscript, was forced to abandon the practice of annotating variants because they were found in every line. A dramatic example of divergences is the passage in which the author discusses her decision to marry Lauzun.[1]

Montpensier seems to have considered her secretary's copy the definitive version. Internal evidence suggests that she used it to refresh her memory when she returned to the project.[2] Furthermore, she entrusted it to her executor, le président de Harlay, whose name is now attached to it. The Bibliothèque Nationale owns several other manuscript copies based on this version, which she probably had made also. One of these supposedly belonged to the duc du Maine, the illegitimate son of Louis XIV to whom she was forced to deed her property.[3] However, the autograph manuscript, minus the first eighty pages, also survived.[4] Thus readers must choose between the "corrected" copy preferred by the author and the autograph manuscript she rejected but mysteriously preserved.[5] The choice reflects the difference between seventeenth-century aristocratic attitudes toward authorship and postromantic scholarly concerns.

The existence of two versions of a woman's text also raises gender issues. It is important to remember that even though all aristocrats relied on their secretaries, women aristocrats were generally far less able to write correctly than their male counterparts. Montpensier's father, Gaston, was an erudite aesthete; and her cousin, Le Grand Condé, had been schooled by the Jesuits. She, on the other hand, was barely literate. She had never learned penmanship or the rules of orthography (that g before a cannot be soft, for instance). In his reply to her letter announcing the capture of Orléans, her father reprimanded her for writing so illegibly and commanded her never again to send him a letter in her own hand.

The disparities between the autograph manuscript and the Harlay copy also reflect the gendered differences between written and spoken language in Montpensier's time.[6] As she herself wrote, "[I]t would seem that I should want to show off my eloquence, and that is what I aspire to the least, but only to say things simply, as I know them, and the most intelligibly that I possibly can" (1985, 1:129).[7] Thus it appears that the original manuscript reflects the feminocentric, conversational style of the salons, whereas the Harlay version incorporates the "educated" manner favored by "men of letters." Verdier points out that in the Harlay version, "Words that are too concrete are replaced with more conventionalized expressions; the logical ruptures are filled in and the conjunctions are varied to make her staccato rhythm more flowing and polished. . . . One of her most striking stylistic traits is corrected, one which grows more pronounced with the passage of time—her use of direct discourse. Speech is often transposed into indirect discourse, narrativized, rendered more distant, the voices smothered" (1983, 18–19).

In her day, the conversational style favored by Montpensier was seen as inferior by "men of letters," a perception that has continued to influence judgments of her text. Sainte-Beuve would later criticize her because she did not conform to "literary" norms. In his review of the Chéruel edition he wrote, "[H]er style is restored here in all the purity of its natural incorrectness" (1851, 3:525). Even Garapon, who has devoted so much scholarly effort to her memoirs, argues that her "unified and sober prose" owed much to Segrais's influence, only to add illogically that Segrais could not have collaborated with her, given her "frequently incorrect expressions" and "awkward turns of phrase" (1989a, 32). Furthermore, he condescendingly defines her "place" in the literary pantheon as that of "a woman memoirist, certainly without pretensions, but of an irreplaceable psychological and documentary value" (261).

The politically subversive nature of these memoirs prevented their publication until 1718, when a first printing was interrupted and confiscated.[8] An edition based on the Harlay copy appeared in 1728. It enjoyed great popularity, and was republished frequently thereafter. Both Petitot and Michaud and Poujoulat reprinted it in their collections of early French memoirs. However, an edition of the autograph manuscript did not appear until the middle of the nineteenth century, when it was transcribed by Chéruel. So far as I can determine, no one has yet had the courage to subject his work to extensive verification. My spot checks reveal his transcription to be amazingly faithful, since in the original sometimes only one or two words on each page can be deciphered without difficulty. Although he did not reproduce Montpensier's orthography, which was illiterate even by seventeenth-century standards, he did make a valiant attempt to indicate discrepancies between the two versions and to provide historical and biographical information.[9] His edition remains the only acceptable scholarly tool. The 1985 reprinting makes it available to present-day readers, but unfortunately does not include Chéruel's notes or variants.

THE MISFORTUNES OF A WOMAN'S HOUSE

Half a century after Marguerite de Valois wrote her memoirs, her ex-husband's granddaughter was inspired to undertake a similar project. "I had read the memoirs of Queen Marguerite," she wrote, "and that, added to the insistence of the comtesse de Fiesque, Madame de Frontenac, and her husband that I should write my memoirs, convinced me to begin these" (Montpensier 1985, 1:299). There is little evidence, however, that Montpensier used Valois's text as a model. A true daughter of the Renaissance, the queen of Navarre had sought a way to tell her story in the literature of antiquity. Perhaps less well read, or at least less focused on classical tropes, Montpensier preferred to imitate her French predecessors, the noblemen who had written to pass down a record of their deeds to their descendants. Arrogantly conscious that the blood of Henri IV flowed in her veins, the heroine of the Fronde was determined to do likewise. She too would boast of military exploits. This would be the story of *her* house, the family romance of which *she* was the *hero*. It was in such a spirit that La Grande Mademoiselle began her memoirs.

However, early French memoirs were a genre written by fathers for sons.[10] They implicitly excluded women as both writers and readers. She cannot write for her descendants, for she has none (since she remains unmarried). Indeed, her incipit foregrounds her rootlessness. She has taken up her pen not to create a dynastic legacy but at the urging of "some people I love." All she can promise is that what she writes "will not be boring" (1:21), a statement that would seem to situate her project in the realm of pleasure rather than history. In fact, in the watershed passage telling how she began to write her memoirs at Saint-Fargeau, she represents herself as "a person who is never bored, always finding something to do, and even distracting myself with reveries." Her project has begun as a diversion after her exile from court life.

But although both this passage and her prefatory remarks seem to define her text as a pleasurable pastime, it becomes clear that this is not her only objective. Like the memoirists of earlier times, she is in fact calling on her readers to render judgment in her favor, to weigh what she has done against the compensation she has received. There is, however, a major difference between her and them: she is not seeking to perpetuate the patriarchal legacy; she is seeking to discredit her father's word and affirm her maternal inheritance. And in so doing she represents herself as a self-reliant woman in charge of her own destiny and no longer in need of a husband to give meaning to her existence.

When she began her memoirs, Montpensier was only in her mid-twenties, an extraordinarily young age to embark on an autobiographical project. Her heroism during the Fronde and the bitterness that followed it led her, however, to painful realizations about the father she had idolized as a child. He had thwarted her dreams of a brilliant marriage and refused to recognize the heroic deeds that had led to her exile. She starts her story, therefore, with a lament for the dead mother who would have done what her father did not do: arrange her "establishment": "The beginning of my house's misfortune came soon after my birth, since it was followed by the death of my mother. The great wealth that my mother left me when she died, and of which I am the only heir, should have, in most people's opinion, consoled me for her loss. But for my part, as I realize today what an advantage her care would have been in my upbringing, and her credit, joined to her tenderness, in my establishment, I cannot regret her loss enough" (1:22).

Despite her exclusion from masculine discourse, she insists on defining these memoirs as the story of her *house:* "Soon after her death, my house[hold] was formed, and I was given more attendants than any daughter of France had ever had" (1:22). This, however, is a house that exists outside the patriarchal order. Founded by a woman's fortune, called by a woman's name, the house of Montpensier was not a house in the accepted sense of the term, for it had neither the past nor the future of a lineage. Because she was an anomalous unmarried woman, Mademoiselle de Montpensier had no predefined place in the social order, which ranked women according to the men they married. Consequently, the word *maison* (house) as she uses it here takes on a different sense. It means nothing more than an *équipage*—a vast assembly of servants. What should have been a story of "good fortune" transmitted by blood has become a *malheur.*

When she triumphantly secured Orléans for Gaston's forces, Montpensier had every reason to believe she had finally won a place in the roster of family heroes. "Everyone says that your action is worthy of the granddaughter of Henry the Great [Henri IV]," her father wrote. Her heroism had produced no permanent change, however, in their relationship. In fact, when the cause had been lost and the Frondeurs were banished from court, Gaston had actually mocked her: "You were so happy to play the heroine and to be told that you had twice saved our party; so whatever happens to you, the memory of all the praise you received should console you" (1:274).

At the time she composed part 1, therefore, she had just passed through a crisis of identity. She had lived through events that should have made her permanently esteemed by the paternal line, only to come face to face with the truth that as a daughter, she could never win her father's respect. "Monsieur never honored me with his confidence. This confession is hard for me to make, more for his sake than for mine, for whoever knows me will judge that I certainly deserve it, and those who will read these memoirs and only know me by them will easily judge that I deserved that honor" (1:216).

Like Valois, Montpensier recalls childhood experiences, a practice that was a hallmark of early Frenchwomen's memoirs. Garapon sees in these recollections her nostalgia for "a lost paradise" (1989a, 179); but such a reading misses the polemical objectives that underlay her project. The constant theme of these pages is her steadfast and ardent devotion to the fickle father who betrayed her, as he did all those who supported him. She portrays herself as a lonely little princess, endlessly waiting for him to return from banishment and forced to defend his treasonous activities to hostile courtiers, as well as to herself. Given the legal battles in which they were embroiled at the time she was writing, there is bitter irony in her memories of how she rejoiced at his brief visits, of her thrill at picking him out of a group of officers, of the "pygmy dance" he organized in her honor, of chasing him up and down the grand staircase at Chambord and having him tuck her into bed at Blois. With the wisdom of hindsight, she also contrasts the delusions of grandeur inculcated in her by fawning servants with what she has since learned about the realities of her situation: "It often happens that children who are respected, and to whom people are always talking about their high birth and their great wealth, are taken in by feelings of false glory" (1:23).

She recalls how she first came to suspect Gaston's true nature when she incredulously watched him enjoy his dinner to the sound of twenty-four royal violins, knowing full well that he had paid for his freedom with the lives of his fellow conspirators, Cinq Mars and de Thou. "I confess that I couldn't see him without thinking of them," she writes, "and that in my joy I felt that his gave me pain" (1:50). Her memories of a childhood visit to Champigny, the Montpensier estate he deeded to Richelieu, are also infused with resentment toward him and a newfound allegiance to her maternal roots. She emphasizes how she prayed fervently for her ancestors, how the local populace lamented the change in ownership, praised her grandfather's goodness, and "testified by their tears and all possible affectionate demonstrations their sorrow at their loss" (1,31).[11]

The account of her fruitless search for a husband, which dominates the early sections of part 1, functions as an indictment of her father, as well as of Mazarin and the *régente*.[12] She describes how her disillusionment increased and her satisfaction with her high birth gave way to anger and frustration as she realized that they had no intention of arranging the illustrious marriage to which she was entitled. Philip IV of Spain and the emperor of Austria were held out to her as tantalizing prospects, but no concrete overtures were ever made. When she learned this, she was overwhelmed with impotent indignation: "I could not help growing more and more angry at the court, and it was a resentment that was all the more painful to bear because I had no way to express it" (1:88). There is a decided similarity between this passage and Valois's description of her silent wrath when her brother rejected her as an ally. In both passages, rage becomes an initiatory threshold on which the writers suddenly confront the realities of their disenfranchisement.

And like Valois, Montpensier traces the transition from innocence to maturity as she describes her gradual awakening to the importance of being "established." When Richelieu vetoed Anne d'Autriche's promise that she would marry the infant Louis XIV, she was not particularly upset: "I was not anxious about getting married. I was much less interested in such projects than I was in dancing and the other diversions of the winter season" (1:41). But a few years later, she was distraught at the death of a potential husband, the régente's brother Ferdinand, "because it was the most agreeable establishment in the world for me" (1:49). At this point, she had already grasped what marriage signified for a woman like her. Aside from Ferdinand's royal birth, she was drawn by "the beauty of the country, its proximity to this one, and the style of life there, which is not too different from that in France" (1:49). At fifteen she knew precisely what the traffic in women exacted of a princess—the loss of home, friends, and traditions, and she sought, above all, ways to minimize these costs. "As regards his personal qualities," she admits, "although I esteemed him greatly, they were what I thought about the least" (1:49).

In describing her growing desire to be "established," she represents herself less as a woman with a body than as the embodiment of a social position. The personal and the physical are eclipsed by her desire to make the royal marriage that is her birthright. Her physical charms matter only to the extent that they reflect this essential aspect of her identity. Nowhere is this more evident than in her account of a ball at the Palais-Royal, where she recalls how she sat on a throne at one end of the theater: "No one missed the chance to tell me that I had never appeared less out of place than on that throne, and that since my birth gave me the right to it, when I had one of my own, where I could remain longer than at a ball, I would be still more at ease" (1:81). It is not the male gaze that interests her but the gaze that sees her enthroned.

By the time she started to write her memoirs, however, Montpensier had begun to appreciate her single status. She insists that she had no patience with romantic notions. When someone suggested she could marry Condé if his wife died, she replied scathingly that while she admired his heroism, she had no intention of doing so: "[I]f you believe that I would marry like the maidens in the stories, and that he will come like Amadis to seek me on a palfrey, striking down all the obstacles he meets on his path; and that I, for my part, will mount another palfrey, like Madame Oriane, I assure you that I am not the type to do such things, and that I consider myself very offended by those who hold such an opinion of me" (1:305). Later, describing how one of her ladies in waiting went into hysterics when her husband arrived unexpectedly, she rejoiced that she had avoided getting into such a fix: "I had always had a great aversion to love, even when it was legitimate, so much did that passion seem to me unworthy of a noble soul!" (1:308).

Garapon believes that these sentiments were attempts to console herself for the fact that marriage was an impossibility while she was out of favor at court. But one should remember that opposition to marriage was in the air, popularized by the *précieuses,* who valued women's independence and regarded marriage as a form of slavery. The letters she exchanged with Madame de Motteville, referred to in chapter 1, show that Montpensier espoused this point of view, and she continued to hold it after her return to court. It is also true that when she was writing part 1 of her memoirs, she had less to gain from marriage than formerly. Having reached her majority at twenty-five, she had come into legal possession of her inheritance. She was now in charge of her own affairs and head of a house(hold) in fact as well as in name. Undoubtedly her aversion to marriage was also related to her heroic adventures during the Fronde, when she came to see herself as self-sufficient and self-reliant. And it was this image of herself that she wanted to project in her narrative.

Though she remembered how the reflected glory of a brilliant "establishment" had fired her imagination when she was a girl, when she wrote this installment of her memoirs she was far more interested in narrating her military exploits. Everything in her account of the Fronde is calculated to portray her in a heroic light. Concomitantly, she wants to disparage Gaston by contrasting his pusillanimity with her courage. She depicts him as forever longing for the peace and quiet of his chateau in Blois, while she did what he should have done. She recounts how she assumed her rightful and inevitable place as his heir. Armed with his authority, she took command of his troops and demanded the obedience owed to his representative. She ignored his skeptical officers and rode out before the army: "It gave the troops great joy to see me. I began from that moment to give my orders" (1:177). When she suspected that the officers were only humoring her, she wrote to her father on the spot, upon which they all protested that they would do nothing without her express orders. To their consternation, she then announced that she planned to go personally to Orléans: "[M]y presence will fortify the spirits of those who are well intentioned toward His Royal Highness," she told them, "for when persons of my quality are seen exposing themselves [to danger], it inspires the people tremendously, and it is nigh impossible for them not to submit voluntarily or by force to those who have a bit of resolve" (1:180). Those who predicted failure and warned her not to go, she disregarded. "That didn't frighten me at all, being naturally quite resolute; which will become apparent enough in these *mémoires,* in the most important actions of my life" (1:181). Her reinvention of herself as hero(ine) is infused, however, with ironic bemusement at the incongruity of actually being one. On the one hand, she claims that as Gaston's scion, she was only doing what was expected of her; but on the other, she was giddily overwhelmed by her own boldness. Told that she was to be present at a council of war, she avows that she burst out laughing.

The words that recur most frequently here are "joy" and "laughter." She tells how she toured the walls of Orléans on foot and persuaded some boatmen to break open a gate on the quai, while she climbed on a mound to watch, scrambling "like a cat, grabbing hold of brambles and thorns, and jumping over hedges" (1:182). When she finally made her way into the city to shouts of acclamation, "Two men took me and put me on a wooden chair. I don't know if I was seated in it or on the arm, I was so beside myself with joy: everyone was kissing my hands and I was dying of laughter to see myself in such a ridiculous state" (1:183).

Once she had won Orléans back to Gaston's cause, she took control of the situation "with absolute power" (1:185). Suddenly nothing seemed beyond her. The next day she found herself "in the last state of embarrassment" before a company of notables assembled at her command—"I who had never spoken in public and who was quite ignorant" (1:186)—informing them of His Royal Highness's orders and inciting them to remain loyal to his cause. Before she spoke, the officers tried to convince her to make a set speech, but she refused: "I know what I have to say; if I thought about it, I wouldn't be able to say anything worthwhile; I must simply say everything that comes into my head." However, she ordered the men to stand behind her because she feared that if she saw them looking at her she would not be able go on.

In the euphoric days that followed, she became the person she could have been, had she been born a man, or had she lived in the Amazonian utopia of her fantasies. She boasted that Condé, the greatest military strategist of the age, affirmed that he would not have altered the orders she issued (1:196). She proudly refused to let Gaston send a written confirmation of her authority on the grounds that everyone obeyed her without question and that such an order would be an insult to her. Upon her return, she became the toast of Paris and was given her own regiment: "I confess that I was like a child and felt quite joyful about it, and that the sound of trumpets thrilled me: never were troops so well dressed as mine" (1:256).

But although she had acted as Gaston's heir, he did not treat her like the heroic son she had impersonated so successfully. "M. le Prince paid me a thousand compliments and told Monsieur that I had done enough to deserve his praise. He came to tell me that he was satisfied with me, but not with as much tenderness as he should have." And she adds, not without malice, "I attributed this to the repentance he must have felt because *I had done what he ought to have done* [emphasis mine]" (1:236). When she wrote about the Fronde, she was without doubt reliving the most gratifying days of her life, but she was also indicting her father, contrasting his spineless behavior with her own valor. The passages devoted to the events of 2 and 4 July 1652 are heavily critical of him. "I begged him . . . to mount a horse and go to help M. le Prince; but in vain, for all the reasons I could muster had no effect on his spirits; and seeing that I could obtain nothing, I begged him to go to bed, for I felt that he should either pretend to be sick or do something" (1:226). That day, she recalls, she wept tears of shame and fury at her father's craven desertion of yet another ally.

She depicts herself as the true upholder of the family honor. It was she who persuaded the town fathers to open the gates, she who supervised arrangements for the retreat, she who sent wine to the troops and watched the wounded and dying enter the city. And when she saw that Condé was about to be cut off at the Porte Saint-Antoine, it was she who ordered the cannons of the Bastille to fire on the royal army. Throughout these pages, she represents herself, the daughter Gaston didn't want, as the true hero who never failed to rise to the occasion, while he proved incapable of honorable action again and again. When he refused to help her escape from Paris and taunted her for playing the hero, she replied with a stinging Cornelian riposte, "I performed both of these actions for which you now reproach me at your command; and if I had to, I would do so again, because it is my duty to obey and serve you. . . . That is why it is better, to my way of thinking, to have done what I did than to have done nothing. I don't know what it is to be a heroine: I am of such a birth that all I do can only be high and grand; and you can call it what you want; for me, I call it following my inclination and my path; I was not born to take any other" (1:274–75).

In representing her heroism during the Fronde, she does not entirely erase her feminine traits, however. She insists instead that her womanly instincts made her especially valuable to the cause. Describing how she succeeded in making peace between Valon and Condé, she adds, "This occasion as well as many others will make known that they were not unfortunate to have me, since I put their affairs to rights. I cannot refrain from saying that the evening and the day after the affair at the Porte Saint-Antoine, I inquired after all the wounded on behalf of Monsieur and M. le Prince and sent my respects to their families. They would never have thought of doing so, and this kind of attention wins hearts" (1:254–55).

Hipp argues that Montpensier's objective was not to bear witness, as did men memoirists, but to express her sensibility and imagination, as well as "her inability to make her life a success" (1976, 294). Yet when Montpensier narrates her actions during the Fronde, it is evident that she is holding herself up before the posthumous tribunal of history. Indeed, although she states in her prologue that she is writing for her friends, she later asserts that her memoirs "will probably never be seen by anyone, at least during my lifetime" (1:148). In this, her memoirs exhibit strong ties to texts like Monluc's *Commentaires,* described by Fumaroli as "a memoir in the financial sense of the term, where the debts of the hero toward the monarchy and the debts of the monarchy toward the hero are weighed with rigor" (1971, 15). What makes Montpensier's memoirs different is her relationship to the family structure. Memoirists like Monluc saw themselves as embodying the feudal houses to which rights and privileges were due in return for services rendered. But in Montpensier's text the relationship between debtor and creditor could not take place at the state level. The conflict lay inside the family itself. She wrote as one outside the line, and her complaint that Gaston had not rewarded her for services rendered was in essence a denunciation of a social structure that made no provision for heroic daughters. But if her exploits did not compel her father to reward her as she deserved, they did give her a sense of self-worth, which she inscribed in her text. Having played a part worthy of Henri IV's granddaughter, she was able to claim a heroic identity.

Just as she had reinvented herself as a hero during the Fronde, so she summoned unfeminine strength of character to meet the challenges of life at Saint-Fargeau: "Who could have said, in the time when I was at court, that I would have known the cost of brick, mortar, plaster, wagons, a day's wages, in brief all the details of construction, and that every Saturday I would settle the accounts; and yet I did all that" (1:356).[13] She also came to identify herself more and more with her mother's line. Her genealogical research revealed to her that the house of Montpensier was "very good and very illustrious and I am very glad to be descended from it" (1:329). It is at this point that she begins to link the textual signs "house" and "money" and to associate them with the Montpensier name. Comparing her father's and her mother's families, she claims that it was the latter who were people of integrity. The riches they left to her they had come by honestly. "I would have very great scruples about possessing the wealth of others, and it would even displease me if mine had come from confiscation," she writes in a gibe at both Gaston's misappropriation of her patrimony as well as the questionable financial practices of the crown. "Thank God," she adds, "I don't have that displeasure. All that I possess has come through the right channels and I would have still more if someone would return to me what is rightfully mine" (1:329).

Montpensier's claims to an independent and autonomous identity did not, however, reflect the realities of her situation. Although she was technically in control of her own house, as a daughter she was still subject to her father's orders. As she brings her narrative up to the time of writing, she appears more and more paranoid about what she perceives as his persecutions. She fears that he will have her incarcerated in a convent. She suspects that he is paying her female companions to spy on her. She falls prey to horrendous headaches and hysterical fits of weeping. Her narrative becomes an endless litany of the suffering inflicted on her by Gaston and the "friends" he has suborned.

The most grievous injustice is his order that she dismiss Préfontaine, the dedicated secretary who taught her to manage her estate and recopied her memoirs. In the passages devoted to these events, probably written down as they occurred, it is clear that her text has become her court of last resort. If she could not force her father to acknowledge her merit, pay back what he owed her, or let her control those in her employ, she could still denounce him to posterity: "I write this with some personal satisfaction," she exclaims, "for I want those who read about the evils that have been done to me and what I have suffered to have compassion for me" (1:426). The autobiographical act becomes an outlet for her rage and a remedy for her helplessness. If she writes as the victim of paternal oppression, she does not write as a passive victim. By translating her grievances into written words, she is able to assume the role of subject.

Inscribing Gaston's unjust acts into the historical record, she subverts commonly held ideas about masculinity. Are men honorable and loyal in friendship? She shows that they are not, whereas she is. Are men brave and daring? So is she. Are only men competent to control women's financial affairs? She has learned to administer her estate better than her father ever did. Almost every word of her text encodes a protest against the discourses that deny women the so-called manly virtues.

Once reconciled with Gaston, Montpensier was allowed to return to court. For a while she continued to record what she had seen and done, but once their dispute had been laid to rest, the real impetus to write disap-

peared. Significantly, she interrupted her memoirs in the middle of a passage that began, "My father came to Paris, where he stayed ten or twelve
days. Every evening upon returning from town he came into my room . . ."
(2:108). She wrote down what he had said. She started to write down her
reply, but she did not finish the sentence. The daughter's words no longer
mattered.

Seventeen years later, while vacationing at one of her estates, Montpensier found her secretary's copy of her memoirs. She completed the sentence she had left unfinished. Then she took a new sheet of paper and re-
commenced. Once again, it was a desire to testify to the wrongs done her
that impelled her to write. At the age of fifty, she was still a victim of the
paternal order. Although her cousin Louis XIV had been no more willing
than her father to arrange a proper "establishment" for her, he had forbidden her to marry the man she had chosen and had subsequently sent him to
prison, where he had been languishing for six years.[14] Once again, the Bourbons were determined to retain control of her mother's fortune, and once
again she found an outlet for her anger in writing. She returned to her memoirs with evident impatience to arrive at the events surrounding her aborted
marriage, although she did not neglect the historical aspect of her project,
recording the royal progress through France, the events surrounding the
king's marriage in 1660, and the early years of his personal reign.

The woman who narrated this installment of the *Mémoires* was not the
disdainful Amazon of Saint-Fargeau. No longer did she view marriage
merely as an "establishment" that would put her on a throne; nor did she
denigrate its emotional compensations. Indeed, her sudden eagerness to
bestow her hand and fortune on a man far beneath her social station has
caused some to see her as a frantic old maid on the brink of menopause, at
once pathetic and awe-inspiring in her ill-fated quest for love: "This passion," writes Bourgoin, "was undoubtedly a physiological effect, determined by the unhappy princess's forty-three years" (1954, 18).

Yet the autograph manuscript shows that in her first draft she made a
supreme effort to represent her decision as rational and logical:[15]

[B]oredom with my estate, although it was a happy one, took hold of me
and with it the desire to marry. I reasoned within myself (for I spoke of this
to no one) and I said, "This is not a vague idea; it must have some object,"
and I couldn't discover who it was. I searched, I pondered, and I couldn't
figure it out. Finally, after having worried about this for several days, I
perceived that it was Monsieur de Lauzun whom I loved, who had slipped
into my heart. I considered him to be the epitome of the perfect gentleman

[*le plus honnête homme du monde*] and the most agreeable person in the world. I saw that the only thing I lacked to be perfectly happy was a husband like him, whom I would love a great deal and who would love me also; that no one had ever admitted to feeling affection for me and that for once in one's life one should know how sweet it is to see oneself loved by someone who was worthy of one's love. It seemed to me that I felt more pleasure in seeing him and talking to him than was usual; that the days when I did not see him, I was bored. I believed that the same idea had come to him but that he did not dare to say so to me; but that the trouble he took to visit the queen, to meet me in the courtyard when she was going out, in the galleries, indeed everywhere where we could see each other by chance, made it apparent enough to me. I was delighted to be all alone in my room. I planned all that I could do for him, **. . .** I thought of how he would be obliged to me, of how much that would redound to my glory. I thought of those who would praise me, of those who would blame me, of how pleasant it would be to remain in my own country, where there were so few above me in rank, which should cure me of any regret I might feel at not being a queen in a foreign land, where the kings were not made like Monsieur de Lauzun. As for being a sovereign, I found that to be the subject of so great a king as ours was equal to being a sovereign. Finally one day I told myself everything that could possibly bring me pleasure from the idea I had conceived. I found it in depriving my heirs of their great hope of having my wealth, which made them wish for my death. (1985, 2:247–48).

Montpensier later revised this passage, adding a flyleaf to be inserted between the asterisks. Such revisions are extremely rare in the autograph manuscript and indicate that she expended far more care than usual on this passage.[16] On this flyleaf she cited a scene from Corneille's *La Suite du Menteur* that speaks of love as ordained by divine providence, and she tells how she sent out for a copy of the play so that she could meditate on these sentiments.[17] But if Montpensier fantasized herself as a Cornelian heroine, she nonetheless makes it clear that she was the initiator and orchestrator of the courtship. It was she who manipulated Lauzun into becoming her sentimental advisor, who tantalized him with hints that she was contemplating marriage, and slipped him a note reading "C'est vous." Even as she refashions herself as a romantic heroine, therefore, Montpensier steadfastly projects herself as controlling rather than controlled.

Of course, it is also obvious that she takes immense pleasure in reliving these experiences, especially the three days when she was blissfully planning her wedding: "If I could never stop thinking about them and believe I was still there, I would be quite content. I recall these moments and make them last as the happiest of my life, having endured very cruel ones since" (2:304). Sentiments such as these, which focus on introspection and emotional satisfaction, certainly evoke sentimental fiction, but they also prefigure another genre—modern autobiography. Thus as the novel and the theater moved Montpensier toward a heightened sense of self, they also moved her memoirs away from the preoccupation with heroism and history that dominated part 1.

There is more than nostalgia and self-dramatization at stake here. Montpensier's changed view of marriage had important sociopolitical dimensions. As Lougee's study shows, there is good reason to believe that the romantic view of marriage disseminated by seventeenth-century novels and plays actually inspired women in salon circles to reject traditional restrictions and marry outside their class.[18] Montpensier was one of these; and her memoirs encode the revolutionary nature of her venture. Structuring her version of the Lauzun affair like a novel, and representing herself as its heroine, Montpensier also inscribes resistance to patriarchal ideology.

If she no longer desires a royal "establishment," it is because she is now unwilling to make the sacrifices such "establishments" require of women, that is, giving up the privileges and pleasures of life at the French court and going to live in a foreign land. The decision to marry Lauzun is above all a decision to put personal happiness before family duty: "to know how sweet it is to see oneself loved by someone." Such an aspiration is inimical to the rules laid down for noblewomen of Montpensier's day, who were expected to have no will of their own in the choice of a mate.

In part 1, she represented herself first as a military hero(ine) and then as the self-reliant head of a household who openly defied paternal authority. The announcement that she would marry Lauzun was another declaration of independence, a refusal to limit her life to the marginal role imposed on her by the royal family. Having been denied the respect and eminence that should have been hers, she was, in effect, claiming the right to live outside the male line.

This is evident in the passage cited above. Despite her assertion that her condition is a "happy one," her words convey just the opposite. She refers to her "regret" that she will never be a queen; she believes herself to be unloved and, worst of all, she suspects that her heirs are waiting for her to die so that they can inherit her fortune. It is this that finally convinces her to go ahead with her plan: to make a marriage that will be tantamount to disinheriting the royal family. Her seemingly innocuous remark—"I was delighted to be all alone in my room; I made a plan for myself of what I could do for him"—unveils the subversive nature of what she is doing. Withdrawal into the privacy of one's room amounted to an infringement of the unwritten code governing court life, for the relentless round of ceremonies and distractions Louis XIV imposed on his followers was specifically designed to eliminate solitude—and the seditious thoughts it might generate. The Princess Palatine, Monsieur's second wife, was suspected of treason because she spent so much time alone writing to her relatives.[19] It was only in the privacy of her room that Montpensier could transform herself from victim to rebel.

"Establishing" Lauzun as the master of Montpensier would effectively disinherit her royal relatives. Commenting on this passage, James Doolittle expresses indignation at her desire to take over Lauzun's life: "She takes no account of the venomous resentment so often bred in the beneficiary of conspicuous charity. He must be *pénétré* by all the wonderful things she will do for him. . . . He must give up even his name; having instructed the notaries to endow him with her duchy of Montpensier in the marriage contract, she displays him to her ladies — . . . 'Voilà M. de Montpensier que je vous présente; je vous prie de ne le plus appeler que de ce nom-là'" (1971, 138). Doolittle's horror at the indignity she will impose on him by changing his name seems somewhat exaggerated, given the fact that French aristocrats routinely changed their names to indicate changes in status. Lauzun himself had formerly been called Peguilin. But he is absolutely right about what she is doing. She is planning to establish Lauzun in exactly the same way that men establish women—in order to found the house of Montpensier.

What is more, her insistence on Lauzun's merits contests the aristocratic belief that power and wealth should only be transmitted by blood, not as a reward for merit. In fact, she recalls that Lauzun himself once said to her, "In my opinion it is ridiculous to base one's worth on one's ancestors. One should base it on one's self" (2:304). In the first part of her memoirs, the matrilineal topos was linked to the preservation of the maternal inheritance, while the patrilineal topos was assimilated to the sign of disinheritance (Gaston's refusal to arrange her marriage, to acknowledge her services during the Fronde, or to take responsibility for her exile) and dishonesty (his misappropriation of her property). Unable to assume the place of a son in the paternal family, she came at that time to identify herself with her mother's ancestors, whom her genealogical research had connected to meritorious conduct. Now she initiated a new kind of opposition to the Bourbon line: redirecting the maternal legacy to a man singled out for his merit. Thus she will repudiate her paternal lineage and refound the Montpensier line.

True, she takes great care to picture herself as Louis's devoted subject. Doolittle remarks that she harps constantly on her "unqualified total adulation of Louis XIV, and the paragon that is Lauzun whose foremost virtue is made out to be that same adulation" (1971, 124). He believes that she intended her manuscript to be read by the king in the hope of persuading him to release Lauzun. Be that as it may, her protestations heighten the contrast between her magnanimity and the king's injustice.[20] Just as in part 1 she stressed her devotion to Gaston in order to show how wrongfully he had used her, so now her elaborate protestations of affection and admiration for her cousin, who is both her sovereign and the titular head of her family, are calculated to put him in the wrong. Once again like the early memoirists, she is drawing up a balance sheet that puts the royal family in her debt.

This part of her memoirs parallels the first, therefore, in its encoding of a matrilineal identity that resists and denies the primacy of the father's line. Needless to say, the royal family had no difficulty deciphering this message, and moved posthaste to thwart her. The king not only forbade her to marry Lauzun, he later found a pretext to incarcerate him. Bitter and heartbroken, when she wrote part 2 she had already been fighting for years to obtain his release. She abandoned this part of her memoirs soon after she learned of his unsuccessful attempt to escape, ending with this melancholy lament, "All these things awaken both pain and tenderness and make the world seem still more wearisome by the pleasure one takes in being alone . . ." (2:379). Still unestablished, the woman of fifty reiterates her preference for the dissident posture, the solitude inimical to her lord and master, Louis.

When she returns to her memoirs in part 3, Montpensier recounts how she was made to understand by Louis's mistress, Madame de Montespan, that in order to win Lauzun's freedom, she would first have to hand over a sizable portion of her estate to the *illegitimate* branch of the Bourbon line. The passage in her memoirs that relates how she agreed to this transfer is followed without preamble or transition by an inordinately long digression on a seemingly unrelated subject: the purchase of an estate near Paris: "All my life I had wanted to have a house near Paris. . . . I was told that there was one two leagues from Paris, in a village named Choisy,[21] above Villeneuve, on the bank of the river Seine. I rushed there in great haste; I found it to my taste. . . . I bought it for forty thousand francs" (2:401) At the very moment when she describes how she was forced to divest herself of the principality of Dombes, the territory that had conferred on her the status of sovereign, this unexpected digression reinvokes the sign of the *house*.[22] In fact, she writes, so irresistible was her desire to possess Choisy that she sold her pearls to pay for it.

The *noblesse d'épée* had been founded on military prowess, not wealth; and as Kavanaugh points out, the true aristocrat had little regard for riches, except as they allowed him to practice the virtue of *largesse*. Montpensier had learned the value of money, however, when she assumed control of her inheritance, a moment that coincided with her reassessment of the principles she had lived by before her exile. And as it became increasingly clear to her that gender and not blood would determine her destiny, she also came to understand wealth as a form of power (a truth that was becoming more and more evident as the king conferred noble titles on the bourgeoisie in return for large sums of money). Accordingly, she had made it her business to keep close tabs on her possessions.

In purchasing Choisy despite her reduced circumstances, she was using the remnant of her mother's fortune to establish herself literally in a house of her own, a place to which she could retreat from Louis, his court, and her Bourbon relations. The dreams of becoming a sovereign, or of establishing herself as the head of a matrilineal dynasty, have been replaced by the vision of an ideal dwelling. Choisy, she proclaims proudly, was entirely her own creation. Not even the king's prestigious architect Le Nôtre could dissuade her from arranging it to suit herself: "I discharged him [Le Nôtre] and had my house and garden laid out *the way I wanted them* [emphasis mine]" (2:401). The five-page digression on Choisy, which interrupts her account of the negotiations for Lauzun's release, clearly signifies the symbolic replacement of the lost Montpensier holdings by a new house, created purely "à ma mode."[23] Time had deprived her of the power and glory she once believed would be hers by birth, as well as much of her fortune, but it had not cured her of seeing herself as a women in charge of her own affairs. She retrenched, but she did not surrender.

Louis XIV constructed Versailles to house under one roof the entire nobility of France. Montpensier gathered under the roof of her new abode a vast collection of paintings. Some of these, as befitted the descendent of Henri IV, were devoted to royal battles, but in the room where she ate her meals, Montpensier hung the portraits of her family.[24] As she enumerates them, she devotes a long passage to her Montpensier forebears, recounting their accomplishments in great detail. In so doing, she incorporates their histories into her memoirs, as she incorporated their representations into the space over which she was mistress. The house at Choisy embodies Montpensier's final solution to the dilemma of her marginality. Her illustrious forebears are enclosed within the walls of *her house*. ". . . I would rather enlarge my house," she asserts, "than not have the pleasure of seeing them there"(2:403). Significantly, her aunts, uncles, and cousins are not arranged according to genealogy or rank, but as *she* wants them to be. And in her father's case, "I myself am over the mantel, holding my father's portrait," she states. "I deemed it preferable to put him there rather than between his two wives, for I did not want to put anyone else in my mother's place" (2:403). Thus, in her house the father who denied her a place in his house is reduced to a painting within a painting, in which it is she who bears him.[25]

The description of the portraits Montpensier hung in her house calls to mind the famous passage in *La Princesse de Clèves* where Madame de Clèves contemplates the duc de Nemours's picture. Here as there, the painted image fulfills the viewer's need to possess iconographically what she has not been able to possess in reality.[26] "It seems, by the details I have entered into concerning Choisy, that I love it; *it is my work: I made it all*" [emphasis mine]" (2:406). Choisy not only consoles her for the loss of her inheritance. It replaces the project of founding the house of Montpensier by deeding her holdings to Lauzun. Just as her portrait collection surrounds the mistress of Choisy, this digression surrounds the message communicated to her by Madame de Montespan: "You must not flatter yourself: the king will never allow you to marry Monsieur de Lauzun as you wanted to do; nor allow him to be called Monsieur de Montpensier"(2:406).

Not surprisingly, Choisy eventually became a bone of contention between her and Lauzun: "He told me one day when I was walking there: 'That is really a useless building. All you needed was a little house where you could come to eat a chicken fricassee and not stay overnight. All these terraces cost immense sums. What good is it?' Someone there told him that it was not too fine for me. He began to swear that it was easy for those it hadn't cost anything to talk like that. I told him that I had done nothing without Monsieur Colbert's advice. He said, 'Will he pay for it? As for me, I have something to complain about, you could have used that money better by giving it to me'" (2:427).

What she had spent years reclaiming from her father and had bestowed so begrudgingly on her cousin she was not about to hand over to a boor. *Her* house at Choisy was her reward for losing the fortune that had made her the most eligible woman in Europe. She had had enough of men telling her what to do with what was hers. She was determined to control what remained of the Montpensier money herself. "It would be a fine thing," she told him acidly, "if I had to come begging to you every time I needed money" (2:433).

Montpensier's marginal status is one of the determining forces behind both the genesis and the composition of her *mémoires*. In part 1, she wrote from a bitter sense of grievance to prove that her father had excluded her unjustly from her rightful place in his house and misappropriated her maternal heritage. In part 2 she narrated her abortive attempt to break away from the passive role assigned to her by the royal family and to found a house of her own. In part 3, she recounted the final chapter in the struggle, her capitulation to the royal will, her realization that she had been mistaken about Lauzun's merit, and her retrenchment to a position in which she was absolute mistress of what was still hers. Over all of Montpensier's chronicle hovers the topos of the maternal inheritance, which funds a house but cannot provide an establishment. In Montpensier's world there was no position of real power for women, no matter how rich or well born. I would maintain, however, that the reader's act of archaeological rehabilitation is not the rediscovery of the lonely princess who never married. The representation of self in these *mémoires* contests and revises what constituted femininity by narrating a princess's struggle to create a house of her own outside the boundaries of patriarchy.

4

Hortense Mancini

Hortense Mancini was reputed to be one of the most beautiful and charming women of the seventeenth century. As a child, she was her mother's favorite; and her uncle, Cardinal Mazarin, found her so appealing that he was delighted when she arrived in France, even though he had not invited her. She soon won the heart of the *régente,* and while her sister Marie was confined to her room, she was treated as a member of the royal family.[1] Both the king of England and the duke of Savoy courted her, but as it turned out Mazarin had to settle for a less illustrious match, bestowing Hortense on Richelieu's nephew, Armand de la Meilleraye, who had fallen desperately in love with her and vowed to marry no one else. Mazarin made it a condition of the agreement that Meilleraye would henceforth be called the duc de Mazarin. In return he bequeathed him the major part of his fortune and his priceless art collections.

The new duke and duchess of Mazarin soon proved to be totally incompatible. Hortense, aged fifteen, had no intention of giving up the amusements of court life or the flattering attentions of her admirers. Her husband was insanely jealous, even going so far as to accuse her of having an affair with her brother, Philippe de Nevers. He insisted that she accompany him on his journeys to the provinces so that he could keep an eye on her. He opposed all her social activities, spied on her, discharged her servants, walled up the passage connecting their living quarters with Philippe's, refused to speak to her until she removed her beauty marks, and forbade her to stage theatrical productions in the palace. He was also a religious fanatic who heard voices and claimed to speak with angels. A famous anecdote states that he once told the king the angel Gabriel had appeared to him with orders to break off his adulterous relationship with Louise de la Vallière. Louis is supposed to have replied, "He appeared to me too, and assured me that you are crazy." So convinced was M. de Mazarin that sex was wicked that he wanted to pull his daughters' teeth to make them unappealing to men. He forbade his maids to milk the cows because it encouraged erotic ideas. Worse still, he obliterated the genitals on the artworks he had inherited from Cardinal Mazarin. Driven by religious scrupulosity, he squandered his benefactor's estate, which he considered ill-gotten gains, and then confiscated the jewels that constituted his wife's only personal wealth.

Arguing that he had acted illegally and that he had jeopardized their sons' inheritance, she demanded a separation. It was granted on condition that she be confined to a convent. Further legal attempts to resolve the couple's differences proved fruitless, and Hortense became convinced that he was about to incarcerate her in Alsace, where she would have no recourse against his abuses. She therefore decided that her only hope lay in a clandestine escape and made her way to Italy, where her sister Marie was living. Her departure gave rise to scandalous gossip, which was fanned by her husband, who accused her of having affairs with every man she met.

Soon after her arrival in Italy, her brother Philippe joined his sisters there. But although the three siblings were happy to be together, they quarreled over Hortense's relationship with Courbeville, a man in her entourage who had accompanied her to Rome. Infuriated, she went to live in the convent where her aunt was abbess, but it did not take her long to decide that this abode did not suit her either, and since the nuns now refused to let her depart, she was forced to stage a dramatic escape with Marie's help.[2] Her problems were exacerbated by the fact that her husband refused to send her any money and she was forced to pawn her jewels to pay her expenses. She therefore decided to return to France and petition the king for financial help. Louis agreed that Mazarin should pay her a small pension, on the condition that she not reside in France. She went back to Italy and soon after helped Marie escape from her husband.

From the south of France, Hortense went on to Chambéry, where she lived under the protection of the duke of Savoy. It was at this time that she composed her memoirs, which are dedicated to him. Upon his death, she took up residence in England and became a favorite of her former suitor, Charles II. In London she presided over a salon frequented by the intellectual elite of both France and England. One of its most distinguished habitués was her devoted friend and admirer Saint-Evremond. In 1689, her husband, who had not ceased to pursue every legal means to force her to return, brought yet another suit against her, charging her with adultery to deprive her of her dowry. It is rumored that she poisoned herself in 1699 in despair because her daughter had supplanted her with a lover.[3] However, she had become a heavy drinker in later life and may have died of alcoholism.

Saint-Evremond composed her funeral oration. Her husband claimed her body, and took it with him on his journeys.

PUBLICATION HISTORY: *MÉMOIRES D.M.L.D.M.*

Hortense's memoirs are the first Frenchwoman's autobiographical text to be published during the author's lifetime. They appeared under the title *Mémoires D.M.L.D.M.* in 1675. The name of their publisher, Pierre Marteau of Cologne, was a pseudonym used by editors who brought out works that were at risk of being censored. The memoirs were an instant success, so much so that they inspired the same "publisher" to print a companion volume purporting to be the memoirs of her sister Marie.

Hortense's exact role in writing the *Mémoires D.M.L.D.M.* has always been disputed. They are frequently attributed to the abbé de Saint-Réal (César Vichard), best known for his historical novels. He was in Savoy at the same time she was, and was supposedly engaged in putting together the duke of Savoy's biography.[4] Her statement that she loved to write when she was a girl (1965, 35) has been cited as proof that she was responsible for at least the first draft. Nonetheless, Prosper Marchand included these memoirs in the 1730 edition of Saint-Réal's complete works. However, the editor of the 1757 edition omitted them. Bayle also disputed Saint-Réal's authorship—"He certainly had merit, he wrote well; but not in the easy manner that appears in these two works [Hortense's *mémoires* and the letter that follows it]" (Bayle 1727, 3:539) Mongrédien agrees, arguing that these memoirs agree in such exact detail with authentic historical documents that only Hortense could have written them. He does not disagree, however, that Saint-Réal may have written them down at her dictation, or "somewhat livened up his mistress's prose" (1952, 115–16). Hartmann also believes that Hortense supplied the contents while Saint-Réal did the actual writing. This would account, he argues, for the fact that this text "is immeasurably superior in wit and vivacity to anything else that Saint-Réal ever wrote" (1926, 146). Renée, on the other hand, argues against Hortense's authorship. He points to Saint-Evremond's statement that while she was a brilliant conversationalist, she wrote badly, and adds, "Several letters of Hortense, which we have had the occasion to read, do not entirely correspond to the idea one has of the intellectual queen of England" (1856, 343–45).[5] Gustave Dulong believes, however, that Saint-Réal's role was limited to making her style conform to the linguistic standards set forth by Vaugelas (1921, 1:223). Although Démoris takes no firm stand on the question, he suggests (1975, 115) that the narrative stance of the author was consistent with Saint-Réal's project in *De l'Usage de l'Histoire*—that is, to envisage the great in their private lives, especially insofar as they offer a bad example. Doscot argues that Hortense was quite capable of composing her own memoirs, having "like all the members of this strange family more style than knowledge of spelling" (1965, 27).

Since there is no autograph manuscript, nor any other primary source to authenticate these memoirs, the question of just how great a role Hortense played in composing them cannot be answered with certainty. The only thing we can know for sure is that she did not object to their publication, as her sister Marie did to the pseudomemoirs attributed to her. The ambiguity surrounding Hortense's authorship highlights yet again the question of what constitutes authenticity in autobiographical writings of this period.

Sex, Lies, and Autobiography

In the memoirs of both Valois and Montpensier, self-representation is determined, at least to some extent, by the public's preoccupation with women's sexuality. However, in spite of the rumors circulated about "La Reine Margot" and the ongoing gossip about Montpensier's marital prospects, their royal birth made it possible for them to see their lives in terms of masculine tropes. Such was hardly the case for Hortense and Marie Mancini. They had been brought to court to marry well. They had no other function there. For the nieces of Mazarin, sexual behavior was, therefore, not the subtext but the very essence of existence. This had a crucial effect not only on the way they represented themselves but on the way their memoirs were read. This discussion of Hortense's memoirs will focus on the way questions about her sexual behavior have dominated reactions to her text, and on the way I, in turn, respond to this phenomenon.

Feminist scholars are constantly encountering commentaries on women's writing that are openly misogynist. It is this triangular relationship between autobiography, feminist reading, and misogynist criticism that I want to explore here. I will set my analysis of Hortense Mancini's memoirs against two other responses to them: one that reads the text to see if it tells the truth, and one that reads it as a form of fiction. My reactions to these commentaries grow out of Foucault's insights into the coercive nature of confessional practices.[6] But whereas he was primarily concerned with their historical role in policing relationships between men, I am interested in how the sexuality of women autobiographers has been policed by their readers and what the proper response to that policing might be.

Truth-telling has often been said to authorize autobiography. Elizabeth

Bruss, for instance, claims it to be a constitutive rule of the genre: "Under existing conventions, a claim is made for the truth-value of the autobiographer's reports. . . . The audience is expected to accept these reports as true, and is free to 'check up' on them or attempt to discredit them" (1976, 7).[7] Those who read this way believe that autobiographers are obligated to render a true account of past thoughts and deeds. But as Foucault saw, this way of reading assimilates autobiography to the Catholic practice of requiring communicants to confess to a priest who is empowered to grant absolution according to a prescribed set of rules. The audience assumes it has the right to authorize the text, passing judgment, like the priest, on the writer and the life.

There is, however, an important difference between autobiography and the sacrament of confession. In the latter, there is a presupposition that the penitent will be constrained to tell the truth because she or he is actually confessing to God, who knows the truth already. To lie or withhold information would not only be pointless but would result in yet another sin. In secular autobiography, an omniscient third party does not guarantee the pact between reader and writer. Consequently, in order to evaluate the life submitted for approval, the reader who is concerned with the truth must either accept what the writer says at face value or authenticate it from outside sources. This places the autobiographer and the reader in an adversarial relationship—the former must justify her or his acts, while the latter can withhold approval pending verification. This method has often been applied to autobiographical texts, and nowhere more so than in the case of Hortense Mancini's memoirs, a fact that raises the more general issue of how women's texts have been read in the past and how feminist readers can read them today.

In the incipit addressed to the duke of Savoy, Hortense immediately foregrounds the problem she faced in writing the story of her life, given the misogynist bias of her readers:

> It is not that I don't know how difficult it is to speak acceptably of oneself; nor are you ignorant of my natural repugnance for justifying myself on matters that regard me: but it is even more natural to defend oneself against slander, especially to those who have done us great favors. They certainly deserve to be informed that one is not completely unworthy of them. In any case, I could not find a more innocent way to pass the time in my retreat. If the things I have to tell you seem more like a novel, blame my evil destiny rather than my inclination. (1965, 31–32)

She then repeats the much-quoted aphorism that sums up the aristocratic ideology of gender: "I know that a woman's glory lies in not getting herself talked about" (32).[8] Not getting herself talked about has clearly not been the case for Hortense, of whom much has already been said, and of whom a great deal more will probably be said as the result of this apology. This statement casts her, therefore, in the role of transgressor—the woman who has gotten herself talked about, and who now defies propriety yet again in order to set the record straight.

This incipit indicates that Hortense wrote her memoirs to deal with the calumnies that had circulated about her after she left her husband—calumnies, she will allege, that were disseminated by M. de Mazarin. She does this in several ways. Sometimes she indignantly denies the rumors outright. Sometimes she offers plausible explanations. But more frequently, like Marguerite de Valois, she makes no reference to them at all, thereby erasing them from the record of her life. The bulk of her story is devoted not to refuting malicious gossip but to justifying her decision to leave her husband and to representing herself as the victim of the unjust persecution that he and his supporters have inflicted on her: "all that the malignity of the bigoted cabal can invent and put into action in a household where it dominates tyrannically against a simple young woman, without guile, whose lack of circumspection constantly afforded her enemies new ways to triumph over her" (47).

Her text was widely read. However, it did not necessarily elicit sympathy for its heroine. As the cynical Bussy-Rabutin put it, "[N]o matter how gallant we may be, we do not approve of a lady leaving her husband and running around the country like the heroine of a novel, unless she does it for us."[9] Later generations continued to give credence to the stories of her scandalous conduct, and scholars have devoted considerable effort to corroborating them. Hartmann, who published a full-length English biography of Hortense in 1926, writes that her memoirs "indubitably form one of the most unreliable productions of this nature that has ever been devised" (1926, 146). She was, he says, "congenitally incapable of telling the truth," and her preamble, quoted above, displays "sheer effrontery." "She would have the world believe that the perpetual limelight in which she lived was focussed on her by fatality and not by any actions of her own" (147). Although not all critics have denounced Hortense's text quite so vehemently, this reaction is typical of the way it has often been read.

What position should a feminist critic take when confronted by such statements? One obvious strategy is to search for historical evidence that will prove the allegations to be false. Eliane Viennot has done this for the much-maligned Marguerite de Valois, painstakingly discrediting the sordid legends of "La Reine Margot."[10] But although such efforts to set the record straight have immense scholarly value, they do not offer a real solution to the problem, for establishing the facts does not address the theoretical issue of what the role of truth should be in autobiography; nor does it resist the underlying assumption that a woman's story should be judged by her sex life.

Just what are the "lies" Hartmann finds in Hortense's text? As Montgrédien points out, much of the material she includes is a matter of historical record; and as Doscot affirms, she is "highly discreet when it comes to her amorous adventures" and "quite truthful with regard to events and the character of her terrible husband" (Doscot 1965, 17). What Hartmann is objecting to, therefore, are her attempts to defend herself from gossip about her amorous liaisons: for instance, her claim that an incriminating letter intercepted by her husband was innocent, her outraged reaction to the charge that she committed incest with her brother, her explanations as to why she refused to discharge the gentleman-retainer Courbeville, by whom she reportedly became pregnant, her erasure by silence of other alleged lovers, and her ambiguous references to her relationship with the duke of Savoy.

Hartmann's remarks would seem to exemplify the theoretical position that autobiography is synonymous with truth-telling; but they also corroborate Foucault's perception that confessional policing is primarily concerned with sexual conduct (1978, 1:61). For Hartmann, truth in autobiography means telling the whole truth and nothing but the truth about what the writer did in bed. Thus any attempt to clear Hortense's name on the historical level would make it necessary to agree not only that autobiography must be authorized by truth-telling but that a woman's autobiography must be judged on whether or not it tells the truth about her sex life. In other words, Hartmann's analysis implies that a woman autobiographer does not have the right to tell the story *she wants to tell*.

A second way of reading Hortense Mancini's memoirs is exemplified by Démoris's remarks in *Le Roman à la première personne*. He argues that her real purpose is not to write an apology, but to give pleasure to the reader by imitating the popular *libelles* and *romans à clefs* of her day.[11] This must be so, he asserts, since as she implies in the prologue, she knew that the very act of publishing her story would be held against her, and since she realized that her reputation was already beyond saving. Indeed, he points out, it is significant that she did not write her apology until after she had given up any idea of establishing herself in France and had resigned herself to living in Chambéry under the protection of the duke of Savoy (1975, 111). Furthermore, he maintains, she herself explicitly conflated her story with fiction when she wrote, "If the things I have to tell you seem more like a novel, blame my evil destiny" (32).

There is no doubt some justification for Démoris's contention that

Hortense Mancini's memoirs have much in common with the fiction of the time. Her story is full of novelistic elements—clandestine escapes, perilous journeys, and transvestite disguises.[12] And in her account of her girlhood at court, as well as in the many other amusing anecdotes, she represents herself as high-spirited, with a flamboyant sense of fun and a penchant for merry pranks. It is she who provides an unprecedented glimpse of what passed for humor at the French court with her anecdote of how her six-year-old sister Marianne was persuaded that she was pregnant and eventually found a newborn baby in her bed. She also relates how, during one of her enforced stays in a convent, she and Madame de Courcelles tried to wash their feet and ended up inundating the nuns in their beds on the floor below. Another time, she says, they hid in the *parloir* behind a grill, from which she proved too plump to escape. She also describes how she loved to play blind-man's buff and indulged in rough horseplay, once injuring her knee so badly while chasing after one of her ladies that it nearly had to be amputated. At times the narrative voice becomes flippant, or downright irreverent. She does not hesitate to report that her brother and sister greeted their uncle's death with the vulgar exclamation "Dieu merci, il est crevé!" [Thank God, he's croaked].[13]

By addressing the question of genre and linking Hortense's story to the rise of the novel, Démoris appears to move toward a more sophisticated theory of autobiography than the one that imposes truth-telling as the chief criterion. He also defines the thematic concerns of these memoirs in terms of a heroic and aristocratic literary tradition, citing the high station of the female narrator, her noble concern for her children's inheritance, and her struggle to live in freedom and to survive (1975, 113–14). It is this, he maintains, that saves her text from falling into vulgarity. Indeed, he argues, if there are hints of the bourgeois here—her tendency to speak of her servants, to mention her financial difficulties, to describe in graphic detail her battles with her husband—they are not her fault, but her husband's, whom he caricatures as a blend of Orgon and Harpagon (113).

But although Démoris's explication is seductive, it too has serious flaws. For one thing, it ahistoricizes both Hortense and her story. Reducing the narrator to a fictional stereotype—"the great lady of easy virtue" who finds herself in a "scandalous situation"—he glosses over the fact that Hortense was a real woman and that the dilemma she found herself in was inevitable if a women left her husband. He makes no attempt to deconstruct the aristocratic scenario he idealizes or to consider that under the ancien régime a great lady, even if she had inherited a fortune, owned nothing, lived nowhere, and enjoyed no status at all without her husband's permission.

What is more, Démoris's formalist analysis is ultimately based, like

Hartmann's, on the presumption that the narrator is lying. He seizes on the very silences intended to erase the rumors about her as evidence that she is guilty, and claims that she more or less invites the reader to supply what her text does not explicitly say (114). He even contends that she derives some sort of narcissistic pleasure from representing herself as a great lady of little virtue who cannot avow openly the true nature of her adventures, but is quite satisfied to have spent her life in an interesting manner—to have *lived* a novel—and is not too vexed, with some precautions, to make it known (114–15).

Corroborating Foucault's statement that women's bodies are "saturated with sexuality" (1978a, 1:104), Démoris, like Hartmann, regards Hortense's story primarily as a narrative of sexual conduct. Accepting as axiomatic the preamble's statement that a woman's glory lies in not getting herself talked about, he concludes, "Hortense is not unaware that the very fact of setting down her memories pleads against her. . . . A woman's situation with regard to memoirs is different here than a man's: as a woman, she only has the right to a negative glory, whereas the political errors of a great lord do not necessarily exclude moral grandeur. To publish one's story is already, in a sense, to be guilty" (1975, 111). This pronouncement has at least one virtue: It brings out into the open the assumption that underlies both his and Hartmann's critiques—namely, that the kind of truth at issue here is sexual and concerns only women.[14] This becomes even more obvious when he uses the example of Marguerite de Valois to back up his assertions: "The only women's memoirs anterior to Hortense's are Marguerite de Valois's, Henri IV's wife, *whose reputation is well-known* [emphasis mine]" (111).[15]

In other words, he implies that only "guilty" women wrote about themselves. Furthermore, since they knew they wouldn't be believed, they indulged in self-narrative primarily for pleasure, their readers' as well as their own. Ergo, their memoirs should be read as fiction. His argument neatly shifts Hortense's memoirs out of the realm of fact/autobiography into the realm of "literature," seeming to assess them on purely aesthetic grounds. But although this circular reasoning seems to skirt the question of whether or not they are *in fact* lies, the entire analysis rests on the belief that they are: "That there was lying in Hortense's memoirs, either by disguise or omission, her contemporaries must have been aware, but this lying was the source of aesthetic pleasure" (115). This text affords its reader the pleasure of enjoying, "a lively story," he concludes, "without debasing himself to the vulgar calumnies and vilifying genres of scandalous writing, in other words, to find pleasure while retaining a sense of cultured dignity" (115).[16] In the last analysis, the real difference between these two commentators is that whereas Hortense's memoirs make Hartmann angry, Démoris finds them amusing.

I want to pursue an entirely different approach to this text. Instead of discussing it as lies/fiction, I want to go back to the question of the signature and reexamine what the means of production can tell us about how we should read it. Although Hartmann and Démoris write as if Hortense was entirely responsible for her memoirs, this is probably not the case. It was common for aristocratic women to ask "men of letters" to correct their texts, as we have seen in the cases of both Valois and Montpensier. And although I believe that Hortense *was* responsible for the *contents* of these memoirs, there is a good chance that Saint-Réal revised them in ways that significantly altered their style or tone. Consequently, I think that everything of a stylistic or rhetorical nature must be viewed with some caution.

I want to concentrate primarily on the contents of Hortense's story, therefore, rather than on the way it is told. In Doscot's edition, it is found on pages 31 through 87. Pages 31 through 40 recount her childhood up to the death of Mazarin and her marriage. Pages 41 through 63 justify her decision to leave her husband. And the last twenty-five pages narrate her peregrinations prior to her arrival in Savoy. If we cull out the topics, ideas, and themes that occupy the greatest amount of textual space, we find that her main concern is to accumulate evidence of her husband's abuses, to record the judicial procedures initiated by both spouses, and to protest the unjust and illegal treatment meted out to her both before and after her departure from Paris.

Only the childhood narrative, written in an archly flippant style and conjuring up an amusing picture of life at the French court, is not devoted to these polemical objectives. As soon as Hortense arrives at her marriage, the tone abruptly shifts. From this point on, she is intent on representing herself as the innocent victim of her odious husband and accumulating evidence of his abuses.

During the three or four first years of our marriage," she writes, I made three trips to Alsace, and the same number to Brittany, not to mention several others to Nevers, le Maine, Bourbon, Sedan, and elsewhere. . . . Several times he made me travel two hundred leagues when I was pregnant and even on the point of giving birth. . . . I could not speak to a servant without having him sent away the next day; I could not be visited twice in a row by the same man without having him forbidden to enter the house. . . . The innocence of my diversions, which would have reassured any man of his humor who had some regard for my age, troubled him as much as if they were criminal, whether it was a question of playing blind-man's buff with my companions or going to bed too late. . . . I could not go out for a promenade in conscience, let alone to the theater. (1965, 43–44)

Through all this, she insists, she imposed on herself a Griselda-like compliance. "He was so determined to keep me near him . . . that three weeks after giving birth I was obliged to leave Paris. Few women of my class would have done so; but what won't one do to enjoy something as precious as peace?" (45).

She insists, furthermore, that her reasons for demanding a separation had nothing to do with her husband's tyrannical obsessions or her desire to lead a less repressed existence. The real reason she opted to oppose him publicly was her realization that he was squandering her son's patrimony:

> If Monsieur de Mazarin had been content to bow me down with sadness and suffering, to expose my health and my very being to the most unreasonable caprices, and to make me spend my best years in unparalleled servitude, . . . I would have been content to groan and complain to my friends. But when I saw that his incredible wastefulness was about to make my son the poorest man in France, when he should have been the richest, I surrendered to the call of blood, and maternal love took precedence over all the moderation I had tried to maintain. (48)

When he confiscated her jewels, traditionally a woman's sacrosanct property, she took action. Her narrative becomes in large part a record of her struggle to convince the courts, the king, and, above all, his hostile minister Colbert that her claims were just and her grievances well founded. This is apparent from the indirect quotations printed in italics and inserted on almost every page. These all pertain to legal evidence, advice, or judgments. The persona who emerges from these pages is energetic and decisive, determinedly defending a just cause. Narrative takes precedence over description or reflection. If she speaks of her emotions, she does so not to analyze them but to prove to the reader that she has been reduced to hysteria by her husband's vengefulness: "Monsieur de Mazarin gave me a choice between living in the hôtel de Conti[17] or in the abbey at Chelles, the two places he knew I hated most in the whole world and for the best reasons. I was so prostrated that it was impossible for me to choose between two such odious propositions. Others had to choose for me" (52–53). She represents her own conduct as not only innocent but virtuous, pointing out that the abbess of Chelles gave her husband "the most favorable testimony of my conduct that he could desire" (53). Furthermore, she asserts, it was he who purposely spread false rumors about her: "Monsieur Mazarin and his adherents did all they could to blacken my reputation in the world and above all to the king" (58).

She describes how she fought to obtain a financial separation that would have guaranteed her an independent income and given her the right to verify her husband's expenditures. For a brief moment, it appeared that she would be successful. A lower court made up entirely of "reasonable young men" awarded her 20,000 francs, and "what was most important, *he was required to produce the documents I needed to prove his wasteful spending*" (56–57; italics in original). When her husband appealed this judgment to a higher court, however, the king convinced her to return to her private quarters in the Palais Mazarin while the case was in arbitration.

She goes on to elucidate and defend her reasons for the scandalous flight from Paris that made her an outcast in a society that consigned unattached women to convents.[18] She explains that she was warned in secret that the court of appeal, composed entirely of old men sympathetic to her husband, was about to order her to return to the conjugal abode. This information, passed to her in strictest confidence by people who made her promise never to reveal their identity, left her no choice but to flee: "Imagine what kind of treatment I could have expected from M. Mazarin, if I had returned to him by court order, having both the court and the parliament against me, considering the reasons he thought he had for his grievances. That was the motive behind my strange and much-blamed resolution to go to my relatives in Italy, seeing that there was no longer any safe haven for me in France" (61).

In the section dealing with the events after her departure from Paris, she frequently offers evidence that corroborates her version of events. She calls attention to an account of her journey that was written by a man in M. de Mazarin's employ and subsequently deposed to the parliament: "I also learned that he had sent a commissioner after me to find out what I had done in every place I had stopped; and this is perhaps the only debt I owe him, since this man's deposition, which is registered with the parliament provides an eternal testimony to the innocence of my conduct during the journey, against all that my enemies have published" (69). She also quotes innocuous passages from her brother's poems to show that her husband's accusations of incest were ridiculous (64, 70–72). Her reaction to this vile accusation is the most vehemently indignant in her memoirs:

> Posterity will find it difficult to believe, should it hear of these affairs, that a man of my brother's standing was interrogated by the law about bagatelles of this nature; that they were taken seriously by the judges, that such an odious use could be made of the commerce of mind and sentiment be-

tween persons so close to each other; that finally my esteem and friendship for a brother of merit as well known as his, and who loved me more than his life, could have served as a pretext for the most unjust and cruel of defamations. . . . The most holy ties, founded in nature and reason, become the greatest crimes to please jealousy and envy; but nothing is impossible to one who professes to be devout: rather than being wrong, he [Monsieur de Mazarin] would have it that the most honest people on earth are the most abominable. (70)

She claims that harsh and unjust measures were deployed against her by a society that regarded husbands' rights as sacrosanct and treated undutiful wives as criminals. Cataloguing M. de Mazarin's attempts to have her hunted down and punished, she charges him with depriving her of her rights, "which is only done to women convicted of the ultimate turpitude" (69). The king's agents, Colbert and Louvois, thwarted her appeals at every turn. She reports that even Louis (himself a notorious adulterer) told her that her conduct had made it impossible for him to help her. Court society sided with her husband, and both church and state decreed that she should be confined to a convent under the harshest conditions. Even her sister the countess of Soissons pressured her to return to her husband and renounce her claim to her jewels. It is difficult to see anything facetious in all this.

The most cruel and potent form of coercion, she asserts, was the widespread prejudice against women who left their husbands, for it guaranteed that even the most vile and outrageous gossip about her would be believed. "I confess to you," she writes, "that if I had foreseen all the consequences, I would sooner have chosen to pass my life immured within four walls and to finish it by the sword or poison, than to expose my reputation to the inevitable slanders incurred by every woman of my age and quality who is separated from her husband" (64–65).

This passage points to the difference between Hortense's agenda and that of the reader who polices the text for truth. While the latter is interested in verifying whether the rumors about her were true, what concerns Hortense is *why they were circulated*. In her view, these "slanders" were the inevitable result of her refusal to live with her husband, which had placed her outside lawful society and endowed her every act with sexual connotations. The rumors about her corroborate her representation of herself as the victim of a power structure deployed to keep women in their place.

But although the narrator vociferously denounces the calumnies that have ruined her reputation, she spends relatively little time refuting them. Her explanation of what passed between her and Courbeville, for instance, never hints at a romantic liaison and occupies less than four pages (73–75, 77). Like Marguerite de Valois, she seems determined to desexualize her story. She says absolutely nothing about her conjugal relations with Monsieur de Mazarin or her love affairs. Instead, she focuses the reader's attention on his reprehensible behavior, both before and after their separation.

If one searches for the topos that dominates these memoirs, one discovers that it is not sex but money. Démoris may consider this vulgar and bourgeois. However, one of the most original and interesting features of these memoirs is the way they explore the relationship between money and an aristocratic woman's freedom. Indeed, it might be said that this is the story of a woman's financial education. As a girl, Hortense confesses, she had no understanding of money. She once spent an afternoon tossing gold ducats out the window, an act that she admits probably hastened her uncle's demise. Later, however, she came to appreciate Mazarin's vast fortune as "the fruit of his labors and the recompense for his services" (48). But although she realized that her husband was squandering her children's patrimony and took legal action to stop him, she still was so naïve that she forgot to bring along jewels and cash when she fled from Paris: "[I]t never even occurred to me that I would lack for money; but experience has taught me that it is the first thing one lacks, especially if one has always had it, and never known its importance, or the need to manage it" (65).

Having always benefited from her uncle's generosity, she had to learn the hard way what it meant to need money. From the moment she abandoned the conjugal domicile, she possessed nothing. It was her husband who controlled Mazarin's estate, and he was determined to force her to return by depriving her of all means of subsistence. When she found herself penniless and forced to borrow from those who took advantage of her plight, she finally recognized the importance of financial independence and decided that her only hope lay in convincing the king that her husband should grant her a pension. And since M. de Mazarin's madness had recently driven him to hack the genitals off all the statues in the Palais Mazarin, she felt that this was a propitious time to plead her case. Louis gave her the option of returning to her husband or receiving a pension of 24,000 francs, promising that if she did the former she would not have to accompany M. de Mazarin on his travels, would have total say in choosing her servants, and would not be obliged to submit to his "caresses." She records her response as follows: *I could not resign myself to return to him; whatever precautions were taken, given his humor, I would endure twenty small cruelties every day, about which I could not importune His Majesty; therefore, I accepted with extreme gratitude, the pension it pleased him to accord me"* (81; italics in original).

Furthermore, she makes it a point to tell how she ignored Lauzun when he predicted that she would spend the entire sum at the first inn she came to. "He did not know that I had learned to manage money," she writes. "It isn't that I didn't see it was impossible to subsist honestly for any length of time on this sum; but . . . I calculated that it would give me time to take other measures" (81). The other measures were, of course, her decision to accept the duke of Savoy's protection. "When my sister started off for Paris, I took the road to Chambéry, where I have found at last the repose I sought unsuccessfully for so long and where I have always resided since, with a great deal more tranquility than a woman as unhappy as I deserves to enjoy" (86–87). Being a kept woman turned out to be the only viable alternative to life with an abusive spouse or imprisonment in a convent.

In the ancien régime, the "aristocrat" supposedly adhered to the noble ethic of *largesse*—lavish generosity and wasteful spending, while the "bourgeois" practiced frugality and thrift. However, a woman who sought to establish herself outside the institution of marriage found herself immediately cut off from aristocratic privileges and forced to renounce the values of her class, as well as the virtues of the "good woman."

Embedded in Hortense's memoirs is a quasi-legal brief, which may well have originally been intended to serve as documentation of her grievances in her request for a pension.[19] This is substantiated by the fact that the king's ruling is the final installment of the financial and legal saga that dominates her narrative. Her memoirs end only five pages later, after she refutes one last false rumor and offers a very succinct account of how she and Marie escaped from Rome and sailed to the south of France, from which she made her way to Savoy.

This is, then, in a very real sense a judicial memoir. During Hortense's stay in Chambéry, she probably revised and expanded it to its present length. The original document, designed to persuade the king of her worthiness, was now dedicated to Philippe-Emmanuel II, the patron for whom she wanted to appear in the best possible light. She may have added for his amusement the lively accounts of her childhood at court, her convent escapades, and the adventures that befell her on her journeys. Or she may have recounted these anecdotes to the duke or Saint-Réal, who convinced her to include them in her memoirs. They portray a lighter side and suggest that she must have possessed considerable skill as a raconteur. They certainly went a long way toward satisfying the requirements of a publisher like "Marteau."

Where does this leave the question of truth and sex in Hortense's autobiography? How should a reader interpret the fact that she tells the truth in great detail about her financial and legal problems, but says nothing of her love life? What is one to make, for instance, of her account of the Courbeville affair, of which she says only that despite her siblings' opposition, she retained him out of loyalty? There are many ways to interpret this silence. Readers like Démoris and Hartmann see it as a form of lying. Feminists like Cixous might see it as the repression of feminine sexuality.[20] As Sidonie Smith argues, "Women had to discursively consolidate themselves as subjects through pursuit of an out-of-body experience precisely because their bodies were heavily and inescapably gendered" (1987, 272). Whether or not Hortense penned them, the opening remarks of this text point to the silence imposed on early women with regard to speaking about sexuality and the body, a silence that goes beyond mere *bienséance* to define the conduct of the "good woman." As Ann Rosalind Jones writes, a woman's speech "was seen as intimately connected to the scandalous openness of her body" (1986, 76). Not only should a chaste woman not get herself talked about, she should have no story to tell.

I would suggest, however, that here, as in Valois's memoirs, this absence of erotic revelations has another significance. I see it not so much as the result of strictures that prohibited women from "writing the body," but as their refusal to engage in the discourse of sexuality, out of resistance to the belief that sex was all that really mattered in a woman's life. Because of their intense interest in feminine sexuality, readers want to find a libidinal confession in the narrative of an "outlaw" woman like Hortense. But her memoirs pointedly avoid that scenario. Instead, they are a protest against the social and political enforcement of conjugal duty. They stubbornly insist on situating the heroine's apology not in the bedroom but in the courtroom, calling on public opinion to ratify her right to autonomy. By not speaking about the body, they contest the construction of woman as *just* a body, and demonstrate that a woman's story does not have to be the story of unchastity that gets her talked about.

5

Marie Mancini

When Cardinal Mazarin summoned the Mancini daughters to France in 1653, their mother, who preferred the prettier Hortense, wanted Marie to stay in Rome. Marie flatly refused. Once they arrived, Madame Mancini insisted, however, that the headstrong Marie spend most of her time in her room. Eventually, her uncle sent her to the Convent of the Visitation to improve her command of French. There she not only learned the language but acquired a love of French literature.[1] She came into contact with the young king in the course of his visits to her mother's deathbed. Attracted by her wit and vivacity, he fell in love with her; and after Madame Mancini's death, the two became inseparable. She is believed to have shared with him her love of poetry and novels. "The king was in much better spirits after he fell in love with Mademoiselle Mancini," comments his cousin, La Grande Mademoiselle. "He was gay, he chatted with everyone. I think that she had advised him to read novels and verse. He had a great number of them, with collections of poetry and comedies; he appeared to take pleasure in them and when he was asked his opinion, he even expressed it as well as someone who had studied and had a perfect acquaintanceship with letters" (Montpensier 1985, 2:101). Marie has also been credited with teaching him the gallant manners for which he was famous.

Louis held her honor in deep respect, for as Hortense affirms in her memoirs, Marie's husband found to his surprise that she was a virgin. At one point the king even seriously considered marrying her. He was obliged, however, to marry the Spanish infanta as a condition of the peace treaty with Spain. Marie and her sisters were sent off to a desolate coastal chateau in Brouage. The heartbroken king deluged her with letters and borrowed money to buy her a string of pearls, which she wore all her life. In another romantic gesture, he sent her a puppy born to his little dog Friponne, with a note that read, "I belong to Marie Mancini."

At this point, Marie realized that she must find a husband without delay. She encouraged Charles de Lorraine to court her, but Mazarin opposed the match. Louis, for his part, treated her with extreme coldness and rebuffed all her efforts to renew their friendship. Marie then reluctantly agreed to marry Lorenzo Onofrio Colonna, grand constable of Naples and scion of the oldest and noblest family in Rome. The arrangements were completed just before the cardinal's death in 1661; and immediately following the marriage by procuration, Marie set off for Italy. She reports that when Louis bade her farewell, he promised always to protect her.

Colonna, who was relatively young and good-looking, was immediately attracted to his new bride. He insisted on consummating the marriage before the nuptial mass. Exhausted by the journey and depressed at returning to Italy, where women were still more oppressed than in France, Marie fell ill and nearly died. Colonna treated her with such consideration, however, that by the time she regained her strength she had come to regard him with affection. During the early years, the marriage seemed amazingly successful, but it deteriorated after the birth of their third son. According to Marie, this was because she broke off conjugal relations with him, fearing she would die if she became pregnant again. Her decision may actually have been motivated, however, by her anger at discovering that he had been unfaithful. In any event, he later made no secret of his extramarital liaisons. As she grew increasingly jealous, he became more and more inflexible. Hortense's arrival in Italy, following her separation from Monsieur de Mazarin, provided a welcome distraction, but her difficulties and the Courbeville affair burdened Marie with a new set of problems.

Eventually, she suspected that Colonna was trying to poison her. On one occasion, she became so violently ill after taking an emetic that she almost died. The local gazettes spoke openly of this episode, and one of Marie's servants intercepted a note to Colonna containing advice on choosing a second wife. Her suspicions were no doubt exacerbated by sinister gossip about the sudden death of Louis XIV's sister-in-law, Henriette d'Angleterre. Marie communicated her fears to the exiled chevalier de Lorraine, then in Rome, and he in turn reported them to the king. Louis was sufficiently concerned to offer her royal protection.[2] She persuaded Hortense to help her escape while Colonna was out of town, and after a series of near disasters, they made their way to the south of France by boat.

There Marie found that the king had sent her a letter of safe conduct, but when she tried to approach Paris she was rebuffed. Frustrated in her desire to speak to Louis face to face, she found herself forbidden to come within sixty leagues of the capital. Her presence in France was unwelcome to the king's wife *and* his mistress. What is more, the French crown could not oppose the legitimate claims of a wronged husband, who had the backing of both Spain and the pope. Colonna, who had been publicly humiliated by his wife's departure, and who was now furious to learn that she had been speaking publicly of his attempts to poison her, was determined to make her pay dearly for her departure.

Unable to comprehend the delicacy of her position, she committed a series of strategic blunders. She was persuaded by her brother to go to Savoy, where the duke received her as hospitably as he had Hortense. Then when they had a falling out, she ventured into the north of Italy and landed in the power of Colonna's agents. They led her north to Flanders, where she was virtually imprisoned. She was finally persuaded to go to Madrid. In 1676, while she was living there under virtual house arrest, the publication of the unauthorized *Mémoires de M.L.P.M.M. Colonne, G. connétable de la royaume de Naples* impelled her to set forth her version of her life story—*La Vérité dans son jour*. After Colonna died in 1689, she was able to return to Italy. She devoted her final years to her sons' interests. She returned several times to France; and in 1706 she even spent some time near Paris, but she declined an invitation to Versailles, some said because she did not want the king to see how old she had grown. She died, aged seventy-five, in Pisa on 8 May 1715, four months before Louis XIV. Only two objects of value remained in her possession: the diamond wedding ring given her by her husband and the pearls given her by the king. At her request, her tombstone was engraved with the epitaph: *Cinis et Pulvis* (Ashes and Dust).

PUBLICATION HISTORY: *LA VÉRITÉ DANS SON JOUR*

The circumstances surrounding the publication of Marie Mancini's memoirs provide yet another example of how seventeenth-century attitudes towards authenticity in autobiography differed from those of today. In 1676, a year after the appearance of Hortense's memoirs, the fictitious "Pierre Marteau" published *Mémoires de M.L.P.M.M. Colonne,* a spurious text based on Roman gossip concerning the Colonna ménage.[3] Two years later "Marteau" brought out an Italian version, preceded this time by Hortense's memoirs, also in Italian, plus the paratextual notices and letters that had accompanied both texts in the first editions. Concentrating on the Italian years, these pseudomemoirs relate a series of dubious escapades in which the narrator represents herself as silly, capricious, and irresponsible.[4] They

provide almost no information about her girlhood or the period that followed her departure from Rome.

Some scholars believe that they contain authentic material that could
only have originated with Marie. Citing the final sentence—"There, Monsieur, you have what you wanted from me and what I was obliged to do in
order to obey you and convince you that I am, etc." (Lever 1997b, 139)—
Chanteleuze speculates that Marie composed them in the form of a letter to
a close friend, who then allowed them to fall into the hands of an unscrupu-
lous publisher (1880, 311 n. 1). Lever, who reedited them in 1997, is not
specific about their provenance but contends that they are an "unauthorized" version of Marie Mancini's story: "Obeying no apologetic exigen-
cies, not held to any obligation of either reserve or glorification, for that
reason they seem to us the most independent, the most open, and the most
creditable" (Lever 1997b, 31).[5] Dulong refers to them as "apocryphal" (1993,
273), but often suggests that what they say about Marie is true.

Marie Mancini objected so strenuously to this unauthorized and inauthentic representation of her life that she wasted no time in refuting it.
Early in 1677, she brought out *La Vérité dans son jour, ou les véritables
mémoires de M. Manchini, connétable Colonne*. A Spanish translation, *La
Verdad en su Luz, o las Verdaderas Memoria de Madama Maria Manchini*,
appeared in Saragossa that same year. It seems to have been slightly revised. This is confirmed by a letter to Colonna on 15 September 1677, in
which she wrote, "I am pleased that the book has been to your liking. It is
much better in Spanish."

In 1678, a writer of pulp fiction, known variously as Sébastien Brémond,
Saint-Brémond, or Gabriel de Brémond, published a reworking of Marie
Mancini's text, which he retitled *Apologie, ou les Véritables mémoires de
Mme Marie Mancini, connétable de Colonna, écrits par elle-même*.[6] Although Brémond followed the story line of *La Vérité* closely, almost every
sentence was rewritten. For instance, in the passage telling of her decision
to marry Colonna, *La Vérité* reads, "[I]t was necessary to leave, therefore,
I hastened my departure and had no rest until I saw myself on the point of
setting off; for in short, when I have resolved something, advantageous or
the contrary, I must carry it out, not being of a humor to renounce it" (M.
Mancini 1998, 44). Brémond rewrote the passage in the third person to
read, "[W]hen one has resolved something, be it favorable or the contrary,
one must carry it out as soon as possible" (Doscot 1965, 118). As a result,
Marie's analysis of why she left France so precipitously is reduced to a
vague platitude.[7]

Many other passages were subtly modified, notably the account of
Marie's romance with Louis XIV.[8] Brémond also suppressed comments on

the dangers to which her sister exposed herself during her pregnancy, details concerning the near-fatal illness from which Marie suffered immediately after her marriage, mention of the jewels and money her husband gave her when she arrived in Rome, her prayers for a son, the precautions taken to protect her from miscarrying before the birth of her second child, and particulars about her husband's journey to Spain prior to the birth of their third child. Although he may have cut some of these passages because he found them tedious, it is significant that many of them refer to gynecological matters; he may have considered them unseemly, because they did not conform to the "classical" rule of *bienséance*. In so doing, he not only flattened Marie's narrative but in essence censored it. Brémond's procedure corresponds to what Hayden White identifies as "overt and covert code shifting by which a specific subjectivity is called up and established in the reader, who is supposed to entertain this representation of the world as a realistic one in virtue of its congeniality to the imaginary relationship the subject bears to his own social and cultural situation" (1987, 193).

It is possible that like Mademoiselle de Montpensier, Marie entrusted a "man of letters" with revising her text. It is also possible that he purloined it. Brémond was in London when *La Vérité* appeared, and someone in Hortense's circle may have given him a copy. Marie's financial and marital problems, plus the fact that she was living as a semiprisoner in Spain, would have made it impossible for her to have much control over what happened to her book. However, there is no evidence that she contested the *Apologie,* as she had the apocryphal *Mémoires de M.L.P.M.M. Colonne.*

In 1677–78, Brémond was living in England. He seems to have produced a first draft there before leaving for Holland. The first and only English translation, also entitled *Apologie,* appeared in England in 1679, published by Brémond's friend Richard Bentley. Curiously, this English translation incorporates some of the minor revisions found in the Spanish version. It may also have been based on a first draft by Brémond, which was subsequently revised still further, for although a number of passages in it were altered or omitted in the *Apologie,* it also includes some that are not found in *La Vérité.*

The existence of one set of memoirs repudiated by its supposed author, plus two others purporting to be authentic, raises many questions. It has even caused some scholars to argue that all three texts were written by someone else—either Brémond or, oddly enough, Saint-Réal.[9] There is really no reason to doubt that *La Vérité* was written by Marie, however. In three letters written to Lorenzo Colonna between March and September 1677, Marie expresses her outrage at the publication of the pseudomemoirs and discusses her progress in composing her version of her life story.[10] A letter by Madame de Villars, wife of Louis XIV's ambassador to Spain, dated 2 November 1679, also confirms Marie's authorship. She writes, "She has made a book about her life, which has already been translated into three languages" (Courtois 1878, 213). Chanteleuze confirms Marie's authorship on historical and stylistic grounds: "The authenticity of these memoirs is not open to question. . . . it would be impossible, after having read the *Apologie,* not to attribute it to its veritable author, so much do the details that the constabless gives on certain particularities of her life agree in all points with letters and memoirs of the time that had not yet appeared. Let us add that it is a completely personal work, evidently written by a great lady, very familiar with our language, well qualified to approach the subjects she treats or suggests; and that everything in it betrays Marie Mancini, including the Italianisms, which she falls into from time to time, and which only add to the charm of her narrative" (1880, 227–28).[11]

Brémond's rewriting was widely circulated and frequently reprinted. It is the version used in the Mercure de France edition, edited by Gérard Doscot. In contrast, only two copies of *La Vérité* are known to have survived, one in the Paris Bibliothèque Nationale and the other in the Madrid National Library. It was not republished until 1998, when Elizabeth C. Goldsmith and I edited it for Scholars' Facsimiles and Reprints. All citations of Marie's text refer to our edition.

CLAIMING IDENTITY

Marie Mancini's memoirs also raise the issue of truth in autobiography, but in a different way from Hortense's. Whereas the latter was essentially engaged in writing what might be called a judicial memoir, *La Vérité dans son jour* is concerned first and foremost with establishing the true identity of the author. Goaded into the autobiographical act by the scurrilous pseudomemoirs that purported to be the true story of her life, Marie's primary concern was to prove that she was neither the author of the spurious text nor the person represented in it: "I do not have to tell those who know me that there is not a single adventure that is not invented and as far from the truth as it is out of character. Those who are familiar with my conduct and my actions will see clearly that the author of this supposed history has made up everything in it, and if it contains some incidents from my life, they are so disfigured as to be unrecognizable" (M. Mancini 1998, 33). Marie also distances herself from the pseudomemoirs by characterizing them as vulgar and lacking literary merit: "I do not even speak of the lowness of his style, although it is impossible for there not to be some connection between his thoughts and the way they are expressed." Accordingly, she makes a pact with the reader to provide "a sincere and truthful account of all that has happened to me since my tenderest youth" (33).

However, there was a compelling reason why she could not carry out this promise in full, namely the fact that she wanted her book to appear while she *and the other characters in it* were still alive, especially her husband, Lorenzo Colonna, and her former sweetheart, Louis XIV, both of whom had the power to make her life still more miserable than it already was. She had to write with great circumspection, therefore, about the portions of her life in which they were involved. In the case of Louis, she had to avoid supplying details of their romance that could embarrass him; and in the case of her husband, she had to avoid accusing him directly of trying to murder her. As a result, she found herself faced with a dilemma: In order to prove the inauthenticity of the pseudomemoirs, she had to supply facts about her life that their author had not possessed; at the same time, so as not to offend the two men who had had the greatest impact on her existence, she had to withhold information about them.

She resolved this by focusing her text on herself, rather than on them, explaining the character traits that had caused her to act as she did and describing what her feelings had been in the crucial moments of her existence. As a result this text concentrates more on the author's personality than the others I have discussed so far. Valois and Montpensier used the tropes of the historical memoir: heroism, glory, and political achievement. Hortense wrote to defend her rights and to justify her request for a pension. Marie Mancini wrote about who she was and why she had done what she did.

In the pages that follow, I will first discuss how her memoirs were shaped by her need to refute the pseudomemoirs without affronting either Louis or Colonna. I will then proceed to the issue of how she tells the truth about herself, and how this has influenced posterity's assessment of her character.

La Vérité can be divided into three parts: her girlhood, her marriage, and her search for a modus vivendi from the time of her departure from Rome up to the time of writing. In each she is engaged in discrediting the pseudomemoirs that appeared the preceding year. In the first section, she challenges them by supplying information proving that she alone possesses the truth about her past. The pseudomemoirs claimed that Hortense had already said all there was to say about the Mancini sisters' childhood. But this was manifestly false. Hortense had said nothing, for instance, about the memorable journey to France that was to transform their destinies. Marie describes it in considerable detail: the Genoan galley on which they were "treated like queens," the pomp and circumstance that greeted them when they arrived on French soil, and finally, of course, their first audience with the royal family, who welcomed them with "extraordinary goodness" (34–35). She goes on to reveal more personal information that the author of the pseudomemoirs could not have known—her unhappy relationship with her mother and her jealousy of her sister Hortense.

A comparison of her text and the pseudomemoirs shows that she goes out of her way to correct them. For instance, she contradicts their claim that she initially refused Colonna's offer of marriage out of a desire for greater grandeur. She asserts that she did so because the separation from Louis had made her lose interest in the things of this world. On the other hand, she states that she encouraged Charles de Lorraine's attentions in the hope that they would lead to marriage (17–18), whereas the pseudomemoirs imply that she was promiscuously flirtatious. *La Vérité*'s version of how she and Louis parted emphasizes his promise that he would not forget her and would always protect her. The pseudomemoirs relate that she tore hysterically at his clothing and accused him of abandoning her.

In her account of her marriage to Colonna—the part of her life with which the author of the pseudomemoirs was most familiar—Marie is constantly occupied with deflecting or refuting their malicious insinuations. The spurious text consistently portrays her as vainglorious, saying, for instance, that she was gratified by the acclamation that greeted her on her journey to Italy because it proved her importance. *La Vérité* says pointedly that nothing of note happened during the trip. It does, however, reveal that when she arrived she mistakenly took Spinola (Balbasès) for Colonna and was so horrified by the former's ugliness that she announced she would not marry him (perhaps confirming the hypothesis that he detested her and commissioned the *Mémoires de M.L.P.M.M.* to punish her).

A great deal of information about the events that took place right after her marriage contradicts assertions in the pseudomemoirs. *La Vérité* corrects and amplifies the facts about her pregnancies and miscarriages and diverges significantly in its version of the initial years of her marriage, insisting that she and Colonna at first loved each other, whereas the pseudomemoirs state that they both agreed at the outset to grant each other sexual freedom. The most glaring disparity between the two narratives is their divergent explanations of *why* and *when* she broke off sexual relations with her husband. *La Vérité* relates that she did so immediately after the difficult birth of her third son because she feared that another pregnancy would kill her. The pseudomemoirs place the rupture much later, after Hortense's first visit to Rome, and allege that Marie wanted to safeguard her sons' patrimony following the marriage of Colonna's brother.[12] The pseudo-memoirs report that Colonna objected to the *séparation de lit* and tried to force himself on his wife. *La Vérité* maintains that he accepted her conditions and faithfully kept his word. Marie also denies explicitly the allegation that Hortense encouraged her to leave Rome, saying that on the contrary she tried to dissuade her. She says nothing, on the other hand, about the chevalier de Lorraine's role in obtaining a passport from Louis, probably because he is supposed to have told Louis that Colonna wanted to poison her.

The *Mémoires de M.L.P.M.M.* draw a malicious portrait of Marie in Rome, attributing to her compromising liaisons with Cardinal Chigi, the chevalier de Lorraine, and, as in Hortense's case, her brother Philippe de Nevers. They claim to explain rumored improprieties (i.e., letters from a lover discovered by her husband, a ladder placed mysteriously outside her bedroom window, a spanking episode in which both her husband and her brother participated), but the justifications they offer are so weak that they have exactly the opposite effect.[13] Marie, like Valois and Hortense, refuses to dignify most of these degrading anecdotes by denying them. Instead she describes at length her innocent if frivolous activities—frequent trips to Venice, hunting, masquerades, and elegant receptions at the Colonna palazzo.

Marie's determination to refute the false information conveyed by the spurious text accounts for many of the facts she incorporated into her version. The pseudomemoirs devote only ten pages to what happened after her escape from Rome; she devotes almost half of *La Vérité* to it, once more underlining the other author's unfamiliarity with her life outside Italy. On the other hand, she purposely avoids going into too much detail about what passed between her and Louis XIV during their romance. Her correspondence with Colonna when she was preparing her memoirs for publication proves that this was a source of anxiety for her. On 4 March 1677, she wrote, "As far as the king is concerned, I could not have explained myself in less detail, because we are dealing with such public events that it would be worse to keep silent about it. Also, everyone knows already of the good intentions that His Majesty held toward me, so if they do not see it, they will gossip about what was a decent courtship." On 29 April, she wrote, "The book is finished and even if everybody had seen it before it is printed, no one could find an excuse to say anything against it. Neither the king nor anyone else could object, as everyone knows about his gallantry, and as I note in my book, I do not go into it out of modesty."[14] Marie had already learned to her cost how important it was not to arouse Louis's ire, either by reminding him of emotions he had long since renounced, or by implying he had treated her dishonorably. It is likely that she was still smarting from the rebuke his ministers had delivered to her when she complained about his refusal to see her. This may be another reason why she expanded her reminiscences about her unhappy childhood: By focusing on what preceded the romance, she could shift attention away from the love story that should rightfully have been the centerpiece of her book.

As for the king's feelings, the reader learns about them only in their most superficial manifestations: gallant behavior, gifts, and letters. She records none of his words, nor does she reveal what they did and said when they were alone together: "The gallant adventures that accompanied our meals and our walks would require a whole volume, and thus I shall pass over them all in silence" (40). She stages their romance as a public divertissement, a series of magnificent fêtes: "Our only care was to amuse ourselves. There was no day, or better said, no moment, that was not given over to pleasure, and I can say that no one ever passed the time more agreeably than we did. His Majesty, wanting to perpetuate our diversions, ordered everyone in our circle to take turns treating us. Thus there was nothing but a succession of fêtes and balls" (39).

She offers only one example of "how delicately the king loved, and how he lost no opportunity to prove it," describing how when the hilt of his sword accidentally struck her as they were walking together, "he drew it brusquely from its scabbard, and threw it away" (40). Perhaps aware that she is disappointing her readers, she excuses her reticence on the grounds of modesty: "This would be the place to speak of the thoughts that *it is said* [emphasis mine] His Majesty had in my favor, if modesty did not forbid it, and for the same reason, I shall not expand on this prince's palpable displeasure when I withdrew for eight days to Chantilly, thinking only of dispatching couriers to me, the first of whom was a musketeer charged with five letters" (41). The only time she actually reports what the king said to her is when she recalls his final words: "[T]he king said good-bye to me, assuring me that he would always remember me and that he would protect me everywhere" (44).[15] This exception to her self-imposed rule of silence may have been inserted to justify her ill-conceived belief that he would receive her personally when she returned to France.

In representing Colonna, on the other hand, she emphasizes her affection for him, in order to counteract the impression that she wanted to defame him.[16] She reconstructs the early days of their marriage as a romantic idyll, depicting him as an ardent lover, who won her affection through patient devotion but subsequently turned against her when she put an end to their sexual relationship. She portrays him as passionately smitten with her from the moment he saw her, so eager to consummate the marriage that he refused to wait for the nuptial mass. She describes how he did everything in his power to please her, while she remained not only unresponsive but hostile. "He forgot nothing that could afford me satisfaction. He was well-groomed and dressed in a fine style. I cannot put into words how attentive, ardent, and considerate he was" (48)—until as a result of his delicate attentions, she gradually came to discover in herself an "inclination" for him.

Marie is pursuing a double agenda here, addressing both the general public, who have received a false impression of the couple from the pseudo-memoirs, *and* the man who holds the keys to her prison. Colonna emerges as gallant, tactful, and devoted in their early days together. How much of what she says about their love is designed to soften his heart and how much is true only she knew. Was she reminding him that she had loved him when she writes of her "incredible displeasure" when he was summoned to Spain, and tells of how he rushed back to her side as she gave birth? Certainly, she was trying to show him that it was not she who had spread the rumor repeated in the pseudomemoirs—that he had forced himself on her after she asked for a *séparation de lit*—"for he religiously kept his word to me all the time that we were together" (53).

Clearly, the most difficult part of her task was to convey her reasons for leaving Rome while withholding the excuse that he had tried to poison her. That is why the passage explaining her decision to escape to France seems so contradictory and inadequate. She mentions his "coldness and scorn . . . which added to my sorrows and discontents." She alludes to her brother's warning that Colonna will eventually lock her up in the fortress of Paliano. She alleges her aversion to the Roman way of life and speaks of her affinity for France, "the country where I was raised, where I had the greatest number of relatives, and where my spirit feels at home," adding quite inconsequentially, "since I love novelties, a gay atmosphere, the clash of arms, subjects who are soldiers, and not a peaceful place and a pacific government" (63–64). Marie obscures the real reason for her clandestine departure—her fear of being poisoned. Her only reference to it is an allusion to a near-fatal attack of colic; and she even blurs that hint by accusing Hortense of being as unsympathetic as Colonna (62).[17]

Marie wanted to refute the pseudomemoirs' misrepresentations, while at the same time placating Louis XIV and Lorenzo Colonna. These strategic moves had a direct influence on the contents of her text, but they also had another significant effect. They forced her to focus her story on *herself* rather than on others. In its focus on private rather than public space, Marie Mancini's *La Vérité* is the most personal and private of the self-narratives I have discussed so far. Unlike her royal predecessors Valois and Montpensier, she boasts of no talent for politics, no ambition for public service;

nor, like Hortense, does she attack the institutions that have persecuted her. For her, the courts of Europe are not the site of history, but of divertissements—magnificent diversions. Her behavior may have sparked crises of international scope, but she limits her recollections to the "feminine" sphere—the trivial occupations and limited spaces of a great lady's existence. She looks inward to the individualized private self, cataloguing, defining, analyzing, and explaining the traits that made her who she was. What is more, like the autobiographers who would come after her, she delineates the dynamics of family relationships, the formative effects of mother-daughter conflicts, the petty resentments and fierce loyalties of siblings, and the evolution of a failed marriage. And like them, her goal, seldom appreciated by her biographers, is to impose form on a chaotic existence.

This turning inward can be explained to some extent, it is true, by the circumstances in which she found herself at the time of writing. But it is also important to acknowledge that there were literary forces at work in this text. If she had few autobiographical models to learn from, she was well acquainted with the fictional narratives so popular with the *précieuses* in her youth.[18] She had arrived in France in 1653, when Madeleine de Scudéry was at the height of her popularity. Indeed, we know that a passion for literature had been instilled in Marie by the nuns who taught her to read French. And in the days when her mother confined her to her room, she must have pored over *Le Grand Cyrus* and *Clélie*.[19] When she was being courted by a king, Marie's life certainly seemed to be turning into a novel, and the fact cannot have escaped her. But if she had once thought she would live happily ever after like the heroines of fiction, by the time she wrote *La Vérité* she was well aware that she had been mistaken. It is important to bear in mind, therefore, that whatever her debt to the narrative techniques of fiction, hers is very much the story of a real woman who lived in the real world, and had learned to her cost the difference between life and fiction.

In fact, most of her text deals with what happened to her *beyond the point* at which novels end. Like almost all sentimental fiction, the pastoral romances of Marie's girlhood had dealt with foreplay. Marriage was not the subject but the goal of the plot. Marriage had one signification in fiction, however, and quite another in the real world of the ancien régime. Novels portrayed women as the wooed and pursued; for a woman in Marie's position, the opposite was more likely to be the case. The Mancinis had little social standing.[20] She had only her uncle's ephemeral power and her own charms to rely on.[21]

Yet this is not the self-representation of a woman who conceives of her identity as that of niece, sweetheart, or wife. Nor does she ever concede, all evidence to the contrary, that in leaving her husband she forfeited the right to live as she pleased. The catastrophic situation in which she found herself at the time of writing may have resulted from her failure to grasp fully her mistake in leaving the conjugal domicile, but her memoirs also inscribe a tenacious sense of self-worth. The very act of responding in print to the pseudomemoirs proves that she believed herself to be an important personage. Her pact with the readers who have been misled by the pseudomemoirs is also a pact with herself—the dysphoric ex-heroine, virtually reduced to the status of nonperson—a vow to claim the identity she sees as still and always hers. In her incipit, she defiantly sets forth a vague but sweeping myth of origins: "I was born in Rome of a family illustrious enough for me to be honored for its renown" (33). As Karro says, "The enunciation of genealogy was the first proof that one was not usurping one's place in society" (1993, 68). In point of fact, aside from her tie to Mazarin, long dead and all but forgotten at the time of writing, Marie's social standing was the result of her relationships with the two men who had loved her, the king of France and the constable of Naples. Yet she constructs herself here as a great lady sui generis, worthy of honor long before a king fell in love with her or a Roman prince made her his wife.

The emphasis she places on her childhood recollections also implies that they were significant because of who she was. They function as a stirring prelude to the episode for which she was most famous, her romance with Louis XIV. These opening pages focus exclusively on the author, revealing what she thought and felt during her years of growing up. To appreciate how far Marie Mancini progressed in the art of self-revelation, it is only necessary to compare her memories of her youth with the pseudomemoir's dismissive words: "[Y]ou know about my upbringing and the whole world also knows about the grand society I lived in with those of my age" (Lever 1997b, 48). Unlike them, Marie engages in a real search for lost time and for its meaning to the totality of her existence. Furthermore, she demonstrates how aspects of her character were already emerging: her stubborn determination to do what she wanted, her hot temper, her defiance, her refusal to play the role of "good girl."

She bitterly recalls the mother who did not love her: "When I was seven, my mother, to whom I seemed less beautiful than my sister Hortense . . . put me into the Campo Marzo, a Benedictine convent, with the intention of having me raised there for the religious life" (M. Mancini 1998, 33). But she also depicts the hot temper and quick tongue she never learned to control—the "vivacity" that would be the cause of many of her later misfortunes. She admits that from the beginning she was always determined to get her way and makes it clear that then, as later, she lacked the political skills that would have tempered her mother's antipathy. She recalls how, overcome with rancor at being excluded from court festivities, she lashed out, causing Madame Mancini to complain that she was totally lacking in docility or deference. And when her uncle delivered a furious reprimand, she refused to take it seriously.

Nonetheless, she understood all too well the psychological effects of her mother's hostility: "Education is the richest gift that fathers can offer children, after giving them their being," she writes, "but it is of great importance that it be accompanied by gentleness: too great severity often serving only to divest them of tenderness, love and fear nearly always being incompatible. I had enough experience of this myself, for it was more than two years after my mother's death, and still my imagination, obsessed by the apprehensions that remained, always represented her in my dreams to me as still living, and even waking, it seemed to me that I saw her, and this thought gave me incredible pain" (37–38).

Only after her release from this antagonistic presence could she change from ugly duckling to swan. After her mother's death, she writes, "[E]njoying all the prerogatives attached to the rights of the eldest daughter, which I now possessed, I lived quite peacefully and began to find life sweeter. Spiritual satisfaction is almost essential for good health. My state at that time was a very convincing proof of that. I was not recognizable; and I can say that this prosperity was as advantageous to my spirit as to my body, and had greatly increased my vivacity and gaiety" (38).

Her contemporaries would have grasped immediately the reasons for this fairy-tale metamorphosis, and would have taken immense satisfaction in perceiving how spectacularly wrong the wicked mother had proved to be. And if the reader was momentarily disappointed at being deprived of a more intimate glimpse of the two sweethearts, she would have been compensated by Marie's description of her own feelings—a joy so intense that she wished for a "traverse" to mitigate it, and an unbearable anguish when they were forced to part—"I cannot remain silent about the pain this separation caused me. Nothing has touched me so profoundly in my life. Everything that one can suffer appeared to me to be nothing in comparison with this absence. There was no moment in which I did not wish for death as the only remedy for my woes" (41). Later the reader would also have been touched by Marie's confession of how she impetuously disobeyed Mazarin's orders and reproached Louis for his indifference, and then resolved never to confront him again when he responded with cold indifference. Yet these passages never go beyond the bounds of good taste. On the contrary, they are remarkable for the sincerity and simplicity of the feelings expressed. And in this they are again markedly different from the pseudomemoirs, where one finds vulgar locutions like, "Thus willed my cruel fate when, capable of being a Venus, I found myself less than one of the Graces. My eyes still swell with tears and my distressed heart snuffs out all contentment when I so much as think of it" (Lever 1997b, 49).

But if Marie seems to depict herself as a romantic heroine, she also shows that she was not the total dupe of her feelings. She does not pretend that she was unmindful of her predicament, or that she refused to envision a solution. She knew very well that she could not remain single once Louis's marriage was formalized and that she must put the past behind her. She tells how she tried to forget him, even ordering Hortense to make a list of his flaws, and how she hoped to replace him with a promising French suitor. It is true that she had refused Lorenzo Colonna's offer while she was in Brouage, but she makes it clear that above all she dreaded returning to Italy, where stricter mores governed women's behavior. When the French prince Charles of Lorraine showed interest in her, she did not hesitate to encourage him.[22] And when her uncle rejected Lorraine's proposal, she understood that she had no alternative but to accept Colonna.[23] *La Vérité* makes it quite clear that she did so for pragmatic reasons. She foresaw that her position would become increasingly precarious, and even though the king grew more friendly after Mazarin's death, she had no illusions about her long-term prospects: "In spite of all these diversions, I did not cease to worry when the articles Monsieur le Connétable was supposed to have signed did not arrive from Rome. And this delay caused everyone to think that doubtless he had changed his mind after His Eminence's death" (1998, 44). Nevertheless, when Louis volunteered to find a husband for her, she proudly rejected his offer, proclaiming that she would enter a convent if Colonna refused to marry her (44). She sees clearly that she did this, however, "as much through spite as through honor." Thus it is Marie herself who understands and admits that she departed for Italy in a fit of temper, doing the very thing she had wanted to avoid. While on one hand she was able to grapple with the realities of her situation, on the other she was unable to maintain a cool head, as her heart constantly vied with her mind for supremacy.

Notwithstanding the unromantic reasons that motivated her to marry Colonna, in her account of the early part of her marriage she once more represents herself as a romantic heroine, this time the reluctant mistress, wooed and won like Astrée by the patient and arduous devotion of a long-suffering Celadon. The passage in which she describes Colonna's efforts to please her call to mind the stages mapped on Scudéry's *Carte de Tendre:* "Soumission," "complaisance," "petits soins," "empressement," "tendresse," "générosité," "respect," and "bonté." She also transforms his natural concern for her recovery into "inconceivable" despair and hopeless devotion.

But her sentimental portrayal of Colonna's initial devotion does not prevent her from perceiving with acumen the true causes of the mysterious malady that struck her down almost as soon as she set foot in Italy: "The fatigue of my journey, my displeasure at finding myself separated from my family, and above all my sorrow at leaving France, which increased as I realized the differences between its customs and those of Italy . . . , put me into the worst possible mood . . . the melancholy that had overtaken me and the effects of a fever that came upon me regularly every day, took from me all taste for pleasure" (45–46). But, she also admits, during her illness her husband had to endure more than his share of her bad temper.

In an age when marriage was a business arrangement between families, Marie manages to construct a narrative in which a husband's steadfast love triumphs over a broken heart. And if she did so in the hope that her story would soften Colonna's heart, undoubtedly it also gave her no small satisfaction to demonstrate that the woman who had once been wooed by the king of France had been capable of inspiring passion *and* falling in love again. Indeed, this part of her narrative could be construed as the real dénouement to the Ugly Duckling's story. If the prince has changed his name, it is here, nonetheless, that the heroine completes the conquest that passes for success in a narcissistic woman's life: "I can indeed say that although he [Colonna] may not be of an extremely tender nature, I am the only women he has ever loved so deeply and for so long" (48).

If, however, *La Vérité* reads like a novel in the sections dealing with her childhood, her romance with Louis, and the beginning of her marriage, thereafter autobiography and fiction inevitably part company, for where fiction imposes closure, life goes on, after the happy ending. It soon becomes evident that the harmony between her and Lorenzo was contingent on her willingness to serve his sexual and dynastic needs. She reports that not only he but his relatives lavished presents on her when their first son was born, and the news of yet another pregnancy sent Lorenzo into paroxysms of joy: "In his life he has never seemed so happy, and believing that to be so perfectly happy he only needed to see me content, there was nothing he wouldn't do to give me satisfaction" (50).

If there was any doubt that the marriage was founded on her willingness to do her conjugal duty, she dispels it when she announces her decision to evict Colonna from her bed because she fears another pregnancy. This decree has aroused a great deal of comment.[24] Dulong, following Perey, believes that the real reason Marie refused to sleep with Colonna was because he had been unfaithful to her: "It was too much for her to bear," Dulong writes, "after having come so close to winning the king of France, to learn that a second-rate Roman prince had been unfaithful to her" (1993,

155). Although Dulong does take seriously Marie's fear of dying in child-birth, she does not believe that Marie and Colonna would have broken off sexual relations so abruptly for this reason.

Dulong is convincing when she argues that Marie concealed the real reason for the *séparation de lit* because she wanted to portray herself as a woman capable of arousing and controlling masculine desire. However, this does not explain why Marie *chose* to attribute her decision to the fear of becoming pregnant, rather than offering the equally face-saving reason set forth in the pseudomemoirs—that she wanted to limit the number of heirs in order to preserve her sons' patrimony. It seems to me that if she used the former pretext rather than the latter, it was because it expressed her deeply felt conviction regarding women's right to safeguard their health by limiting pregnancies. After all, Marie grew up in France during the de-cade when women were asserting their reproductive rights.[25] Furthermore, the publication of the abbé de Pure's *Prétieuse,* in which Eulalie complains of "a youth that is too fecund and too abundant, . . . which exposes her every year to a new burden, to a visible peril" (1938, 1:285), coincided with the death of Marie's older sister, who died at twenty-two following the birth of her third child. This tragedy may well have impressed the va-lidity of Eulalie's arguments on Marie and made her vow to avoid a similar fate. Her husband's infidelity could well have provided her with an excuse for putting Eulalie's principles into action. And the fact is that she had good reason to do so. In less than six years she had borne three sons and suffered two miscarriages.[26] At this crucial point in her life history, I be-lieve, Marie *chose* to represent herself as the *précieuse* she had once been. Rejecting the patriarchal argument that her sons' patrimony must be safe-guarded, she published her adherence to the profeminist doctrines of the salon movement.

The *séparation de lit* marks the point of no return in her narrative. Until then it has wavered between representing "real" life and romance, but now Marie embarks on an unsentimental analysis of the events and emotions that had led to her incarceration in Madrid. Whether Colonna's infidelity preceded or followed her decision to end their conjugal relations, it had a profound impact on her. As always, she is explicitly honest about her emotional state. She writes that in the wake of her decision she fell prey to jealous doubts, which proved all too founded: "[T]he pain of seeing that others were profiting because of my political sterility, gave me very bad moments, and had already reduced me to a pitiful state" (1998, 54).

Her initial jealousy gave way to a growing resentment toward her hus-band, exacerbated by the fact that he was now less willing to satisfy her whims or indulge her in the "divertissements" she adored. Instead he insisted that she submit to the hated Italian mores. Nonetheless, she is not unmindful of the fact that her hot temper and willfulness were also partly to blame for the deterioration in their relationship. She admits that when he denied her permission to accompany Hortense and Philippe to Venice, she could not contain her anger: "This refusal and the manner in which he gave it so irritated me, *for I grow bitter if I am resisted and especially when I know that someone is taking pleasure in opposing me* [emphasis mine], that I would have walked out then and there, if the marquise Spinola had not overcome my resentment and made me see reason" (57).

Another unattractive facet of her personality emerges in these pages. She depicts herself as a woman in desperate pursuit of frivolous amusement.[27] Of course, this aspect of her character is nothing new. Her disputes with her mother grew out of Madame Mancini's refusal to let her enjoy the pleasures of court life; and she describes her romance with Louis as an endless round of amusements. One should also bear in mind that when she was composing her memoirs, she was not even allowed to go for a ride in her carriage, which may have caused her to exaggerate the value of worldly distractions. Yet ultimately Marie's unquenchable thirst for distraction must be understood for what it is: the reflection of the pettiness and futility that permeated aristocratic women's lives. Once the challenge of making a brilliant marriage and the duty of producing male heirs had been met, a woman like Marie had no purpose in life. Her husband was occupied with overseeing his property and carrying out his administrative duties. She had nothing to do but keep herself amused. Gambling, hunting, concerts, promenades, balls, and masquerades were all she had to fill up the empty hours.

She offers no account of serious or fruitful activity. Indeed, in her preoccupation with "divertissement," Marie Mancini seems to be willfully suppressing the intellectual dimension of her existence. In France, she had been known as a bluestocking. Somaize described her as a women who had read all the good books. Her letters show that she wrote far more legibly and correctly than many women of her circle. What is more, during the years spent in Italy, she produced a book on astrology.[28] Yet in *La Vérité* she never mentions any of this. In this most feminine of self-representations, intellectual accomplishments are carefully concealed, and the narrator's persona is constructed within the prescribed boundaries of the womanly. The "perle des précieuses" reveals herself only in the literary tenor of her story and the profeminist stance she assumes on reproductive rights.

The sections I have just discussed make up only the first half of Marie's narrative. The second half is devoted to what happened to her after she left Colonna. Again, one reason for this is her determination to prove that she is the only person authorized to write her life story, since only she can provide such detailed information about these years. However, there are other reasons for the length of this section. Her inability to understand what had brought her to such a sorry pass may also explain why this portion of her story is so long. This is an obsessive re-creation of a tumultuous journey, swinging progressively out of control. Picaresque peregrinations were, of course, a staple of the novels to which both Hortense's and Marie's memoirs have been compared;[29] and it is possible that this also influenced this part of her story. My own opinion, however, is that although picaresque elements are certainly present in her chronicle, it should be construed first and foremost as an autobiographical act. This account is driven by a compulsive need to transcribe exactly what happened, what Marie and all the other actors in her drama said and did, to sort out these confusing events, and to impose at least chronological order on the most incoherent portion of her existence.

With the frankness that pervades her entire narrative, she makes no attempt to hide the naïve frame of mind in which she set out for France. She admits she had assumed she and Hortense would be allowed to live in their uncle's palace, despite the fact that it was now occupied by Hortense's husband and that Hortense had agreed not to reside in France. Nor did it occur to Marie that the king would refuse to see her, or that her presence would be less than welcome, or that political considerations would prevent the French government from supporting her cause. Throughout this account of miscalculations, intrigues, betrayals, and mishaps, Marie records her appalling lack of insight into the people she comes into contact with. She shows how she alienated those who tried to help her and entrusted her fate to those who sought her downfall. If she recognizes her blunders, it is always in retrospect—"I repented, albeit later."

She is constantly declaring how her shortcomings worked against her. "I have a character that is irritated by contradiction"—a fact she blames on a malevolent fortune. But whereas Valois saw Fortune as an external force, Marie blames it for inspiring her to make mistakes: "[A]s fortune cannot suffer me to enjoy for long the good I possess, she decided *to use me against myself* and to trouble my repose with spiteful and sorrowful sentiments, *making me write a letter* complaining of His Majesty's lack of sympathy for me [emphasis mine]" (73–74).

As was true for the other writers studied here, the issue of Marie's self-representation has been obscured by the propensity to confuse biography and autobiography. All too often, critics have concentrated more on Marie's life than on her text. And of course, the innuendoes of the pseudomemoirs have been given more credence than *La Vérité*. This is not too surprising, given the widespread tendency to assess a woman's life in terms of her sexual conduct, and to assume that silence on that subject is tantamount to lying. What is surprising is the fact that the frankness and honesty with which Marie analyzes herself have also been turned against her; and the very qualities that set her text apart have caused her to be denounced as a foolish woman. Even sympathetic biographers like Perey, Mallet-Joris, and Dulong have criticized Marie for her inability to act sensibly, while failing to acknowledge that if she appears obtuse and headstrong, it is because she confesses her flaws so candidly. As Dulong exclaims in exasperation, "The historian sometimes experiences considerable discouragement when confronted with heroes and heroines whose destiny and character, unlike the novelist, she cannot change. Every time Marie opens her mouth, one would like to cry, 'Shut up!' before she has a chance to speak. But alas! . . ." (1993, 222). And later she writes, "Marie lived only in the moment, forgetting a misfortune as soon as it was behind her, never foreseeing the next one" (254). Never does Dulong give her credit for the rare honesty and self-awareness with which she compiled this relentless catalog of mistakes.

Yet if her critics come away infuriated by her stupidity, it is because Marie constructed a narrative that fuels their reaction. Were it not for her unflinching willingness to retrace her mistakes, the reader would not be able to judge her and her blunders so harshly. Thus, it seems to me that in the final analysis, the weakness of her character is transposed by her honesty into textual strength.

I would also like to point out that those who call Marie obtuse or foolish do so because they agree implicitly with the patriarchal structures that denied rights to women. Ladies in Marie's situation could not circulate freely in society unless they cohabited with their husbands. The most they could hope for was to be allowed to reside in a convent. And there, living conditions were imposed by authorities whose principal function was to maintain the patriarchal institutions that granted virtually unlimited power to husbands. This is the bitter truth that was forced on her progressively in the years after she left Rome.

Like Hortense's memoirs, *La Vérité* inscribes the progressive narrowing of her expectations. As she treks back and forth across Europe, her dream of returning to Mazarin's palace gives way to the search for a safe haven where she could enjoy a modicum of comfort, until, in the final pages, she finds herself bargaining for the right to ride out in her carriage once a week. If her biographers have criticized her actions, it is because they have implicitly judged them by the patriarchal ideology of her time. They have not found merit but stupidity in her efforts to resist the system that denied freedom and autonomy to women. Yet from the very first pages to the final episodes, Marie's story is a cry for freedom.[30] As a child she fights not to be sent to a convent. At court she is forced to stay in her room. While Louis goes off to be married, she is sequestered in a lonely château on the French coast. She flees from Rome fearing that her husband will lock her up, only to end up behind convent walls, first in France, then in Madrid. Her story is an early woman's endlessly fruitless search for a place where she can live life on her own terms. These words, which she set down in the final pages of *La Vérité,* sum up the determination with which she pursued this goal:

> [A]s I reflected from time to time on the violence with which they tried to keep me in the convent under unpleasant conditions that were very differ-ent from those I had been led to hope for, I was filled with cruel uncer-tainty. I did not, however, lose courage because the two attempts I had made to deliver myself had failed so badly, and knowing that liberty is the richest treasure on earth, and that there is nothing a great and generous spirit should not do to win it, or recover it when it has been lost, I once more applied myself to regaining it. (90)

6

Jeanne Guyon

Madame Guyon was born into a pious family of Montargis in 1648. Neglected by a mother who favored her younger brother, she spent much of her childhood in convent schools. There she acquired religious knowledge that her father delighted in displaying to visitors, including the exiled queen of England. At twelve she experienced a religious conversion and decided to enter the Visitandine Order, but was forbidden to do so by her father. When she was fifteen, he married her to Jacques Guyon, a wealthy citizen of Montargis twenty-two years her senior. The marriage was arranged without her consent and she signed the nuptial contract without knowing what it was. She bore five children to Guyon, of whom two died in childhood. Her married life was miserable, due in large part to her mother-in-law, a penny-pinching harridan who criticized everything she did. Her husband, himself given to irascibility and violent jealousy, consistently took his mother's side against her. Realizing that if she was to maintain her sanity she must find some way to make her life bearable, she resolved to seek mystical union with God and undertook a rigorous program of devotional exercises and ascetic self-discipline. Her efforts met with little success until a hermit advised her to seek God within herself. This revelation formed the basis of her meditation practices and teachings.

Following her husband's death in 1676 (she was twenty-eight), she was free to devote herself to religion. In 1681 she made a financial settlement on her children, reserving only a pension for herself, placed her two sons under her mother-in-law's guardianship, and set off for Thonon on the Swiss border, accompanied by her younger daughter and her spiritual director, the Barnabite priest François La Combe. There she entered into an informal association with the Nouvelles Catholiques, an order devoted to converting Swiss Protestants to Roman Catholicism. Soon after, she experienced an overwhelming urge to write and composed *Les Torrents* (published by Poiret in 1704). In all likelihood, she also produced the first draft of her autobiography during this period.

As it became clear to the ecclesiastical authorities that she had no intention of becoming a nun or endowing a religious community, she fell into disfavor and was forced to leave the area. In 1685, she published *Le Moyen court de faire oraison,* a practical guide to mental prayer, which immediately gained a wide readership but was viewed with suspicion in some ecclesiastical quarters. For a while she traveled in Savoy, northern Italy, and the regions around Marseille and Grenoble, visiting those who shared her interest in meditation practices. Then, in July 1686, she returned to Paris, where Louis XIV, determined to impose order and unity through the suppression of religious dissidence, had just revoked the Edict of Nantes and increased pressure to stamp out nonconformism. In 1687, questions about Guyon's orthodoxy redoubled after Innocent XI sentenced Miguel de Molinos, a Spanish priest, to life in prison and condemned as heretical his doctrine of quietism (the belief in a passive spirituality attained by contemplation). Her brother, who had tried unsuccessfully to gain access to her money, denounced her and La Combe to the religious authorities, accusing them of heresy and sexual misconduct.

Although the quietist controversy was rooted in theological controversies and later expanded into a personal struggle between Fénelon and Bossuet, it is evident that Guyon's status as an unattached female was in no small way responsible for her problems. In the same way that the Mancini sisters were regarded as outlaws when they left the conjugal domicile, Guyon's insistence on retaining control of her financial resources and her refusal to take religious vows made her seem highly suspect. When this was added to the fact that she moved about freely, accompanied by a man who was not her husband, *and* that she had set herself up as an authority on religious practices, it was almost inevitable that church and state would take steps to curb her. And, as had been the case with Valois and the Mancinis, her accusers assumed that her guilt must be at some level sexual in nature.

In January 1688, Guyon was sequestered in a Visitandine convent and forced to submit to a series of interrogations regarding her conduct and her beliefs. None of the charges against her could be substantiated. She was released at the end of the summer and even enjoyed a brief moment of favor with the king's morganatic wife, Madame de Maintenon, who invited her to Saint-Cyr. It was at this time that Guyon began her correspondence with Fénelon, soon to be appointed tutor to the crown prince, for whom he composed his best-known work, *Les Aventures de Télémaque.*

Before long, however, accusations of quietism resurfaced. She was banned from Saint-Cyr; Fénelon was attacked as her defender; and she was subjected to harsh questioning by Bossuet, who eventually had her arrested by the royal police. On 31 December 1695 she was incarcerated in Vincennes. The next year she was moved to a convent on the rue de Vaugirard; then, in June 1698, to the Bastille, where she remained until March 1703. She was handed over to the custody of her elder son and allowed to live near him in Blois. Although there is absolutely no evidence that she and La Combe ever had a sexual relationship, he confessed under torture to having been her lover. He eventually went mad and died in the prison of Vincennes in 1715.

During her last years in Blois, Guyon was visited by Protestant admirers from England, Scotland, Holland, Germany, and Switzerland; but although she made them welcome, she always maintained that she was a true daughter of the Catholic Church. She died on 9 June 1717 and was buried as she requested in the Church of the Récollets in Blois.

Guyon was a prolific writer. She claimed that she produced her texts automatically under divine dictation. In addition to her devotional books and spiritual and biblical commentaries, she produced two autobiographical works, *La Vie* and *La Relation de Madame Guyon*.[1]

PUBLICATION HISTORY:
LA VIE DE MADAME GUYON ÉCRITE PAR ELLE-MÈME

La Vie was composed in several stages. Gondal believes that a first draft of what is now part 1 was written in about 1682. It covered events up to her arrival in Thonon. This draft, which Guyon claims was rejected by her spiritual director because it was incomplete, she revised and expanded in 1688 during her first detention. It covers the years on the Swiss border, her subsequent peregrinations, and her battle to defend herself from the charges against her. She completed it on 21 August 1688 while she was still sequestered in the Convent of the Visitation. Although she claims that it was written out of obedience to her spiritual director, the urgency of defending herself from the charges against her was evidently uppermost in her mind and she undoubtedly intended it to be read by her interrogators. In addition, she was certainly concerned about the effect her arrest would have on her followers and hoped that they would be reassured by it.

Two short sections added in September describe her release and her first meetings with Fénelon. After her incarceration in the Bastille, she composed a brief final installment. It recounts Bossuet's interrogations and her imprisonment, but provides few details. During her last years, she prepared *La Vie* for publication and entrusted it to A. M. Ramsay, an English admirer. He arranged for its publication in Amsterdam by Pierre Poiret in 1720.

The manuscript on which Poiret's edition is based, although not in her hand, was supposedly authorized by her. It is now in the Bodleian Library at Oxford. A second edition in 1791 was essentially a reprinting, with the addition of a long "Discours sur la vie et les écrits de Madame Guyon" by Dutoit. In 1962, Jean Bruno reedited the first section, which covers the years 1648–81, for the *Cahiers de la Tour Saint-Jacques* along with an introductory essay, a bibliographical summary, and a chronology of Guyon's life. Bruno's great contribution was to restore passages cut from the Oxford manuscript in the Poiret edition (notably accounts of an adolescent romance and an emotional entanglement with a Jansenist priest), but due to space limitations he was forced to make extensive cuts in some other passages already published by Poiret.[2] Bruno speculates that the expurgated sections were deleted at the family's request, but it is also possible that one of her followers decided to suppress them. Bruneau suggests that it was her daughter who opposed their publication.[3] Although Bruno promised to publish the entire text at some future date, he never did so. As a result, there is no scholarly edition of Guyon's text. Dervy-Livres reprinted the Poiret edition in 1983.

Gondal believes that a manuscript in Saint-Brieuc may be a copy of the version Guyon completed in 1688. It contains passages that correspond to erasures in the Oxford manuscript, as well as episodes that do not appear there. Gondal describes it as "more prosaic and more colored," whereas the published version puts more emphasis on the author's inner life. In Gondal's view, the Oxford manuscript was destined for the public at large, whereas the more personal and detailed Saint-Brieuc manuscript was intended for those closest to the author.[4] Her theory is corroborated by the fact that another autobiographical work, the *Relation de Mme Guyon,* provides details about Guyon's arrest and imprisonment that she explicitly excluded from *La Vie*. Gondal has published this text under the title *Récits de captivité*.

I will cite the Dervy Livres edition of *La Vie,* supplementing it with passages from Bruno's additions from the first part of the Oxford manuscript.

"A Life as Miserable and Extraordinary as Mine"

La Vie de Madame Guyon belongs to a different branch of autobiographical writing than the memoirs I have discussed so far. It is a spiritual autobiography, a genre that traces its origins back to Augustine's *Confessions* and, due to the popularity of Saint Teresa of Avila's *Vida,* had become a popular medium for women in the seventeenth-century. Guyon worked diligently to make *La Vie* conform to the conventions of this genre: There were political reasons for this. When she rewrote her text in 1688, she was defending herself from charges of heresy and fornication. By representing her life story as a spiritual journey, she hoped to convince her interrogators as well as her followers that she was both innocent and saintlike. But just as the Valois and Montpensier narratives did not follow traditional models of life-writing, so her story broke out of the bounds of spiritual autobiography as it had been practiced before her. Unlike most other spiritual autobiographers of the period, she was not a cloistered nun but a secular woman who had never belonged to a religious order. In addition, she was endowed with a rebellious spirit that made it difficult for her to accept the restrictions that the genre placed on representing the feminine condition. The act of representing her femininity causes her text, like the memoirs already studied, to resist generic conventions and defy the gender ideology they encoded.

Foucault has argued that the "genealogy" of modern autobiography can be traced back to early Christianity, when ritual practices of self-examination and confession created a "technology of the self." Foucault was not the first to notice life-writing's debt to early Christianity, but his perspective is original in that it emerges from his perception of the way ideology shapes autobiographical discourse. Foucault defines "genealogy" as the "union of erudite knowledge and local memories which allows us to establish a historical knowledge of struggles and to make use of this knowledge tactically today" (1978, 83). This definition implies that the "genealogy" generated by confessional practices should be conceptualized as a history of subversively political struggles for rights, an interpretation that is corroborated by his insistence that genealogy is an "insurrection of subjugated knowledges" that must discover what has been silenced or forgotten (81).

There is something missing in Foucault's analysis, however. It is hard to see how spiritual introspection, in and of itself, produced the sense of uniqueness that characterizes the modern "self." Augustine, for instance, in no way thought of himself as a unique individual. As Weintraub argues, "the indications are that he saw in the story of *one* Christian soul, the one he could know best, the *typical* story of all Christians" (1978, 45). Early spiritual autobiography followed a predetermined script, and the self it represented was allegorical and exemplary, not unique and individualized.

Other factors were at work in the construction of the individualized/ modern self, as opposed to the allegorical/exemplary self, and in the emergence of self-conscious self-representation. One of these was gender (a category Foucault did not consider). When a woman wrote her spiritual autobiography, she could not write as universal "man," nor could she, as Weintraub claims Augustine did, see the whole history of "mankind" in her life story. Her story was necessarily imbued with the sense of being excluded from universal discourse.

A woman's *difference* was the result of her lack, not of male genitalia, but of autonomy—the right to decide her own destiny. Augustine was free to choose chastity, if and when he decided to. A woman was not. As Mason writes, Augustine's use of the conversion narrative, with its "climactic victory" of spirit over flesh, is prototypical of masculine autobiography (1988, 210). A woman's body was controlled by her family, and her life's scenario was prescribed by her obligation to marry the man chosen for her and to bear his children. The lives of women saints bear witness to this. They proved that they were holy by wresting control of their bodies away from their fathers and suitors so that they could offer them to God.

Cloistered nuns like Teresa of Avila were exempted from the biological destiny of wife and mother and could identify themselves at least to some extent with universal mankind, but this was impossible for a secular, married woman. In Guyon's narrative, therefore, living as a woman in the world functions as a "technology of the self," producing a sense of individualized identity. Just as the other writers analyzed here departed from the established conventions of historical memoirs, so she explored aspects of her existence that lay outside the traditional boundaries of spiritual autobiography. However, she did not do so without experiencing acute anxiety at the scene of writing.

To be sure, the project of spiritual autobiography was always fraught with misgivings for women writers, who were inevitably torn between the moral imperative of self-abnegation and the necessity for placing themselves at the center of the text. Typically they justified doing this by claiming to be writing at the order of a spiritual director, thus shifting responsibility onto an ecclesiastical authority and defining what they were doing, as Foucault points out, as a function of sacramental confession.

Guyon explicitly invokes this convention in her incipit, which is addressed to her spiritual advisor (presumably Father La Combe, although he is nowhere mentioned by name): "Since you wish me to write a life as miserable and extraordinary as mine; and you thought the omissions I made in the first one too considerable to leave it in that state, I want to obey you with all my heart and do as you desire" (1983, 15). Her pledge articulates the paradox that runs through her text: to fulfill the vow of obedience, she must write about matters that she does not want to discuss. Although she does not state their nature here, she will later reveal that they concern "uncharitable" revelations about those who were responsible for her "crosses" (misery). She makes this clear when she launches into the story of the cruel treatment she endured from her husband and mother-in-law: "It would be painful for me to write to you about this kind of thing, which cannot be done without appearing uncharitable, if you had not forbidden me to leave anything out, and if you had not absolutely commanded me to explain everything and to put in all the details" (53).

If Guyon is uncomfortable about including these "details," it is not only because they make her seem "uncharitable." It is because they go against the conventions of spiritual autobiography, which traditionally regarded external experiences as irrelevant and kept information of an anecdotal or intimate nature to a minimum. Marie de l'Incarnation, when pressed by her son to elaborate on the marriage that she had regarded as a form of captivity, would say only that its purpose had been to bring him into the world (1929b, 482). Likewise, Marguerite-Marie Alacoque refused to reveal the names of those who had persecuted her in her youth (1920, 32–33). By placing the responsibility for speaking of her unhappy marriage on her director, Guyon is exonerating herself for doing what spiritual autobiographers are not supposed to do.

In point of fact, however, her claim that she is including this contested material because her director has ordered to do so is problematic at best. When she revised her *Vie* in the summer of 1688, she had been forbidden to have any contact with La Combe, let alone obey his orders; and she was certainly not writing under obedience to him when she prepared her text for publication shortly before her death. These words are not, therefore, proof of her obedience, but a screen to conceal her unwillingness to suppress questionable material. Her victimization as a wife constitutes both gap and excess, a story that should not be included but cannot be left out.

Which brings me back to what I said about the difference between spiritual autobiography as written by a man like Augustine and spiritual autobiography as written by early modern women. The information Marie de l'Incarnation and Alacoque did not reveal, and that Guyon did, was the direct result of the fact that they lacked autonomy—the right to decide to follow a spiritual vocation. What was at stake was not so much "Christian charity" as the double bind that forced them to choose between duty to parents and what they perceived as duty to God. As dutiful daughters and conformist spiritual autobiographers, they submissively refused to discuss these matters. But Guyon did not bow to the code that silenced women's complaints about their disenfranchisement.

There are indications, however, that she continued to agonize over this question. Her letters to Fénelon, written soon after she had completed the

1688 revision, show that she was still of two minds on the subject. In them she complains that she cannot get away from writing about the "particular," and that she finds herself blocked when she tries to write about her spiritual state: "I can speak only of particular facts, or of what can be expressed, which is the least part of the state I sustain" (Masson 1907, 24). The following year, eager for him to read her *Vie,* she offers to abridge it "and leave in only what relates to the interior, along with the exterior conduct indispensably necessary to make myself known" (Masson 1907, 203).[5] Bruno's discovery of the differences between the Oxford manuscript and the Poiret edition and Gondal's research on the variant manuscripts provide further proof of Guyon's ambivalence about communicating the details of her "external" life. Yet, as even the expurgated Poiret edition makes clear, in the end she did not suppress them. Up to and including the time she was preparing her book for publication, she was never able to eradicate the details of her "miserable life."

The scene of writing conjured up in Guyon's opening sentence—in which a female penitent submits without question to a male director—is more than a little fictitious, therefore. Not only does her unexpurgated story tacitly call into question the gender roles and theological doctrines that it overtly upholds; it undermines the very premise of obedience to masculine authority that it seems to reinscribe. As we shall see, this is a highly formulaic text, yet in its graphic depiction of episodes that represent her as the victim of gender oppression, it goes much farther than other examples of the genre. As a result, it is continually shifting between imitating and subverting the generic conventions of spiritual autobiography.

It does this through strategies that separate narrative from didactic discourse, inserting digressions in an authorial voice, in order to distance the writer, at the time of writing, from the past events she is narrating. This results in the representation of two selves: the self written about (the past self who lived the story she is telling), and the writing self (the present self who passes moral and spiritual judgments on the acts, attitudes, and experiences of the past self). In this way, the author not only transmutes the events of the narrative into edifying exempla (thus further justifying their inclusion), she represents herself as conforming *at the time of writing* to the patriarchal ideology that her narrative seems to call into question.[6] Her text is thus an amalgam of shocking disclosures and pious disclaimers, the latter relating the spiritual journey of an allegorical/exemplary self, the former supplying a wealth of details about a woman's miserable and extraordinary life. As a consequence, her text complies on one level with the conventions of the genre, while on another it resists them, a fact that contributes in no small measure to the many tensions and contradictions inscribed in it.

I will concentrate here on how the sections of *La Vie* that deal with her childhood and marriage contest and expand the conventions of spiritual autobiography by replacing its repression of gendered experience with the story of a spiritual journey undertaken in a female body.

In one sense *La Vie de Madame Guyon* comes the closest of all the texts studied here to modern definitions of autobiography.[7] Yet a modern reader finds it difficult to appreciate this, due to its ostentatious prudishness, pious self-abnegation, and pervasive paranoia. One must bear in mind, however, that such attitudes were not peculiar to Guyon. They were prevalent in the Counter-Reformation and are found in many other spiritual autobiographies of her time. Following the Wars of Religion, and inspired by Teresa of Avila, mysticism flourished in seventeenth-century France. As had been the case in Spain, a high percentage of these enthusiasts were women: Madame Acarie, Marie de l'Incarnation, Jeanne de Chantal, Marguerite-Marie Alacoque, and Antoinette Bourignan, to name the most celebrated examples. Brémond believes this was so because the Catholic hierarchy, which jealously excluded women from all priestly functions, paradoxically regarded their visions and raptures as a source of inspiration to the faithful, so long as they remained devout daughters of the Church, deferred to the recommendations of their spiritual directors, and practiced the virtue of self-renunciation.[8] Bowman, who made a comparative study of French seventeenth-century spiritual autobiographies, affirms that they commonly incorporate persecutions, mortifications, and diabolic possessions (1976, 24). He also identifies four recurrent "themes": "the consumption of disgusting matter and vomiting; the rejection of sexual activity and especially horror at sexual penetration; the fear of a fall through space; the refusal of the edenic myth of childhood" (26).

Such works had a threefold agenda: didactic, hagiographic, and apologetic. Their ostensible aim was to edify and instruct the reader with an exemplary account of the (saintly) author's spiritual journey. But to accomplish this, their authors first had to prove that they possessed valid spiritual credentials. What is more, since mystics were regarded with suspicion by both church and state, particularly if they were women, they had to insist heavily on the orthodoxy of their beliefs and the probity of their practices. As Weber shows, this was one of Teresa of Avila's main concerns.[9] And it was especially true for Guyon, who was rewriting her autobiography while she was undergoing interrogations for her beliefs and behavior.

The hagiographic focus of her text is immediately apparent in her claim that she is descended from a long line of "saints," particularly on her father's side, and in her insistence that like the saints of old, she had to endure excruciating physical afflictions or "crosses." She gives a harrowing account of her entry into the world. Born prematurely, she nearly died of an abscess that caused gangrene in both thighs. While her father rushed frantically back and forth, she was alternately given up for dead and revived: "Such an unexpected malady at such a tender age should have been fatal," she writes, "but oh my God, as you wanted to make me the subject of your greatest mercies, you did not allow it. This abscess, which gave off such frightful puss, symbolized, it seems to me, oh my love, the corruption in me that you had to expel" (1983, 22). Nor did her physical afflictions end in infancy. She characterizes her childhood as "a tissue of ills" (25)—"In the evening I would be well, and in the morning I would be found swollen and covered with bruises; other times I had high fevers. At nine I was taken by such a furious fit of vomiting blood that I was expected to die" (31).

With the same intent, she portrays herself as precociously devout. She offers cloying examples of pious acts, telling of how she gave her breakfast to a statue of the Christ child and distributed alms to the poor. "I liked to hear people talk about God," she claims, "to be in church, to dress myself as a nun" (23). She tempers this by making a scrupulous list of her childish sins: "I became a liar, I lost my temper, and was not devout" (29). In one anecdote, undoubtedly intended to refute the accusation that like the quietists she did not believe in hell, she tells how at four or five she began to suspect that the idea of hell had been invented by the nuns to promote good behavior. A nightmare about hell convinced her of her error. In another episode, probably inspired by Teresa of Avila's story of how she tried to run away to have her head cut off by the Moors, she relates that she professed such a strong desire for martyrdom that the nuns offered to cut off her head, until she reminded them that she couldn't be martyred without her father's permission. A third anecdote telling how she fell down a well shaft corroborates Bowman's identification of the fall into darkness as a common trope in this literature. Guyon sees this adventure, which she survived by perching on a board, as yet another prefiguration of her spiritual life: "Oh my Love, was this not a symbol of my future state? How many times have you left me, with your prophet, in a *profound, muddy abyss* from which I could not escape? . . . but you have saved me by your goodness alone" (30).

But although precocious piety in the hagiographic tradition is a pervasive trope, Guyon's childhood narrative goes far beyond the traditional texts in narrating this aspect of her existence. She provides vivid and detailed analyses of her early feelings and experiences. Mallet-Joris calls these pages "A true portrait of a gifted child, affectionate in spite of her misfortunes, who has her childhood sins but also a mischievous gaiety" (1978,

101–2). Like Marie Mancini, Guyon understood the influence of parental attitudes on psychological development. She too portrays herself as the victim of a censorious, unloving mother, but, unlike Marie, she identifies herself with her father, who, she believes, despite overwhelming evidence to the contrary, doted on her. She is also highly conscious of the role of gender bias in her mother's rejection: "My mother, who did not much like girls, neglected me somewhat and left me too much in the care of servants, who also neglected me" (1983, 2); "She consistently preferred my brother to me, which was so obvious that everyone thought it wrong: for when I was sick and had a craving for something, my brother would ask for it, and although he was perfectly well, they would take it away from me and give it to him. . . . I was jealous of my brother, for there was never a time when I didn't notice the difference in the way my mother treated him and me. No matter what he did, he was always right and I was always wrong" (34).

Her bitterness toward her mother is a striking example of her inability to portray herself consistently as humble and submissive. It is obvious that even at the time of writing she was not willing to forgive her mother. In an outspoken authorial digression she denounces such "unjust preferences that single out one child over another," calling them "the cause of divisiveness and ruin in families, where instead equality should unite hearts and maintain charity." She even asserts that mothers like hers are responsible when their daughters go astray (23). Likewise, although her discursive voice suggests that she should have profited spiritually from her mother's "crucifying" conduct, it is evident that she has never resigned herself to it: "I was not guilty of anything, *it seems to me* [emphasis mine], but making cute remarks (or so I thought) that made people laugh" (27). This statement introduces a key theme: Guyon's struggle to be acknowledged as an autonomous speaking subject. Not only does this struggle play itself out in her childhood and later in her married life, it is the subtext of her entire project, for what is at stake in the interrogations she undergoes as she amplifies her autobiography is her right to be the author of a spiritual guidebook.

Here and in the pages that follow, she goes out of her way to depict Madame de la Mothe as the negative force in her life: "It was certainly akin to murder to bring me up so badly, for I was by nature strongly inclined to good and I loved good things. I was suited to reasonable conduct; I let myself be won over easily by gentleness" (36). Paradoxically, although she denounces her mother for not treating her as she deserved, in fact she internalized Madame de la Mothe's gender bias, attributing her access to speech to a male authority figure, her father. She also credited him with bequeathing her his saintly lineage and saving her from death in the first hours of her life.

Thus she claims that he rescued her from her neglectful mother by sending her to a convent school, where she was taught by *his* daughter from a previous marriage. It was this half-sister who nurtured her intellectual and spiritual capacities, whereas her mother had stifled her wit and charm. Under her guidance, she learned so much that when she returned home, her father displayed her to guests, including the exiled queen of England, who was so taken with her that she wanted to take her home to be her daughter's maid of honor.[10]

Guyon also blames her mother for teaching her the sin of vanity:

> My mother, seeing that I was very big for my age, and more pleasing to her than had been usual, thought of nothing but producing me in public assemblies and dressing me elegantly. Unfortunately she encouraged the beauty that you had given me, Oh my God, solely to proclaim your praise and blessings, and which, notwithstanding this, inspired in me pride and vanity. A quantity of suitors presented themselves, but as I was not yet twelve years old, my father did not want to hear from any of them. (37)

This minisermon on vanity presents a clear example of how she uses narrative as a pretext for moralizing.[11] Later Guyon would write extensively of her efforts to eradicate this most feminine of sins, which she saw as the greatest impediment to her spiritual progress. But something else is also happening here. Not only does she, like Marguerite de Valois, conflate growing up with the construction of the female body as an object of desire; in describing how her mother "produced" her as a marriageable commodity, she puts her finger on how and why feminine narcissism was instilled in the women of her class. And what is more, she shows how the sexualization of her body placed her in a double bind, forcing her to choose between playing the dutiful daughter and doing what she perceived to be God's will.

Guyon's analysis of her adolescence is particularly rich. She describes a series of typical phases: religious enthusiasm, first love, an obsession with novel reading. Her religious phase was precipitated by reading the life of Saint Jeanne de Chantal:[12] "All the vows she had made, I made too. . . . I began to scourge myself as well as I was able. One day I read that she had put the name of Jesus over her heart . . . and that she had applied a red-hot iron on which that holy Name was engraved; I was very afflicted because I couldn't do the same. I had the idea of writing this sacred and adorable Name in big letters on a piece of paper; with ribbons and a big needle I attached it to my skin in four places and it remained fastened in this manner for a long time" (40).

Religious vocations that aroused violent parental opposition occur commonly in saints' lives, and Guyon's narrative is no exception. Predictably, she decided that she wanted to become a nun; her father violently opposed her project; and she resisted his edict with fervor. But whereas the saints of hagiographic literature either succeeded in having their way or died in the attempt, Guyon reached an impasse. When her family ordered her confessor to deny her absolution until she stopped seeing the Sisters of the Visitation, she was terrified. "I did not stop weeping until the next day, when I went at daybreak to find my confessor. I told him that I could not live without absolution, that . . . there was no penitence I would not accept to obtain it" (41). Curiously, she expresses no outrage at being brought to heel by this spiritual blackmail. Nor does she question the priest's right to withhold absolution from her. The incident arouses the reader's sympathy and indignation, but she herself takes no stand on it. Instead, she abruptly drops the subject of her religious vocation and switches to an account of how she nursed her father through a serious illness, dwelling on the fact that she personally emptied his slop jars as a token of her love. The episode that begins by assimilating her life to the lives of the saints veers off into a representation of filial debasement.

This anecdote points up the anomaly of a secular woman trying to construct a life story on a model traditionally used by nuns. It also shows the extent to which she identified herself with the father's law, which she saw as the key to her identity as a speaking subject. Faced with the dilemma of obeying her father or entering a convent, she surrenders to him. Concomitantly, the contradictions inherent in this impasse cause the authorial voice to distance itself from the events she recounts. Her narrative portrays her as the victim of both church and family. Her discursive voice remains silent.

In less ambiguous situations, on the other hand, the author reproaches herself vigorously for doing things in her youth that she disapproves of at the time of writing. She admits, for instance, that she was "besotted" with novels, which, like the theater, were frowned upon in devout circles: "I read day and night, so that for many months I got entirely out of the habit of sleeping. The books I read most often were novels. I loved them madly, I was hungry to find out how they ended, thinking that I would find something there, but I found nothing but a hunger for reading." She now condemns such books as "strange inventions that are harmful to youth, for even if they do no worse than waste time, isn't that too much?" In fact, so convinced is she of their deleterious effect that she condemns novel reading as "the worst thing I did." What is more, she asserts, her family was remiss in not putting a stop to it. "No one stopped me," she complains, "people think that they teach the art of conversation" (48).

It is obvious that Guyon is going out of her way to underline her adherence to the strictest and most repressive codes of behavior. Here too she may be imitating Teresa of Avila, who writes that she once loved chivalric romances, but later found them condemnable. But Guyon's diatribe must also be placed in the historical context of the mid-seventeenth century, when the novels of Madeleine de Scudéry were at the height of their popularity. What Guyon is admitting here is that as a young girl she was thrilled by the protofeminist novels of the day, with their implicit and explicit critique of the feminine condition. Furthermore, her remark that she was encouraged to read them because "people think that they teach the art of conversation" suggests that, like the women memoirists studied here, her linguistic and social skills were influenced by attitudes toward women's speech advocated in salon circles. Nonetheless, the author of *Le Moyen court* now decries reading in her effort to edify her followers and confound her critics.

A passage, which was inexplicably deleted from Poiret's edition, demonstrates even more dramatically the extent to which the discursive author now identifies herself with patriarchal oppression. It tells of her romance with a young cousin to whom she became secretly engaged.[13] She describes him as "the very model of a virtuous gentleman . . . very devoted to the Virgin, as he still is today." She stresses his appealing qualities and his deep devotion to her: "As he was good-looking, gentle, clever, and agreeable, I loved him too. There was nothing I could have desired in all the world that he would not have given me . . . his love was very chaste, as was mine, and we had no other thought." Clandestine engagements were, however, a breach of filial duty, and clandestine marriages were forbidden by law; and since the last thing Guyon wants is to appear to approve of either, she reports with satisfaction that she broke off the affair when her cousin revealed their relationship to her father: "I was so offended (for I was beginning to know my own heart and to understand the principle of honor) that my feelings for him changed to aversion." She goes out of her way here to affirm her adherence to this "principle of honor," asserting that it has often served her well "by holding me to my duty when fear of you no longer had power over me, oh my God." Her nostalgic portrait of the young man seems to betray her regrets, but her commentary steadfastly condemns not only his breach of honor but the entire concept of romantic love. "Oh my God," she exclaims, "if these loving and faithful hearts were attached to you, . . . with what goodness would you reward them; instead they are so

blind as to love miserable creatures who only repay them with ingrati-
tude." She then disparages her cousin's practice of saying the Office of the
Virgin, claiming that it made her stray from the practice of mental prayer
and caused a period of spiritual dryness: "[A]ll my former faults returned;
and I added to them a frightful vanity. The love I began to feel for myself
extinguished what remained in me of your [God's] love. . . . Oh my God, if
people knew the value of such prayer and the advantage that accrues to the
soul in conversing with you, and how important it is to their salvation,
everyone would become assiduous in its practice" (45).

Once again, Guyon's concerns are apparently didactic and apologetic.
She reiterates the superiority of her contemplative practices and represents
herself yet again as an upholder of the repressive codes that regulated
women's conduct. Yet if one sets aside the moralizing discourse, she is
obviously telling a heartbreaking tale—of how she was prevented from
marrying a man she loved and was forced to marry one she didn't. Furthermore, her description of the cousin suggests that she still regrets losing
him, even though the "principle of honor" decreed that she must give him up.

She uses the same strategy in relating the conditions under which she
married Jacques Guyon. She never complains directly that her father co-
erced her to enter into the marriage without her consent.[14] Yet she does not
hide the fact that Jacques Guyon was everybody's second choice. Although
he had sought her hand for some time, she says, her father had heretofore
always rejected him. She attributes his change of heart to his fear that she
would leave the region. It appears, however, that financial considerations
were what really led her father to agree to the match "in spite of all his
repugnance as well as my mother's." Indeed, a few lines supplied by Bruno
that are missing in the Poiret edition suggest that, like Molière's Harpagon,
Monsieur de la Mothe may have accepted Jacques Guyon on the condition
that he settle for a very small dowry, for, she reveals, before their wedding,
he broke off his betrothal to a woman "who had received almost twice as
much [as a dowry], and who was from a good family of the *noblesse de
robe*" (1962, 19 n. 16).[15]

Guyon is both shrewdly perceptive and obdurately complicitous in
analyzing her reactions to the match. She admits that Jacques Guyon's
manners "were somewhat opposed to my vanity," but she blames not him
or her father but herself—for not having the right attitude, "although the
match made for me was more advantageous than I deserved, I did not believe it to be so . . . and as I only consulted my vanity in all things, I could
not bear anything that did not flatter it" (1983, 52). And, of course, she
finds a justification for the marriage in God's will: "I was sought by many
who appeared to offer me advantageous situations, but you, oh my God,

who did not want to lose me, did not let them succeed. . . . for if I had married those men, I would have been extremely exposed to danger and my vanity would have increased" (51). Again and again she affirms that she acted rightly, making it clear to those who may doubt her probity that, as always, she placed duty above selfish desires. She did as she was told, she states, so as to avoid public humiliation or bring shame on her family. "My vanity . . . kept me from falling into those disorders that cause family ruin. I would not have wanted to do anything outwardly that could have rendered me blameworthy; and I kept up appearances so well that no one could criticize my conduct" (52). If there is a hint here that her filial duty was inspired more by vanity than by true virtue, she nonetheless steadfastly maintains that this marriage was part of God's plan for her. Although she does not hide the fact that she married unwillingly, she firmly repudiates her regrets and makes every effort to situate her unhappy marriage within the larger context of her spiritual journey. But the reader is hardly taken in by these disclaimers, since she also reveals that she signed the marriage contract without knowing what it was, or ever having met her future spouse. She also states that she was beset by premonitions of disaster, "extreme confusion" and sexual anxieties arising from "that natural modesty that I never lost." And finally, she describes her misery on her wedding day—"There was universal rejoicing over this marriage in our city, only I was sad. I could not laugh like the others, or even eat, I was so downhearted" (52)—and her reaction to her wedding night, when she sobbed hysterically, and repeated over and over that she had wanted to be a nun.

The passage from girlhood to womanhood presents an obvious site on which women autobiographers can construct textual awareness of the self. In the early modern period, even more than today, this passage was almost exclusively identified with marriage, which authorized participation in sexual activity and legitimized motherhood, both of which were confirmed by a new title (madame) and a new family name (the husband's). After marriage a woman became a different person to society and to herself. Guyon analyzes how this crucial passage affected her sense of identity. Narratives of married life were almost nonexistent in spiritual autobiography. Most of its practitioners were cloistered nuns; and if they had once been married, like Marie de l'Incarnation, they passed over their conjugal experiences in silence.[16] Even women memoirists who said far more about marriage than did their male counterparts did not go into its intimate aspects.[17] Guyon's discussion of her marriage is unique, therefore. But it is also crucial to her project, because it justifies the crisis of identity that forced her to fashion a new sense of self.

Ironically, although she states that she included this part of her story only out of obedience, the narrative and discursive voices are less at odds with each other here, and didactic digressions intrude less frequently. These pages are a cry from the heart, infused with righteous indignation at the indignities and injustices imposed on her in the Guyon household:

> I had no sooner arrived at my new husband's home than I knew that for me it would be a house of misery. It was absolutely necessary for me to change the way I behaved, for their style of life was very different from what it had been at my father's. My mother-in-law, who had been a widow for many years, thought of nothing but scrimping; whereas at my father's we had lived in an extremely noble manner: everything was on display, everything was done properly, and all the things that my husband and his mother thought of as showing off, and that I saw as good manners, were observed. . . . My surprise was still greater when I saw that I would have to give up the accomplishments I had acquired with such difficulty. In my father's house, everyone had to behave with great politeness and speak correctly; everything I said was applauded and noted. Here I was only listened to so that they could contradict me and find fault. (53)

Her words convey vividly how marriage cut her off from the person she had been and made her into someone else. She discovered to her horror that her husband and his mother did not approve of the conversational skills her father had encouraged her to acquire. And undoubtedly her disarray was heightened by her sense that the Guyons' disapproving attitude toward women's speech was related to their inferior social status. They belonged to the old-fashioned bourgeoisie that valued economy above *largesse* and heartily condemned the newfangled manners of the salon movement. "If I spoke well, they said I was preaching at them; if there were guests and a subject was being discussed, whereas my father would encourage me to speak up, there if I wanted to express my opinion, they said that I was contradicting them and shamed me into silence."

Thanks to the elder Madame Guyon, she soon became subject to fits of uncontrollable weeping and even began to stammer: "She found the secret of extinguishing my vivacious spirit and making me seem quite stupid; I became unrecognizable. Those who had not seen me said, 'What! is this the person who was supposed to be so intelligent? She can't put two words together'" (55). Within six months she was reduced to such despair that she was on the verge of cutting out her tongue: "One day, beside myself with anguish . . . I took a knife when I was alone to cut off my tongue, so that I would no longer be obliged to speak to those who only made me talk so that they would have an excuse for being angry with me" (57–58).

Although the author has piously denied her desire to indulge in these revelations, her narrative manifestly contests the idea that a good, charitable, Christian woman should be made to suffer in silence. Bruno characterizes these sections as "a long, monotonous complaint," which stretches "across the greater part of the chapters, from her marriage in 1664 until fourteen years later, when she bought a house which finally allowed her to be free of an insufferable presence [her mother-in-law]" (Guyon 1962, vi). Guyon may plead that she writes against her will, but her list of grievances is lengthy, detailed, and passionate; and she shows little forbearance for those responsible for them. In the end, it is hard to imagine that anything could have deterred her from including these bitter outpourings. Only by writing about what was done to her could Guyon end the silencing that once nearly drove her to cut out her tongue.

Even here, however, her discursive voice intervenes, assuring the reader that her suffering was divinely ordained: "You made use of all these things, oh my God, for my salvation. You arranged matters in your goodness so that I subsequently saw that you made me die to my vain and haughty nature. I would not have had the strength to destroy it myself, if you had not worked it out in the wise economy of your providence" (1983, 59). Had it not been for these "crosses," she asserts, she would not have sought God as a way out of her misery. "It was in this deplorable state . . . , oh my God, that I began to understand how I needed your assistance" (56).[18]

Although Guyon's effusive outpourings can seem excessive at times, she nonetheless takes great care to present her conversion as a rational choice, arrived at after a realistic assessment of her situation.[19] She does not represent herself as the recipient of an apocalyptic vision but as a pragmatist: "As my age was so different from theirs (for my husband was twenty-two years older than I), I saw very well that there was no likelihood that they would change their humors, which had become stronger with age. I had masses said so that you would give me the grace, Oh my God, to adjust to them" (57). Furthermore, she explains, she turned to religion because it was an acceptable alternative to having an extramarital affair. "Outside my home I found only admirers and people whose flattery could lead me to perdition, and it was to be feared that at such a young age and among such strange domestic torments, I would turn completely to the outer world and take the path of misconduct" (56). Once again, it was the "principle of honor" that prevailed: "At the start of my marriage you made use of my natural pride to hold me to my duty. I knew that an honorable woman must never give umbrage to her husband" (56).

Up to this point, Guyon has emphasized the piety and orthodoxy that predestined her for the spiritual life, offering the events of her life as didactic exempla. She now describes the various obstacles she had to overcome along the path to enlightenment. The most important of these was the vanity instilled in her by her mother. "I was quite happy to be gazed at," she writes, "and far from avoiding opportunities, I went to the public promenades, albeit rarely, and when I was in the streets, I removed my mask out of vanity, and also my gloves, to show off my hands. . . . I also sometimes went to balls, where I vainly displayed my dancing skills" (62). Even when she went to church, she says, it was less to pray than to be seen (64). If one compares these "confessions" of Guyon's with Augustine, one is struck by the extent to which the sins of the two autobiographers were gendered. The masculine sin of Augustine was lust; the feminine sin of Guyon was vanity.[20] He battled against his desire for the female body, Guyon struggled not to see her body as desirable. "I hated passion," she states, "but my outer being could not hate the part of me that aroused it, although my inner being ardently desired to be delivered from it" (113).

Guyon tells of Draconian efforts not to conform to fashion. She refused to curl her hair, or to put anything on her face; she read the *Imitation of Christ* and François de Sales while her servants were combing her hair. But the habits instilled in a beautiful daughter by an ambitious mother were deeply engrained: "People still found me beautiful, and my vain sentiments were constantly being aroused" (64). To make matters worse, Jacques Guyon placed great store in his wife's beauty and demanded that she dress elegantly, in a manner befitting her age and station (84). He was especially insistent that she wear fashionably low-cut gowns; and since it was his wish, her spiritual advisors ordered her to do so: "They hardly regarded as a fault what displeased you infinitely, oh my God. . . . Oh if confessors only knew the harm they do to women by such laxness" (114). She solved this dilemma with the help of a female advisor, la mère Granger, who suggested she cover her bosom with a handkerchief (the very remedy Molière's sexually queasy Tartuffe tries to impose on the servant Dorine). At last, Guyon writes, a disfiguring attack of smallpox put an end to her beauty and consequently to her vanity. She used this misfortune to make herself appear as unappealing as possible. Refusing to use pomades to conceal the ravages of the disease, she exposed her face to the elements, so that her pockmarks would become permanent. She also went out of her way to display them in the street, "to make my humiliation triumph in the same way as had my pride" (125). Confirming the exchange value of feminine beauty in the patriarchal economy, her husband no longer found in her "the pleasures that softened his harshness and calmed his temper." As a result, he became so irascible and demanding that she trembled at his approach, "for I well knew that nothing I did would please him" (138).

Her narrative consistently demonstrates that it was her marital status that prevented her from reaching her spiritual goals. She was continually trying to reconcile the ethics of the "good wife" and the conduct of the "holy woman." At the heart of the problem was her sexual relationship to her husband. As a married woman, she was required by both canon and secular law to submit to his sexual demands. Yet Catholic Christianity equated chastity with holiness.[21] Post-Reformation writers like François de Sales had made some attempt to depict marriage as an honorable estate, but post-Reformation Catholicism did not really view sexual relations as a desirable manifestation of human love. Women were ordered by their spiritual advisers to give themselves without question to their husbands, but only for the purpose of procreation. And they were strictly warned against taking pleasure in the sex act.

To counter the charges that she had engaged in sexual misconduct with LaCombe, Guyon had to provide a highly intimate glimpse of what went on in the bedroom. She emphatically represents herself as frigid, but insists that she nonetheless always fulfilled her obligations as a wife. Yet, she states, sexual contact grew increasingly repellent to her—a fact that did not escape her husband, who complained that her love for God had caused her not to love him. She concurred with enthusiasm:

> It is true, Oh pure and holy God, that you impressed on me from the beginning such a love of chastity that there was nothing in the world I would not have done to possess it; I preached nothing else to him, although I tried not to make myself unaccommodating and to do as he wished in all that he could exact of me. You gave me then, Oh my God, such a gift of chastity that I did not have so much as a bad thought, and marriage burdened me greatly. He said to me sometimes, "It's easy to see you never forget about being in God's presence." (96)

In another passage, which was crossed out in the Oxford manuscript and omitted from the Poiret edition, she confesses poignantly how she responded to his sexual advances in the early years of the marriage:

> [A]s soon as my husband was alone with me, he entered into a violent state of passionate desire for me . . . I confess also that I was so beaten down by misery that I was not very receptive to his ardor; although I did not let it show and tried to do as I was supposed to do. It is also true that being still so young, the distress did not go as deep as it does at a more advanced age,

and I let myself be won over by his caresses, hoping that he would love me better afterwards and would be less hard on me. (1962, 22 n. 19)

Nonetheless, she states, she took advantage of every pretext to avoid engaging in sexual relations, affirming that chastity was the one virtue she was *never* tempted to abandon: "God put so far from my heart all sensual pleasures that marriage was for me in every way a rude sacrifice" (1983, 144). Unfortunately for her, Jacques Guyon did not share her repugnance. In spite of his failing health, he seems to have retained his sexual appetites to the end. His long-suffering spouse gave birth to a daughter only a few weeks before his death.

Yet, if Guyon went to such lengths to prove that she had always *desired* to remain chaste and had *never* experienced sexual pleasure, it was not only because she wanted to make her image conform to that of cloistered autobiographers, it was also because she had to convince her accusers that she could not possibly have had sexual intercourse with La Combe: "Beneath the question formulated in terms of the illicit hides another question that is not formulated, but is no less important," writes Bruneau. "Has she ever felt desire for another, pleasure with another, even if he were her husband? . . . Jeanne is not mistaken about this and her reply indicates her adversaries' unformulated question. . . . She takes God as her witness and says that such things have never interested her and that her husband even complained that he had married a nun" (Bruneau 1983a, 103). Her revelations function apologetically to exonerate her of the charge of licentious behavior.

Yet here too she finds herself on the horns of a dilemma, for she also has to portray herself as a dutiful wife. Just as she affirms that she broke off her engagement to a man she loved because women were not supposed to fall in love without parental permission, and just as she entered into a nonconsensual marriage for fear of creating a scandal, so she emphasizes that she faithfully carried out all her conjugal duties.[22] In fact, she makes a point of claiming that when a priest advised her not to have relations with a husband she had not consented to marry, she indignantly sought a second opinion from a Jesuit, who disagreed, "which greatly consoled me, for the other [priest] had made a mortal sin of what my duty obliged me to do and would have made it necessary for me to shirk my duty" (Guyon 1983, 115).

She also insists that she was a model wife in other respects, patiently nursing Jacques through attacks of gout. And when her mother chided her for sacrificing her youth to an elderly invalid, she replied that it was her duty to share his miseries as well as his possessions. Nor did she indulge in illusions about what life with a different husband would have been like. "As for his quick temper," she writes, "there are few men without one, and it is a woman's duty to be reasonable and to suffer peaceably, without making it worse by wicked rejoinders" (59).

On the other hand, there can be little doubt that her decision to pursue the spiritual path was in large part a strategy of resistance that made her as unpleasant to be with as were the Guyons. She whipped herself with iron points that drew blood; she wore belts of horsehair next to her flesh; she tore her skin with brambles, thorns, and nettles; she put pebbles in her shoes, doctored her food with bitter-tasting additives, ate barely enough to sustain life, and was always either sick or chronically fatigued. She delighted in a terrible abscess in her eye, had healthy teeth pulled, and poured molten lead and hot wax on her bare skin. "Everything was too weak to placate my desire to suffer. Although my body was very delicate, it seemed to me that the instruments of penitence tore into me without hurting me" (80). Most revolting of all, she forced herself to eat spittle and to lick the pus from bandages. "I was not surprised that the martyrs had given their lives for Jesus Christ. I found them so happy that I envied their happiness, and for me it was martyrdom not to be able to be a martyr" (102–3).

To some modern readers these passages indicate a pathological state. Bruneau writes, "The mystical enunciation is in good part the putting into discourse of masochistic desire: the erotics of pleasure in pain" (1983a, 104).[23] But it is important to remember that Guyon's description of her ascetic exercises carry out the apologetic objectives of her text on the authorial level, situating her within a hagiographic tradition that conflates holiness with heroic suffering. As Bowman points out, all the spiritual autobiographers of her time engaged in such practices. Marie de l'Incarnation writes of forcing herself to lacerate her naked body when it was so cold that she could barely move her arm and then putting on a hair shirt because its stings were particularly painful. The Visitandine nun Marguerite-Marie Alacoque pushed needles into her fingers, bound herself with ropes and chains that cut into her flesh, and swallowed vomit.

Naturally, Guyon does not admit that she was engaging in passive resistance to her husband and his mother when she did these things. She construes herself as an innocent and long-suffering victim. She accuses her husband and his mother of forbidding her spiritual practices and spying on her from morning to night. If she went to the window with her sewing, she charges, they watched her to make sure she wasn't praying. She, in turn, got up to pray at four in the morning and walked to mass in her stocking feet so that they would not find mud on her shoes. Although she punctiliously let her husband have his way with her, she contracted a spiritual marriage with the Infant Jesus. And to add insult to injury, she responded to the Guyons with complete silence, carrying out the lowliest tasks for them and begging their pardon when they accused her unjustly. Most infuriating of all, when the disgrace of Fouquet the finance minister placed the family fortunes in jeopardy, she refused to pray that they be saved from ruin and eagerly envisioned going to the poorhouse: "It seemed to me that there was no estate so poor and so miserable that I would not have found it sweet in comparison to the constant persecution I endured at home" (63).

Reinventing herself as a holy woman not only provided an alternative to being driven mad by the Guyons, it gave her a way to defy them. The more they tormented her, the more she could outsmart them by playing the martyr. Religious piety enabled her to carve out for herself an autonomous space in which she could take refuge from the miseries of her marriage.

Thus, Guyon used the hagiographic tradition of heroic suffering to depict herself as a submissive saint on the discursive level, but on the narrative level she represented herself as the victim of patriarchal oppression. On both levels, however, as she traced her efforts to replace the "lost" self of her girlhood with the "interior" self who achieved union with God, Guyon constructed herself as a subject possessing agency.[24]

Guyon's representation of her search for spiritual enlightenment comes to an end in the pivotal episode describing how she discovered the secret of mystical union with God. The passage is remarkable in the way it is framed by the two topoi that have consistently informed her sense of who she is— her relationship with her father and her consciousness of gender bias. She writes that in spite of all her efforts, she continued to be incapable of experiencing God's presence until she turned for help to her father, who advised her to seek out a holy hermit. However, here as elsewhere, the father's word puts her on the horns of a dilemma: "I never had anything to do with monks. I believed that I was duty-bound to avoid them so as to observe the most rigorous rules of virtuous conduct" (72). On the other hand, as a dutiful daughter, she was morally obliged to do as her father told her. "My father's insistence was as good as an absolute commandment. I believed I could not find myself in the wrong, if what I did was to obey him" (72).

Guyon restages this crucial interview with the hermit as an erotic confrontation hovering on the perilous fringes of impropriety. She tells how the holy man, who had avoided contact with women for five years, was speechless when he saw her, overwhelmed by her "exterior." For her part, she refuses to be dissuaded from pursuing her goal: "I nonetheless proceeded to speak to him, explaining in a few words my difficulties in praying." He turns to flee to his cell, but he tosses over his shoulder as he departs the words she has been seeking: *"Madame, what you are searching for on the outside is inside you. Acquire the habit of seeking God in your heart and you will find him there"* (73; italics in original). The effect of his words is instantaneous. "They were like an arrow that pierced my heart through and through. I felt at that moment a very deep wound, both *delicious and amorous* [emphasis mine], a wound so sweet that I desired never to be healed. These words placed in my heart what I had been seeking for so many years, or rather, they made me discover what was there and what I had not enjoyed because I had not been aware of it. Oh my Lord, you were in my heart and you only asked a simple return to the interior to make me feel your presence!" (73).

This is the climax of Guyon's narrative, for it reveals how she arrived at the contemplative method she later imparted in her *Moyen court.* Yet until she reports the hermit's lapidary utterance, she focuses almost entirely on the sexual chemistry of their meeting, emphasizing how the monk's fear of her female body nearly deprived her of the enlightenment she was seeking. What is more, she goes on to reveal that when she later asked him to become her spiritual advisor, he at first refused for the same reason: "my exterior, which caused him much apprehension, my extreme youth, for I was only nineteen years old, and a promise he had made to God because he mistrusted his own weakness, which was never to take on the direction of a member of the opposite sex, unless our Lord particularly charged him to do so in a vision" (74). Eventually God did send the required vision, instructing the hermit to make an exception for Guyon—*"Do not be afraid to take charge of her, she is my wife"* (74; italics in original)—albeit in terms that assigned to her yet another gendered role.

The way Guyon presents this pivotal episode demonstrates how deeply conscious she was that her female body set her apart from *universal man.*[25] Most of what she says here has no real bearing on the hermit's message. It would, indeed, have been perfectly feasible for her to report his words and her reaction without saying anything about his misogynistic demurrals, for ultimately gender had nothing to do with the truth he imparted to her. Yet throughout this account of her spiritual journey, she constantly emphasizes the gendered nature of her experience.

Seventeenth-century spiritual autobiography belonged to a discursive system that interpreted all human experience as the expression of God's will and imposed submission to his earthly surrogates—church, state, and family. In Guyon's *Vie,* the politics of self-representation are necessarily grounded in this worldview and shaped by its ethical imperatives. Never does she openly question the duties imposed by patriarchal law. Indeed, she consistently endorses them on the discursive level, and represents herself as not only conforming to them willingly but condemning departures from them. Considering the conditions under which she was writing, any deviation from this stance would have been unthinkable. The story of her spiritual journey adheres closely, therefore, to the hagiographic and didactic traditions of the genre. Its purpose is essentially apologetic—to prove to her followers that she is a holy woman and to prove to her accusers that she is innocent of the charges leveled against her.

Yet as a woman who has refused to enter a religious order and has published a book of spiritual teachings, she has already defied the mores that governed women. Furthermore, this refusal to stay within the prescribed boundaries has inevitably been assimilated to sexual misconduct. Gender is, therefore, a primary issue in this text and functions alongside the confessional topos as a technology of the self. The mystic's spiritual journey is doubled and subverted by the writer's struggle to resist repression. The tension between the two is never resolved. They coexist one beneath the other as two stories, text and subtext, discourse and narrative.

7

L'Abbé de Choisy

François Timoléon de Choisy was born in Paris in 1644. Although he spent his life at court, he was not descended from royalty or even from the *noblesse d'épée*. His forebears had been bourgeois merchants who eventually used their wealth to infiltrate the lower echelons of the nobility as civil servants. According to Reynes, a Choisy ancestor who was a wine merchant established the family fortunes by astutely losing to the king at chess. Tallemont des Réaux asserts that Choisy's grandfather was a tax collector who lined his own pockets. His father Jean de Choisy held a number of government posts including *conseiller d'état, intendant* of Languedoc, and *chancelier* to Gaston d'Orléans. His mother came from the same social background, her grandfather having been the chancelier de L'Hôpital.

Madame de Choisy exemplified the upward social mobility of her class. A fixture at Louis XIV's court, she was famous for wit, charm, and an aptitude for intrigue. "My mother," writes Choisy, "although she had married *un homme de robe,* received the visits of the entire court every day; we lived in a fine house near the gateway to the Louvre" (1966, 218).[1] She is supposed to have informed the king in his youth that if he wanted to become a true gentleman *(un honnête homme)* he should converse regularly with her. He took her at her word, scheduled biweekly meetings, and bestowed on her a pension of eight thousand pounds. She was a close friend of La Grande Mademoiselle, who mentions her frequently in her memoirs. Somaize listed her in his *Dictionnaire* under the name "Célie," and Segrais also portrayed her in *La Princesse Aurélie* as "Uranie." She counted the future queen of Poland, the duchess of Savoy, and the queen of Sweden among her regular correspondents.

She instilled in her youngest son the precepts that had guided her in negotiating her place in court society. "I know very well that your fathers and grandfathers were *maîtres des requêtes* and *conseillers d'état,"* he quotes her as saying, "but you must learn that in France only the *noblesse d'épée* is recognized. The nation, which is completely warlike, has placed its glory in arms: therefore, my son, so that you won't be a braggart, never see anyone but people of quality . . . you will grow accustomed from the start to good manners, and all your life you will retain an air of civility that will make you loved by everyone" (24). He states that he followed her advice faithfully and never had anything to do with the *noblesse de robe,* except for his own relatives. According to him, his entire life was spent "at court with my friends, or in privacy with books" (24–25). Madame de Choisy also understood the king's importance for the advancement of her class, for her husband's loyalty to Gaston had resulted in financial loss and political disgrace. "She never stopped preaching to her children that they should attach themselves to no one but the king; and in her will she insists on that above all else" (76).

She gave birth to François Timoléon when she was over forty, and because "a child of eight or nine who went everywhere with her made her seem still youthful" (219), she dressed him as a girl, and kept him constantly at her side. What is more, with her sure instinct for the politically expedient, she used his cross-dressing to ingratiate herself with Mazarin, who was believed to be fostering effeminacy in the king's younger brother, Philippe. Both Choisy and the little prince were encouraged to dress in women's clothes when they played together. Thus it was thanks to his mother that Choisy acquired the insider's view of the court that qualified him to write Louis's history, and the habit that led him to engage in his transvestite masquerades.

As the youngest of three sons, he was destined for the ecclesiastical life, tonsured at eighteen, and named abbot of Saint-Seine in Burgundy (thus the title *abbé*). However, he was not ordained to the priesthood until many years later. In 1666 he ran away to Bordeaux, where he played women's roles in a theatrical company. Later he lived as a woman in the provinces near Bourges and in the Paris suburb of Saint-Marceau. Van der Cruysse believes that these two transvestite episodes took place after the death of his mother in 1669. He probably lived in Bourges between 1670 and 1671, returning briefly to Paris in December, at which time he witnessed Montpensier's abortive attempt to marry Lauzun. In 1671–73, he seems to have carried on a love affair with Bossuet's sister-in-law Renée. He embarked on the Saint-Marceau episode after his brother's death in 1672. In between these escapades, he continued to frequent the court and to indulge in its favorite pastime, ruinous gambling. As he reports in his historical memoirs, he was present at the Rhine crossing in 1672. He underwent a religious conversion following a serious illness in 1683, but according to his friend and biographer the abbé d'Olivet he never completely abandoned his love of feminine attire. A prolific and facile writer, Choisy produced not only his two sets of memoirs but numerous historical books, a travel journal of his trip to Siam, a series of pious meditations and theological studies, as well as an eleven-volume history of the Church. This did not stop him from publishing anonymously in the *Mercure galant* of February 1695 a novel about a romance between a man and a woman who are each cross-dressed *(L'Histoire de la marquise-marquis de Banneville)*. He was elected to the Académie Française in 1687. He died on 2 October 1724.

PUBLICATION HISTORY:
MÉMOIRES POUR SERVIR À L'HISTOIRE DE LOUIS XIV AND
MÉMOIRES DE L'ABBÉ DE CHOISY HABILLÉ EN FEMME

Choisy's *Mémoires pour servir à l'histoire de Louis XIV* and *Mémoires de l'abbé de Choisy habillé en femme* appear together in the Mercure de France series Le Temps Retrouvé. The first is an amalgam of fragments put together by the marquis d'Argenson, who wrote that he had culled what "seemed good or passable" out of "a quantity of useless papers" (Mongrédien 1966, 17).[2] Originally the marquis had not intended to publish them, but only to allow them to be read aloud at social gatherings. However, a copy fell into the hands of Choisy's biographer, the abbé d'Olivet, and he published it in 1727. D'Argenson's truncating of Choisy's manuscript demonstrates once again how seventeenth-century memoirs were shaped and censored by their editors. In this case, it is probable that d'Argenson's definition of what was "good or passable" resulted in the suppression of many autobiographical passages.

In Mongrédien's edition, these historical memoirs comprise twelve books. The first four, probably composed around 1685, discuss the Fronde, the beginnings of Louis XIV's personal reign, and the trial of the finance minister, Fouquet. Finding it boring to write of such "far-off things," Choisy then skips seventeen years to the year 1678. Book 5 is devoted primarily to the revocation of the Edict of Nantes (1685). Books 7 and 8 are concerned with 1686 and, after another lacuna, with 1691. The project was then put aside until 1707, when he composed book 8, which discusses the abbé de Cosnac, chaplain to Louis XIV's brother, Philippe d'Orléans, and subsequently bishop of Valence and archbishop of Aix. Books 9 and 10 deal with the marquis d'Arquien and the cardinal de Bouillon. Early editions end here, but in the nineteenth century, Monmerqué added books 11 and 12, containing particulars about Jean Sobieski, king of Poland, the Turkish siege of Vienna in 1683, and other odds and ends.[3]

The second set of memoirs, known as *Mémoires de l'abbé de Choisy habillé en femme,* were originally published separately as "Histoire de Madame la comtesse des Barres," which appeared in 1735, and "Histoire de Madame de Sancy," which did not appear until 1839, when it was included in the introduction to the *Mémoires pour servir à l'histoire de Louis XIV.* Mongrédien added a short fragment, "Les Intrigues de l'abbé avec les petites actrices Montfleury et Mondory," which may refer to events that occurred during the interlude in Bordeaux.

It is difficult to date these "Histoires," or to situate them chronologically in Choisy's life, but there is considerable internal evidence that the "comtesse des Barres" episode, which follows the "Madame de Sancy" in published editions, actually took place first.[4] Some scholars have used these chronological discrepancies to argue that the events Choisy narrated were all fantasies and never happened, but d'Argenson stated categorically that they were true and that Choisy always took great pleasure in recalling them.

MISREPRESENTATIONS

I have chosen to end this study with Choisy's two sets of memoirs because read together they offer a unique insight into how the politics of feminine self-representation intersected with the arbitrary limits imposed on men's historical memoirs. His *Mémoires pour servir à l'histoire de Louis XIV* purports to conform to the genre's accepted norms, while his *Mémoires de l'abbé de Choisy habillé en femme* manifestly does not. In point of fact, both texts call into question the view that life-writing should be a record of public and political acts.

The opening sentences of the *Mémoires pour servir à l'histoire de Louis XIV* seem to position the work firmly in the masculine domain of memoirs purporting to be history. Like Plutarch, who served as a model for early modern life-writers, Choisy will record for posterity the heroic deeds of a "great man." He claims to be writing "the memoirs of the most beautiful of all lives, the one most full of extraordinary events, the one most worthy of being passed on to posterity," which is, of course "the *Life of Louis XIV,* king of France, whose peoples have dubbed him *the Great*" (1966, 22). Ostensibly, this is a biographical text; and the author's role will be limited to that of chronicler.

What is more, he proclaims, it will comply with the accepted definition of masculine memoirs: his grand theme will be "cities captured, battles

won, states conquered, and all the horrors of war" (22). And to justify such
an undertaking, he invokes the most classical and unimpeachable of motives—
not personal honor or profit, but the education of princes: "History is the
best and surest manner of teaching the princes of the world the sometimes
hard truths that one would not dare to tell them otherwise" (21). He does,
in fact, deliver what he promises, providing important information concerning Mazarin, Fouquet, the religious controversies of the 1680s, and the
rise of Madame de Maintenon. In addition, he sketches a portrait of the
Sun King based on personal observations and anecdotes gleaned from his
mother. The result is a record of Louis's reign that is both intimate and
accurate, a fact appreciated by Saint-Simon, who used him as a source.[5]

If, however, his preamble seems to situate his text within the historical
project, he makes it crystal clear that it has neither the pretensions nor the
limitations of the king's official history: "[M]y plan is not to write the grand
history of his reign; I am not one to interfere in someone else's business:
and since two great minds [here he inserts the names of Racine and Des-
préaux (Boileau) after an asterisk] . . . have been charged with such a great
task, I do myself justice and am persuaded that they will give a better history than I could create, if only for the reason that they have at hand all the
most secret memoirs, and have been working on them for more than fifteen
years" (22).

He will concentrate on the "particularities" of the king's life, depicting
him with his friends, in moments when he is "more friendly and perhaps no
less grand than at the head of his armies." Nor will he omit his pleasures
and pastimes or most ordinary activities, without, of course, neglecting his
"heroic actions" (23). Furthermore, he promises, "I shall forget, to the best
of my abilities, none of his virtues; but also I shall forget none of his faults.
Made of the same clay as Caesar and Alexander, he will have weaknesses
as much as they, and sometimes the hero will allow a glimpse of the man"
(24). Thus his text will differ from the "grand history" of Louis's historiographers not only in subject matter but also in veracity, a "brave if not inso-
lent" commitment that prompts him to declare that these pages will not
leave his study during his lifetime. "Thus, without giving in to flattery, the
ruling vice of all centuries, I shall set down on paper all that I know which
is most secret and most true; and I can boast that I know a great deal" (24).

The boast that he knows a great deal about his subject is based on a
long and intimate familiarity with Louis's court, going back to his childhood when his mother was one of its prominent members. His primary
sources are his own memories and her stories: "Here is how I go about
writing my memoirs: first, I write down everything that I know at first hand,
and everything that my mother told me." This he supplements with what he

has learned from conversations with other courtiers of her generation: "Then I question the people who were involved in the affairs in question, and I do it without seeming concerned, in an ingenuous manner, out of simple curiosity. . . . I use what one says to get the next one to talk; I compare these diverse lessons; and when several agree without having consulted each other, I believe that I have the truth. I perceive every day that this way is admirable for learning about the most secret things" (35).

Choisy's proclaimed methods and intentions are diametrically opposed to the principles laid down by Pellisson.[6] Rather than imposing an official and univocal interpretation on events, he compiles a polyvocal sampling that eventually authenticates a version of the facts on which there is general agreement. Furthermore, authenticity is not conferred by the sovereign. It is the product of a devious strategy that *denies* the biographer's real intentions and dissimulates itself behind a reputation for harmless scribbling. "No one is suspicious of me; I have not raised the banner of king's historian: everyone thinks that I am working on the *History of Charles VII*" (35). Yet, he contends, he has acquired information not known to the king's historiographers. To prove his point, he tells how when old Monsieur Roze began to recount some little-known details of Mazarin's death, he tricked him into continuing by pretending to be thinking about Joan of Arc. "'Ah,'" Roze exclaimed, "'what wouldn't Monsieur Racine give to be here: he's tried several times to get me on this subject, but I have never been willing to talk to him. It would be a sorry business for me to have him misquoting me all over the place.' I began to laugh," says Choisy, "and told him about one of my Siamese adventures: but as soon as I had left him, I wrote down on my tablets everything he had said about the cardinal" (36).

Choisy supports the claim of veracity, an essential component of historical memoirs, by the concomitant claims of authority and incorruptibility. But in so doing, he hints at a subversive agenda; for the claim of veracity, guaranteed by the author's access to superior sources of information, calls into question the trustworthiness of the history being prepared under the king's supervision; the promise that he will not publish these secrets during his lifetime implies a fear of censorship or reprisal that can only reflect badly on the régime of "Louis le Grand"; and the mention of flattery suggests that the king's history will be tainted by its authors' obligation to please him.

However, if these half-serious, self-mocking revelations about his methodology conceal a serious challenge to the king's history, a second declaration of authorial intent destabilizes it much more. Soon after his grandiose prologue, he suddenly shifts gears and informs his reader that he is writing not only the king's life but his own. This announcement is hardly consistent with either the subject matter or the high moral tone he has just enunciated. As he admits, "It will make quite a contrast, but it will afford me pleasure, and I am willing to run the risk that people will say, *He is forever mingling praise of a fop with praise of a hero*" (25). Indeed, as he pursues this train of thought, he contradicts the claim that he is writing for the edification of princes and states that he is writing for himself: "What I am offering myself here is an innocent pleasure. When I am very old, I will have these memoirs read and reread to me, and in a way, I will grow young again, as I recall the happy times of youth, when one thinks only of enjoying oneself" (34–35). Such a baroque intrusion of the particular/personal into the king's life is highly irregular. It constitutes an astonishing shift away from the announced theme of heroic glory and introduces as textual aims "pleasure" and "innocence" (both of which figure prominently in the *Mémoires de l'abbé de Choisy habillé en femme,* where they are explicitly linked to the ahistorical nature of the project).

It is true that early memoirs hover between chronicle and self-narrative, slipping back and forth between event and narrator. One can never be sure whose story is being told or by what discursive voice it is being shaped. But in this text, the authorial "I" goes much farther in problematizing and ultimately crossing over the invisible line between author and subject. By characterizing his own story as that of a "fop," Choisy draws flagrant attention to his alienation from the heroic ideal his text purports to affirm, thereby setting up his own life story as a foil to the king's history.

Crossing the boundary between the public/political and the private/autobiographical, Choisy contradicts his stated purpose—to write a narrative of "cities captured, battles won, states conquered, and all the horrors of war." And this generic deviation seems even more astonishing when the reader learns that what he really wants to reveal is that he is a transvestite: "You will laugh to see me dressed as a girl until the age of eighteen; you will not excuse my mother for having wanted it so" (25). The self-narrative that he inscribes, and to which he always returns, is the story of gender trouble.[7] What is more, each time he shifts to the autobiographical mode, he runs through the same signifying chain: Beginning with his mother, the "maîtresse-femme" who was, "more by her intelligence than by the state of her fortune, quite well-versed in the secrets of the court," he links himself to the milieu that authorizes him to write a chronicle of Louis's reign. The memoirist enters the domain of "extraordinary events" via the boudoir, hidden by and in a lady's skirts. He tells of how from the age of ten on, he spent two or three hours every morning copying out letters to his mother's illustrious correspondents:[8] "It was in this way that I was initiated at an early age into the mysteries of politics" (25). Women's gossip and not councils of state was the source of his knowledge, a fact that immediately makes his text different from those of soldiers or statesmen.

Choisy links himself to the royal family in a yet more startling way. In the section devoted to his friend and patron the cardinal de Bouillon, he reveals that when *le petit monsieur* (Louis's younger brother, Philippe d'Orléans) came to visit, Madame de Choisy would dress the two of them in women's clothes. As soon as Philippe arrived, "his hair was rearranged. He had an embroidered corset to maintain his figure: his *justaucorps* [a long vest] was removed so that he could be dressed in women's cloaks and skirts" (219). It was on these occasions, Choisy says, that he learned to delight in "pierced ears, diamonds, beauty marks, and all the other little niceties to which one becomes so easily accustomed and which it is so difficult to do without" (219).

The reason behind these masquerades, he explains, was that Mazarin had resolved to feminize Philippe, "for fear that he would do harm to the king as Gaston had done to Louis XIII." In other words, Choisy connects his adult desire to dress as a woman with a political plot designed to eliminate the inherent threat to absolute control embodied in the monarch's younger brother. This was the threat that had destabilized the reigns of the last Valois kings (Charles IX and Henri III), as well as that of Louis XIII and the early part of Louis XIV's, when Gaston d'Orléans's supporters had come very close to seizing power.

In a political system that transmitted sovereignty by inheritance, the rule of primogeniture left far too much to chance when it came to the ruler's ability either to reign justly or to produce legitimate heirs. Since the same "blood" ran in the veins of younger sons, conspirators were always tempted to propose them as substitutes, if they judged the eldest son unsatisfactory. Such attempts presented a double danger. They not only destabilized the rule of a particular monarch; they undermined the basic principle of the divine right of kings by implying that human beings were more qualified than God to decide who should reign.

It should be noted that the Salic law, which denied daughters the right to succeed to the French throne, served the same purpose as the law of primogeniture: it preserved the firstborn male's hegemony. Without it Marguerite de Valois and Mademoiselle de Montpensier could have stood in direct line to the throne. According to Choisy, then, Mazarin, bent on disarming the sibling rival, deliberately regendered him as feminine, a strategy that in effect collapsed the Salic law and the rule of primogeniture into a single category.

In her biography of Philippe, Barker dismisses this allegation as "preposterous," claiming it was spread by La Porte, a former servant of Anne d'Autriche, "who detested Mazarin and would do anything to blacken his reputation." She admits, however, that it was widely accepted, and that some version of it is found in many contemporary documents (58).[9]

What concerns me here is not so much whether Mazarin did in fact corrupt Philippe (and Choisy) on purpose; it is the author's revelation that his gender identity had been engineered for political reasons, for this allegation opens a new perspective on his claim that this is his story as well as the king's. The assertion that it was his cross-dressing that lay behind the Sun King's unchallenged supremacy makes Choisy's life as a transvestite essential to the history he is constructing. It represents him as an innocent pawn of the royal family, a sacrificial victim offered up on the altar of the *raison d'état*. His cross-dressing is no longer merely a matter of maternal vanity; it has become an affair of state.

Choisy's accusation points to the fact that where kings were concerned, history was really a family romance. Under an absolute sovereign, public events were often determined by what the French call *la petite histoire*— the loves, hates, jealousies, and intrigues played out in the private quarters of palaces. Indeed, contests like those waged among the royal brothers and cousins were prototypes of the family romances analyzed by Freud; for by its very nature, a political system in which power is transmitted by lineage is subject to sexual entanglements and fraternal struggles. When lesser families squabbled, it stayed behind closed doors; when the Bourbons did so, it reverberated across the kingdom and beyond. Sexuality and gender could never be private matters in a state founded on primogeniture and the Salic law. And this, of course, is also the subtext of the women's memoirs that treat "particular history."

By assigning to his cross-dressing a crucial role in the establishment of the absolute king, Choisy deconstructs the sources and foundations of Louis's power. If, as he implies, the seventeenth-century French aristocracy understood political behavior in terms of male/female stereotypes— the former being construed as aggressive and warlike, the latter as docile and self-absorbed, then this explanation of his transvestism unveils the forces that were at work constructing the gender identities of biologically female noblewomen, who were also cut off from the political arena and transformed into unresisting objects of marital exchange.

Choisy's revelation implies that Louis's greatness rested on sacrificing to the *raison d'état* not only his brother (and Choisy) but many women as well. They included, to name only a few, his first love, Marie Mancini; the bartered Spanish princess, Marie-Thérèse, who became his bride; his two sisters-in-law, Henriette d'Angleterre and the Princesse Palatine, whom he forced into unhappy marriages with his brother to win diplomatic advantages;

and his cousin, La Grande Mademoiselle, whom he forbade to marry Lauzun, and whose fortune he confiscated to provide for his illegitimate son. Louis's power was thus dependent on the devaluation and exploitation of the feminine—a fact that confirms Foucault's insights into the way sexuality became an instrument of political control in his reign.[10]

Philippe never became his brother's political rival. "His inclinations conformed as much to women's occupations as the king's were far removed from them" wrote Madame de Lafayette (1965, 25). The story purporting to celebrate Louis-le-Grand's greatness is thus doubled by the fragmented story of two little boys who were regendered as feminine to assure the monarch's unchallenged possession of the phallus.[11] As Kate Millett argues in *Sexual Politics,* a feminine-identified homosexual necessarily reveals "the arbitrary and invidious nature of sex roles," causing masculine and feminine to "stand out as terms of praise and blame, authority and servitude, high and low, master and slave" (274–79). Similarly, Choisy's allegation interprets the behavior of Louis and his brother on the basis of masculine and feminine stereotypes—the former being construed as aggressive and warlike, the latter as docile and narcissistic. Gendered conduct is understood to be independent of genital identity. It can be instilled by education, regardless of a child's biological sex.[12]

Cross-dressing in Choisy's historical memoirs functions as a sign of the cracks and chinks in the absolute monarchy. Like Marguerite de Valois, Gaston d'Orléans, and Mademoiselle de Montpensier, Philippe represented an alternative to rule by the eldest son, for he was Louis's heir for eighteen years. In fact, when the king fell dangerously ill in June 1658, a cabal of ex-Frondeurs immediately formed around Philippe. And one of the ringleaders was Madame de Choisy! There is no evidence that Philippe actively encouraged this conspiracy, but it is known that she and he carried on a secret correspondence at this time.[13]

Choisy never breathes a word of Philippe's pretensions to kingship; but he does contest the widespread belief that he was unfit to rule, portraying him as heroic in spite of his effeminacy: "for when he had to fight, he proved that he had the blood of France in him and won battles" (219). Furthermore, he describes him as far from happy with his marginal status and eager to convince Louis of his seriousness.[14] In one moving passage, he tells of how Monsieur tried to earn the king's gratitude by preparing trenches for a military siege, not even stopping to eat. Unimpressed, Louis laconically ordered him to get some rest. He also relates that Philippe's chaplain begged the king to name his master governor of Languedoc, a post that had been Gaston's. Louis replied, "The princes of the blood are never well off in France except at court, and as for the governorship of

Languedoc, I beg him to remember that he and I have agreed that he should never have a governorship" (189). Like a woman, Philippe was expected to stay at home and not concern himself with serious business.[15]

Choisy's own ambitions were likewise blighted by his effeminacy. He was never appointed to a significant post: "He [the king] has never listened favorably to me; and whenever I have asked him for some slight favors, he has refused them all" (29). Dedicated to the task of extolling Louis, he seemingly accepts this unobliging attitude, and excuses it on the grounds of his transgressive behavior: "He was not really wrong; I have brought about my own exclusion, and my hidden and irregular conduct is justification enough for the way I have been treated" (29). Yet he was well aware that given his connections at court, he should have prospered: "[I]t was within my power to make a considerable fortune. . . . I can only say in my own defense that out of false tenderness my mother raised me as a girl: how can you make a great man out of that!" (38).

The passages connecting his and Monsieur's marginalized status to their effeminacy reveal that gendered stereotypes underlay the age's attitude toward political leadership: a "great man" was virile. Those like Choisy and Philippe who crossed over to the "feminine" sphere were excluded from the power invested in the phallus. Nevertheless, these memoirs show that their story was the subtext of Louis's. Thanks to their "femininity," a serious threat to his rule was eliminated. Choisy's apparent lack of bitterness at his failure to win Louis's favor indicates that he himself subscribed to the ideology that conflated "greatness" with masculinity. He appears to find it perfectly normal that men like him and Monsieur should have been relegated to the margins of history.

Yet as he weaves his unheroic life into the king's story, Choisy disrupts and deconstructs the master narrative he seems to be promoting.[16] The absolute power supposedly earned by glorious deeds is shown to rest on a very questionable base; the outlines of a personal and highly inappropriate subtext subtly emerge, by way of anecdote and digression; and most shocking of all, the faintest suggestion that Louis's story might have been Philippe's (as, Choisy implies, it is also his) manages to insinuate itself into the reader's mind.

In the *Mémoires pour servir à l'histoire de Louis XIV,* Choisy intrudes his life into the "great man's" history, thereby undermining the principle that the personal was not important enough to be written down for posterity. In the *Mémoires de l'abbé de Choisy habillé en femme,* he departs altogether from the idea that life-writing must be devoted to public affairs. His opening statement is a word-for-word parody of the opening statement of the *Mémoires pour servir a l'histoire de Louis XIV*. Here, he writes, the reader will find "neither captured cities nor victorious battles, politics will not shine here, any more than war. Bagatelles, small pleasures, childishness, don't expect anything else; a happy naturalness, sweet inclinations, nothing dark-spirited, joy everywhere, the wish to please, lively passions, faults in a man, virtues in the weaker sex" (289). This preamble mocks the limits and pomposities of historical memoirs, his own included. Clearly Choisy was cognizant of the conventions of historical memoirs, and conscious of the unconventional aspect of what he was about to relate. As he says to his addressee, "You order me, madame, to write the history of my life; surely you can't be serious" (289).[17]

In fact, he seems bent on turning life-writing on its head by breaking with a number of its accepted procedures. Historical memoirists affirm that they are telling the truth.[18] He, however, will not be concerned with facts, but with pleasure and joy (a word that in French also signifies sexual climax). "Innocent pleasure," which invaded and disrupted the king's story with the subtextual motif of feminized transgression, now completely displaces any other justification for writing. Words like "natural," "happy," "gentle," and "joy" suggest opposition to the horrors of history and the genre that recorded them, implying that this is a kinder, gentler text *because* it is marked with the sign of the feminine. Here what would be called "faults" in a man will be seen as "virtues." Likewise, the promise of "small pleasures" seems to assume a gendered difference between the reader of the *Mémoires pour servir à l'histoire de Louis XIV,* who wants to be informed about war, and the reader of the *Mémoires de l'abbé de Choisy habillé en femme,* who seeks only innocent amusement. What purports to be a joke, therefore, is actually a radical departure from the conventions of life-writing.

Choisy will not compose a linear account, organized chronologically. Just as he skipped over a past that no longer interested him in the *Mémoires pour servir à l'histoire de Louis XIV,* he will now narrate only disjointed episodes: "Allow me, madame, to obey you only in installments; I shall write about certain acts of my comedy, which have no connection with the rest" (289). Likewise, he rejects the conventional beginning for a life story— the narrative of origins that situates the author in relation to a family tree, ancestral accomplishments, or childhood intimations of greatness. His account of life dressed as a woman is thus cut off from the ties that normally bind human beings to their past and future.

Instead of tracing himself back to his roots, he begins by analyzing why he cross-dresses, making it clear that "Madame de Sancy" and the "comtesse des Barres" did not come into being in the normal way.[19] His episodic narrative begins, therefore, with a psychophilosophical analysis of why he cross-dresses. He impersonates women, he explains, because he wants to recreate himself as an object of the admiring gaze. He transforms himself into a beautiful woman because it allows him to experience what it feels like to be God. In his historical memoirs, transvestism cuts him off from the source of power; here it confers "ineffable pleasure" and numinous benefits. Dressed as a woman, the author can reinvent himself not as a mere king like Louis, but as God himself:

> I have tried to discover where such a bizarre pleasure came from. It is this: To be loved, adored, is a property of God; man, to the extent permitted by his weakness, has the same ambition; now, since it is beauty that gives birth to love, and beauty is ordinarily the lot of women, when it happens that men have, or believe they have, beautiful features that may cause them to be loved, they try to increase them with women's finery, which is very flattering. In that way they experience the ineffable pleasure of being loved. I have felt more than once what I describe as a sweet experience, and when I have found myself at balls or the theater wearing beautiful dressing gowns, diamonds and beauty patches and have heard whispered around me, "There is a beautiful person," I have tasted within myself a pleasure so great that it can be compared to nothing else. Ambition, riches, love itself do not equal it, because we always love ourselves better than we love others. (292)

Significantly, he does not say here, as he did in the *Mémoires pour servir à l'histoire de Louis XIV,* that it was his mother (or Mazarin) who was responsible for his behavior. He assigns agency and full responsibility to himself alone.

It is this very sense of rootlessness that somehow renders his constructed personae artificial and incomplete. As Ackroyd comments, "His prose does not connect in any way with a substantial or recognizable reality. His style is fanciful, his tone coquettish and . . . the deliberately gay and superficial nature of his memoirs bears all the marks of a repressive mechanism erasing the actual content of his obsessions" (142). These "histoires" do not resemble historical women's memoirs. They seem closer to the pseudo-memoirs that enjoyed a considerable vogue around the time Choisy wrote: fictive parodies like Villedieu's *Mémoires d'Henriette Sylvie de Molière,* whose superficial and suggestive manner seems to mock and denigrate genuine autobiographical narratives.[20]

There is, however, no real story line. He is largely preoccupied with the mechanics of cross-dressing. The stories he tells of "Madame de Sancy" and "la comtesse des Barres" are basically detailed descriptions of the procedures that transformed him into a woman. He is also seriously concerned with describing the social gatherings he arranged for his new acquaintances in Saint-Marceau and Bourges, as well as recounting his love affairs while dressed as a woman.

The story of "Madame de Sancy" gives a step-by-step account of how he went about impersonating a woman: having purchased a house in the unstylish suburb of Saint-Marceau in order to live among those who would tolerate his eccentricities, he began by blurring the line between masculine and feminine.[21] First he put on beauty spots and diamond ear pendants.[22] Next he wore unisex dressing gowns, which were doubly ambiguous because they also resembled priestly garb. Later, he progressively appropriated clothing and accessories that were metonyms of femininity in his day, but had no real connection to the female anatomy or its biological functions: powdered wigs, bonnets, trains, and ribbons to mark the waistline. As his neighbors grew accustomed to seeing him like this, he gradually allowed the hem of a satin gown to peep out from under his robe and displayed his shoulders, which had remained white, "thanks to the great care I took of them all my life." Finally, he replaced his *hauts de chausses* (breeches or knickers) with petticoats, whereupon even he believed that he was truly a woman (293).

As for the more difficult problem of beard and breasts, which generally serve as visible markers of gender, he claims that he had no beard at all: "From the age of five or six I had been carefully rubbed every day with a certain water that kills the hair at its root, provided it is done early enough" (324).[23] Likewise his breasts were sufficiently developed to pass for a girl's: "My corset was very high and stuffed in front to make it look as if I had a bust, and truly I did have as much as a girl of fifteen. In childhood, I had been made to wear corsets that were extremely tight and pushed up the flesh, which was plump and well-rounded. . . . one would never have guessed that I was not a woman" (332).

Besides revealing the skill and artistry with which he brought his illusory heroines into being, he also describes minutely what he wore on each occasion. He tells of spending his days in the company of young ladies, endlessly repositioning his beauty marks, rearranging his hair, and trying on jewelry. His stories of how he "played the beauty" demonstrate the performative nature of femininity and the way in which it is constructed within the codes and fashions of the day. For Choisy, beauty marks ("mouches"), ear pendants, and "cornettes"[24] were its sine qua non.

As he blurs and then passes over the boundary that separates the masculine from the feminine, a concomitant transformation occurs at the linguistic level. His neighbors begin to address him as "madame," and he now refers to himself in the feminine. However, although he is perceived as a woman by himself and others, in Saint-Marceau he does not hide the fact that he is a biological male. Everyone knows his true identity, and his neighbors are only too ready to tolerate his presence in their midst and to accept his hospitality. In Bourges, on the other hand, he goes to great pains to conceal his true identity, and successfully convinces the townspeople that he is a biological woman. Indeed, his masquerade is so effective that he manages to get a daughter of the local gentry into his bed, and even receives a marriage proposal from a penniless aristocrat in search of a rich wife.

Dressing as a woman not only enables Choisy to satisfy his desire to be admired, it permits him to create social spaces dedicated to the "feminine" qualities announced in his preamble: "bagatelles, small pleasures, child-ishness . . . a happy naturalness, gentle attractions, nothing dark-spirited." The intimate gatherings he organizes evoke the ideals and aesthetics of *préciosité*. Indeed, Choisy's mirror-lined drawing rooms were undoubt-edly inspired by the salons his mother had once frequented. His vivid ac-counts of the luncheons, supper parties, musicals, and amateur theatricals over which he presided offer glimpses of the food, drink, clothing, diver-sions, interior decoration, and social customs prevalent in this milieu, and probably give a far more accurate picture than Molière's *Précieuses ridicules*.

In "L'Histoire de la comtesse des Barres," he tells of a reception he arranged for a provincial official (341–43). The day's amusements include a tour of the house and gardens, followed by an "enjoyable and delicate" luncheon. After a concert at which the "comtesse" plays the harpsichord, the guests are led to a boat on the river bank, where they find a collation of summer fruit. Finally she and a young guest entertain the others with read-ings from *Polyeucte,* in which the "comtesse" plays the role of Pauline.

Choisy reigns over these gatherings as Louis reigned over his king-dom. He assumes the role of expert and authority, demonstrating his mas-tery of everything from hairdressing to tragic declamation, to keyboard artistry. The bourgeois artisans and provincial gentry he invites to his home revolve around him as the planets revolve around the sun, constantly ad-miring his *toilettes* and deferring to his savoir vivre. At the center of a miniature realm complete with adoring subjects and elegant rituals, he lives enshrined as the godlike creature he aspires to be.

What there is of a plot consists of equivocal love affairs that suggest the inherent ambiguities of cross-dressed and same-sex relationships. In-deed, Charlotte, "Madame de Sancy's" first lover, implies as much when she explains that she has fallen in love with him because when he is dressed as a woman he does not represent a sexual threat. "I did not defend myself from you as I would have from a man: I saw only a beautiful woman, and there was no reason not to love her. What an advantage your woman's garments give you! The man's heart that impresses us is in them, but on the other hand, the charms of the fairer sex suddenly carry us away and keep us from being on our guard" (298).

In two of his four amorous adventures, he dresses his partners as young boys, assigning to himself the role of wife. In the two others, he genders his partners as feminine while he plays the role of a double transvestite, that is, a man playing a woman playing a man. He dresses Charlotte, one of his neighbors in Saint-Marceau, as a boy and renames her "Monsieur de Maulny." He marries her/him in a mock ceremony, after winning over a disapproving aunt by inviting her to come and live with them. His next partner, Babet, is an orphan girl whom he literally buys from the lingerie maker to whom she is apprenticed. She too is given a new name ("Mademoiselle Dany"), but unlike Charlotte, she is not masculinized. Instead she is hyperfeminized, fetishistically dressed in exquisite feminine attire—down to her most intimate undergarments—and instructed to call "Madame de Sancy" "mon petit mari." In Reynes's view, Choisy moves closer to a "normal" heterosexual relationship in this affair (1983, 178–79); but if it is true that the parties involved are biologically male and female, it is also true that the male is gendered as a woman and calls himself/herself "Madame de Sancy." The relationship is thus performed as a love affair between an older and a younger woman.

In the two love affairs situated in Bourges one partner is again gendered as a boy, while the other is not. Since, however, the "comtesse des Barres" does not reveal her/his identity, cross-dressing is represented less as a source of self-fulfillment than as a pretext for libertinage. The first couple is made up of two women gendered as feminine, one of whom is, unbeknownst to the other, a biological male who conducts herself/himself as a man although still pretending to be a woman. Passing as a "real" woman, Choisy invites Mademoiselle de La Grise, a daughter of the local gentry, to spend a week with him, ostensibly to give her lessons in hairdressing and tragic declamation. Then, like a veritable Valmont, he takes his young house guest to bed and initiates her into the pleasures of love, all the while keeping up the pretense of being a woman: "I kissed her breasts, which were very beautiful; I had her put her hand on the little bit I had to reassure her that I was a woman" (1966, 337). The effect of this quid pro quo is heightened by the girl's reply when she is cautioned not to tell her mother of their activities. She quickly agrees, exclaiming, "She would be jealous, for we almost always sleep together and never have such contentment" (338).

The heroine of the other love affair is Roselie, an itinerant actress handed over to the "comtesse" by an accommodating "aunt." Less innocent than

his other partners, she quickly sees through his disguise, and enters enthusiastically into the masquerade. Like Charlotte, she is dressed as a boy:
"She was a very pretty cavalier, and it seemed to me that I loved her more
that way; I called her my little husband; she was called the little count or
'M. Comtin' wherever we went" (357). The affair ends in a pregnancy.
Ironically, it seems that passing for a woman, rather than merely dressing
as one, enables Choisy to prove his virility by inseminating his partner.

The equivocations inherent in the transvestite's relations with women
are heightened by the presence of spectators. Lovemaking in these
"histoires" is triangular, consisting of the various combinations of feminine and/or masculine personae he creates, plus the audience before whom
they perform. As Garber comments, "The life of Choisy is fascinating in
the ways in which it manipulates and calls in question the stability of categories like audience and actor, politics and theater, male and female" (1992,
256). During his "marriage" to Charlotte/"Monsieur de Maulny," he invites merchants to show him their wares in their bedroom, "so that they
would see me in bed with my dear husband" (303). Describing how he
made love to Babet/"Mademoiselle Dany," he writes, "I put her on the
outside of the bed, so that Mademoiselle Dupuis could get a better view; I
lifted her nightgown from behind and pressed myself against her little body"
(316). Sex as performance reaches its height in the adventures in which he
masquerades as the "comtesse des Barres." S/he makes love to Mademoiselle de La Grise in full view of his landlords plus the local priest: "Under
the pretext of kissing her, I took the position necessary for our true pleasures. The people looking on increased them still more; it is very agreeable
to deceive the public eye" (346).

None of these spectators seems to find anything unseemly in these activities, or in their role as witnesses. In fact, everyone treats it as a joke.
After a long embrace, the "comtesse" informs the priest that Mademoiselle
de La Grise is her/his little wife, and the latter also cries out that the
"comtesse" is her little husband. The priest readily gives the couple his
blessing; and not to be outdone, the landlord offers to support all the children born of the marriage. Apparently, the idea of a woman making love to
a woman does not disturb either of them. Behavior that would raise eye-
brows in many quarters today seems to be accepted or overlooked here,
although it is hard to tell whether this is the "real world" of seventeenth-
century France or the product of the author's transvestite fantasies. The
situation is rendered still more ironic by Choisy's suggestion that only Mademoiselle de La Grise's timely marriage averted an unhappy disclosure.

His insistence on the presence of an audience suggests that the gaze of
the other, which validates the femininity of the cross-dressed persona, is

also necessary to confirm the reality of the act that is the final test of gender identity. There may also be historical and cultural factors at work here, however. Admitting guests to the bedroom was much more common in seventeenth-century France than it is today. Several decades earlier, the *précieuses* had chosen the bedside as the privileged site of social intercourse. But in Choisy's text, the bedroom scenes do not call to mind the *chambre bleue* so much as they do the king's chamber. It was the monarch who rose in the morning and retired at night in full view of his courtiers. And when he had successfully fulfilled his conjugal duties, the queen so informed those present by clapping her hands as the bed curtains were drawn. Making love surrounded by complaisant viewers, Choisy again represents himself as the king's equal.

Choisy dressed as a woman seems to lead an idyllic life in utopias of his own creation. His cozy retreats are never disturbed by serious matters. Cut off completely from public events, his cross-dressed "ladies" take no notice of what transpires in the outside world. Beneath the shimmering surface of his fantasies, however, lie the outlines of a darker story. History cannot be banished from this purportedly ahistorical text. Just as Choisy's transvestism interrupts the glorious life chronicled in the *Mémoires pour servir a l'histoire de Louis XIV,* so the royal presence invades the cocoon he spins around his feminine creations.

The adventures of "Madame de Sancy" come to an abrupt halt when the king's housing superintendent, Mansard, informs him that unless he returns immediately to court, he will lose his rooms in the Luxembourg Palace. Likewise, the "comtesse des Barres" comes into being after he is obliged to leave Paris altogether, following a humiliating encounter at the theater with the dauphin's preceptor, Monsieur de Montausier. Although, Choisy asserts, the crown prince greeted him amiably, Montausier delivered a stinging rebuke: "I admit, madame, or mademoiselle (as the case may be), that you are beautiful, but truthfully, aren't you ashamed to wear such clothes and play the woman when you are fortunate enough not to be one? Go, go and hide yourself. The prince finds you very offensive" (326). Deeply chagrined, but unable to give up his habit, Choisy conceals his true identity and installs himself near Bourges, where he will not encounter members of the court.[25]

Transvestism destabilizes the patriarchal ideology of gender by demonstrating that the biological categories of "man" and "woman" are arbitrary and artificial.[26] But as both the *Mémoires pour servir à l'histoire de Louis XIV* and the *Mémoires de l'abbé de Choisy habillé en femme* show,

seventeenth-century apparatuses of state control were at work to counteract this threat. The royal preceptor's rebuke suggests the extent to which
French aristocrats perceived the masculine as superior to the feminine; and
his determination to shield his charge from Choisy's transgressive posture
indicates that Louis pursued Mazarin's politics of gender construction to
ensure that phallic power would be vested in the heir to the throne. In Louis
XIV's world, the feminine body was the excluded body, beautiful but offensive; as was the female body, whose forbidden charms threatened the
blueness of the royal blood and had therefore to be excluded from the dynastic succession (re: Marie Mancini). Consequently, the transvestite's feminized body was exiled to the fau (false) bourg (community), and *barred*
from the royal presence. Choisy's encounter with Montausier not only confirms the monarchy's commitment to phallic power, it attests to his society's
conviction that women are by nature inferior to men, an ideology of gender
that is clearly internalized in the author's own construction of the feminine. The male dressed as a woman portrays himself as a misfit; and the
superficiality of the personae he creates reinforces his culture's perception
of women as narcissistic and shallow.

What is more, his disguise does not pass without negative reactions.
The cardinal calls him on the carpet. Appearances in public give rise to
sarcastic compliments. Anonymous letters accuse him of moral turpitude.
His uncle reproaches him for making a spectacle of himself. The parish
priest, urged on by his embarrassed relatives, takes him aside and delivers
a warning. Only in the company of social inferiors can he do as he pleases.
That is why he must hide in out-of-the-way places like Saint-Marceau and
Bourges—"among people who would not find anything to criticize, whatever I did" (290). And when one of these new friends wants to protest
because Choisy has not been identified by name in a *Mercure galant* article
about him, Choisy moves swiftly to discourage her, pointing out that although he may dress as a woman among friends, he does not do so in the
city: "Society is so wicked, and it is so rare to see a man wanting to be a
women, that one is often exposed to ugly jokes" (293–94).[27]

Although he proved in his own life that the so-called masculine and
feminine could coexist in the same person, he was unable to jettison the
stereotypes attached to gender labels. If his friends in Saint-Marceau and
Bourges passed no judgments on his behavior, his own uneasiness pervades his paean to life lived as a transvestite. He may have passed as a
woman in the suburbs and provinces, but he was always and everywhere in
exile.[28] Here as in his historical memoirs, history is a present and powerful
force, invading and shaping the narrative that purports to exclude it. The

transvestite's story decenters the *Mémoires pour servir a l'histoire de Louis XIV,* only to be itself decentered by the long arm of the monarch who imposed his will on his subjects in both the public and the private spheres.

The figure of his childhood friend Monsieur links these two spheres as he links the two sets of memoirs. Appearing in both texts, he bridges the gap between the public domain of the virile Louis and the private havens that shelter the cross-dressed abbé. Choisy points out that when Philippe was in Paris, he always invited him to the Palais-Royal: "He was always very kind to me because our inclinations were the same; he would have liked to dress as a woman too, but he did not dare to because of his dignity. (Princes are the prisoners of their grandeur.) Every evening he put on *cornettes,* ear pendants, and beauty marks, and gazed at himself in the mirror" (325).

Reduced to a secondary role by his shameful "inclination," Monsieur is nonetheless prevented by his royal birth from practicing the unabashed cross-dressing Choisy indulges in. He is a "prisoner" in the palace. Only at his annual Carnival ball can he satisfy his desire: "Monsieur led the dancing with Mademoiselle de Brancas . . . and a moment later he went to dress as a woman and returned in a mask. . . . He made some difficulties about removing his mask, but secretly he was glad, for he wanted to be seen. Words cannot express how far he pushed his coquetry in admiring himself" (325–26).

Choisy may not have suffered from the constraints of princely grandeur, but both sets of memoirs make it clear that there was a bitter taste to his "small pleasures." If he idealizes the gentleness and innocence of the life he led as a woman, his behavior is nonetheless perceived as an embarrassment to everyone, including himself—"You will be ashamed as you read, what then will I be as I write? I will search in vain for excuses in my bad upbringing, I will not be excused" (289). The male who dresses as a woman is represented as a misfit, unable to function outside the charmed circle he draws around himself.

This is the significance of the repeated references to his addictive gambling. Both of these "histoires" terminate with financial ruin. In the first, after he is summoned to court by Mansard, the fatal "rage" inevitably takes hold of him: "In the evening I went to M. Terrac's, where they do nothing but gamble; I returned to playing and lost immense sums, I lost all my money and then my ear pendants and my rings; I could no longer play the beauty. Madness seized me, I sold my house in the faubourg Saint-Marceau, I lost it; I no longer thought of dressing as a woman and took to traveling in order to hide my shame and misery and attempt to dispel my gloom" (319). The second episode ends the same way. Persuaded by embarrassed relatives to give up dressing as a woman, he goes off to Italy. His reminiscences break off with this bitter reflection: "One passion chases away another: I began to gamble in Venice, I won a great deal, but I have more than paid it back since. The madness of gambling has possessed me and ruined my life. I would have been far happier had I always played the beauty, even if I had been ugly! Ridicule is preferable to poverty" (360). The vice that always followed his transvestite interludes provided both a substitute and a punishment for cross-dressing. On the other hand, he absolutely forbade it when he was "playing the beauty" in Saint-Marceau and Bourges.[29]

Gambling was encouraged by the king, who used it to keep potential *frondeurs* both occupied and impoverished.[30] Moreover, Kavanaugh argues, in the time of Louis XIV gambling was still considered a noble pastime, signifying the lordly disdain for money that was the sign of the true aristocrat. "As one of a number of substitute affirmations of nobility, high-stakes gambling held the appeal not only of proving one's willingness to confront risk with equanimity but also of proclaiming the individual's superiority to the ever more imperious rule of money" (1933, 44). He cites as an example the king's readiness to pay the duc de Bourgogne's gambling debts; the king wished to prove that nothing involving "only money" should ever be a matter of concern to persons of their rank. "This contempt for the anonymous power of money as money," Kavanaugh continues, "is important because it points to the nobility's grounding of its personal identity in a fixed, inherited sense of self that brought with it a freedom of thought and action far greater than that available to those whose social status depended entirely on acquired wealth and a compulsive mimicry of aristocratic conduct" (47–48).

Kavanaugh's thesis raises again the question of how the ideology of class determined the concept of selfhood in the seventeenth century. Choisy's family did not have its roots in the ancient *noblesse d'épée,* whose "sense of self," in Kavanaugh's words, "was based on personal ancestry, on an inherited title held over time, and on its identification with a geographically specific estate providing the individual's name and social identity," and for whom, "money . . . was regarded as a means, a pure instrument useful only for the duty of 'living nobly'" (49). On the contrary, as I mentioned above, a Choisy ancestor who was a wine merchant supposedly established the family fortunes by losing to the king at chess. Putting together what Choisy says about gambling, financial ruin, and cross-dressing, one sees a hidden connection between his sense of social inferiority, his attitude to money, and the habit of feminine impersonation. Dressed as a woman, he engages in pastimes associated with the *précieuses,* a group who, as Lougee argues, subtly undermined the old aristocracy's obsession with "blood" and accepted members of the upwardly mobile bourgeoisie who were clever enough to acquire courtly manners. When he was forced to return to the court circles to which he had gained entry via his politically astute mother, Choisy was obliged to give up playing the beauty and play instead the *grand seigneur*—gambling away his fortune to prove his adherence to aristocratic values. Since, however, the king did not reimburse *his* gambling debts, Choisy's losses had serious consequences. They made it impossible for him to finance his transvestite lifestyle and reinforced the reality of an inferior status that was not derived from blood but from money.

Having analyzed the two sets of Choisy's memoirs, I must now turn to the question that remains to be answered: How do they fit into a study of women and self-representation in the seventeenth century? Like the women who wrote self-narratives in the seventeenth century, Choisy introduced the personal, the particular, and the worldly into life-writing. In addition, his texts reveal, perhaps more clearly than those by biological women, how gender was constructed in upper-class France.

Yet in spite of the insights they provide into both femininity and the memoirs genre, I do not think that these "histoires" written by a man dressed as a woman belong to the same category as the autobiographical texts produced by women who were biologically and historically female. Women expanded life-writing to include feminine experience. And even more important, they displayed a more developed sense of personal and private selfhood than did the more celebrated male memoirists; Choisy, on the other hand, veered off into a shallow and fantasized brand of self-invention that emphasized the external and the superficial, which he conflated with femininity.

Although his texts confirm the constructionist view of gender, they invalidate the lived experiences of the female body. Femininity is represented in them not just primarily but exclusively as a performance that depends for its very existence on validation by an audience. To Choisy, a "woman" is nothing but what is seen of her—jewelry, makeup, and clothing. He represents femininity as a sign system in which the "woman" and her observer communicate according to a preestablished code; and since femininity is only skin-deep, anyone, male or female, can reproduce and represent it through purely cosmetic means. Such an appropriation of the "feminine" erases both the female body and the experiences of biological women, rendering invisible their oppression and their struggles to overcome it.

Still more disturbing is the way these "histoires" document, but do not contest, the condition of historical women whose poverty or lack of family connections made them vulnerable to sexual exploitation by the privileged classes. Choisy's wealth and social status allowed him to play the dominant role in all his romances. He takes it for granted that lower-class women like Charlotte, Babet, and Roselie could be acquired for money and used to act out sexual fantasies. When Charlotte's aunt objects to their "marriage," her niece points out that "Madame de Sancy" has given her "a hundred small gifts," and is in a position to make her fortune, adding, "[Y]ou know, my dear aunt, that we are not rich" (1966, 301). Later, he tells of examining Babet as if she were a horse before purchasing her from her mistress: "I had her come closer, I looked at her teeth, her bosom that was beginning to show; her arms were a bit skinny" (312). Roselie is likewise acquired from an "aunt," who is only too glad to see her so well established.

He also makes no effort to deconstruct the relationship between women's class and their sexual behavior. Yet it can be clearly inferred from his text that those who were poor or of low birth were subject to very different treatment and were expected to behave very differently from those who were wealthy or enjoyed higher social status. The actress Roselie is de facto assumed to be a woman of easy virtue, who can be impregnated with much more impunity than a Mademoiselle de La Grise. If Choisy chooses to provide for her and their child, he is not impelled to do so either by the laws or the mores of his time. Furthermore, when Roselie chooses security with the actor Rosan, his bitterness at her defection reflects an unwillingness to understand the economic realities of her situation.

In representing the sexual/social codes of his century, Choisy writes not as a woman, but as a rich male aristocrat. As Rowan observes, "On many occasions he assumes a feminine voice without becoming either a feminist or a female. In the final analysis, he never renounces his loyalty to the world of masculine power and aristocratic privilege" (1991, 230). Nowhere does he question the traffic in women. The "comtesse des Barres" who finds herself/himself courted by a penniless chevalier is amused and embarrassed, until s/he discovers that this suitor has risked a year's revenue to purchase a costume for the ball. Then s/he is so moved that s/he slips him a hundred gold louis, suggesting that at heart Choisy has far more sympathy for the fortune hunter than for his prey.

By disguising himself as a rich widow, he locates himself in the one category of early women who had some measure of control over their lives and fortunes. Although there was a very compelling reason why the "comtesse des Barres" could not consider marriage to the chevalier, her refusal nonetheless underlines the advantages of her position—"I am happy and mistress of my own actions, I do not want to become a slave" (350). It also suggests the unhappy condition of biological women within the institution of marriage. Dressed as a woman, he does not, however, run the risk of being bartered to a cruel spouse. Nor is he subject to a tyrannical father or a jealous husband. It is important, therefore, to state that although this text shifts gender traits from the biological to the discursive and implies that "masculine" and "feminine" are not mutually exclusive, it still inscribes masculinist and classist sex/gender biases.

This said, it is nonetheless true that the *Mémoires de l'abbé de Choisy habillé en femme* is a vehicle of resistance to the ideology that privileged the "public" over the "private," the chronological over the episodic, and the "heroic" over the "feminine"; it parodies the phallocentric discourses of the age and deconstructs the technologies of gender that assured their survival. Excluded from the centers of power by his unvirile propensities, Choisy changes the subject of life-writing. The "fop" steps into the limelight and leads the reader away from the bloody battlefields and palace intrigues of historical memoirs to safe houses in suburbs and provinces, where "nothing dark-spirited" interferes with the pleasures of parlor games and pretty clothes. In so doing, he discards the commonly held notions of his time about what constitutes a "life" and how it should be recounted. These rambling monologues inscribe a discourse of "self" outside the limits of both gender and chronology. The transvestite's texts destabilize the assumptions that underlie life-writing by demonstrating the extent to which existence can be fragmentary, unintegrated, and marginalized. The transvestite's performance destabilizes the categories of man and woman by demonstrating the extent to which they are constructed and arbitrary.

8

Conclusion

Having considered how Choisy's transvestite memoirs point to the dramatic difference between representing life lived *like* a woman and life lived *as* a woman, I want to return to the question I raised at the beginning of this study: How did biological women of this era free their self-reflections from the masculine gaze and answer the question, "Who am I?" Although it would be foolhardy to draw sweeping conclusions from this sampling, I believe that it is possible to make some generalizations about how these autobiographers represented themselves and how they approached the autobiographical act. I think it is evident that they not only possessed an individualized sense of self but imposed meaning on their experiences. I believe it is also arguable that this sense of self was rooted in the sense of difference imposed on them by the gender ideology of their milieu.

Beginning with Marguerite de Valois, these self-narratives contest the scenario of life-writing that had come down from Plutarch, through the medieval chroniclers, to the historical memoirists and spiritual autobiographers of their times. They countered the presupposition that the only life worth writing about was that of a "great man." They believed what others had not believed—that lives lived in the feminine sphere deserved to be written down in book form. It is this conviction that gave birth in their texts to the representation of selfhood. Uncomfortably aware of their exclusion, they did not remain silent. Unwilling to remain invisible and mute in the hope that they would "not get themselves talked about," they asserted the politics of individualism defined by Irving Howe as "a claim for space, voice, identity" (1992, 253).

Ironically, it was women's exclusion from the mainstream of history that forced them to turn inward to tell the story of private life. What was considered "weak" and "indiscreet" in men's memoirs gave birth in theirs to uniqueness. Thus they speak of what others did not mention: "real life" as it was lived in the female body (childhood, puberty, marriage) and they analyze what others ignore (the impact of parents, siblings, and spouses on personal identity). They represent themselves as the woman they see reflected in the mirror, the person who, in the words of Marguerite de Valois, "knows the most and has the greatest interest in describing the subject" (1999, 72 [1971, 36).

This in brief is my answer to the central questions of this study; but before I close, I also want to address another issue that up to this point has been more implicit than explicit, despite the fact that it is included in my title. This is the *political significance* of these texts.

It has been a feminist truism to maintain that the personal is the political, but I believe that this is especially so in the case of the six self-narratives studied here. They are united by a common thread, the theme of alienation and exile. In fact, these narratives emerged from the experience of arrest and banishment: Marguerite de Valois isolated in a desolate castle in Auvergne; Mademoiselle de Montpensier confined to her ancestral estate in Saint-Fargeau; Hortense Mancini forced to seek asylum in Chambéry; Marie Mancini incarcerated in a Spanish convent; Guyon, interrogated in a Visitandine convent, later condemned to the Bastille; and Choisy, his transvestite personae barred from the royal presence and exiled to the suburbs and provinces.

Although these texts explore many scenarios of private life, they are all political in the way they publicly contest the silencing and subjugation of women. Guyon and the Mancinis do so by challenging the false representations deployed against them for refusing to submit to the constraints of patriarchy; Marguerite de Valois, Mademoiselle de Montpensier, and the abbé de Choisy by inscribing the threat that the feminine represented to the legitimacy of the Bourbon dynasty and the mythic power of the absolute monarch.

The Bourbon dynasty rested on a very fragile base. The power that made Henri de Navarre a viable candidate to succeed his second cousin and brother-in-law, Henri III, did not really lie in his blood but in his position as chief of the Protestant party, which made him the opponent of the crown's most virulent enemies, the ultra-Catholic Guises. In actual fact, his ties to the royal family were *through the maternal line* (his grandmother Marguerite de Navarre, who was François I's sister, and his wife, Marguerite de Valois, who was the sister of Charles IX and Henri III), while his descent on the paternal side was extremely tenuous. (It was necessary to trace the Bourbon line back to the thirteenth century to prove that he was next in line to the throne.) Although in principle he was legitimized by the Salic law, therefore, his succession was really a negotiated settlement, and years of warfare were necessary to consolidate his hold on the kingdom.

Although the sacred body of the Sun King was validated by the Bourbon blood transmitted to him by his father, Louis XIII, and his grandfather, Henri IV, had it not been for the Salic law, Marguerite de Valois, and not Henri de Navarre, would have been the legitimate heir to the throne. In addition, it is possible to imagine a scenario in which the younger son, Gaston d'Orléans, backed by his mother, Marie de Médicis, could have forced the childless Louis XIII to abdicate, had Gaston's daughter, Mademoiselle de Montpensier, been legally able to succeed him. The threats of feminine rule and feminine succession, both allied to the threat of the younger son, were thus very present during the first half of the seventeenth century.

What is more, by the time Louis XIV reached his majority, the principle of male rule had been further destabilized by the fact that between 1560 and 1660 the actual governance of France had thrice been handed over to women: Catherine de Médicis, Marie de Médicis, and Anne d'Autriche. In addition, across the Channel, the reigns of Mary Tudor, Elizabeth I, and Mary Queen of Scots had provided disquieting evidence that women could govern not only as regents but as crowned heads of state. These threats are present in the subtext of Marguerite de Valois's and Mademoiselle de Montpensier's memoirs, both of which represent lives that *might have been powerful,* had it not been for the disenfranchisement of royal daughters. They are also implied in the two sets of memoirs composed by the transvestite abbé de Choisy, who, like his mother, had strong ties to Mademoiselle de Montpensier and to Louis's younger brother, Philippe d'Orléans.

The subtext of Valois's and Montpensier's stories is the disenfranchisement of the feminine, which played such a crucial role in founding the Bourbon line. The former writes literally and the latter figuratively of living as queens in exile, surrounded in their banishment by shadow courts. Proudly conscious of their royal blood and convinced that they possessed the intelligence, strength of character, and political skills to reign, they represent themselves as talented and astute actors on the political scene, claiming a role for which they were naturally endowed by both intellect and royal blood, but which they were prevented from attaining by their gender. As has already been seen, all memoirs constituted a threat to the myth of the divinely appointed monarch because they presented dissident versions of history, but the threat concealed in these women's life stories was ultimately far greater, because of the way they used self-representation to imply a dynastic model in which power could be wielded by women.

Valois's and Montpensier's memoirs inscribe a direct challenge (and Choisy's an indirect one) to the monarch's legitimacy, but in subtler ways, all the texts I have studied contest the phallocentric ideology that sustained his kingdom. Patriarchal control of women's reproductive capacities and of their access to wealth was essential to the functioning of the ancien régime, as is clearly shown by Louis's efforts to restrict and manage the movements of Hortense and Marie Mancini. Nor could women be allowed to usurp, as had Guyon, the prerogatives of the religious institutions that undergirded his authority. Just as Valois's, Montpensier's, and Choisy's texts resist and subvert the Salic law, the Mancinis' and Guyon's protest the institutional control of women's bodies and speech. Through self-representation, they denounce publicly the injustices imposed on the feminine condition, and in so doing they validate and justify women's lives.

Notes

Chapter 1. Introduction

1. Brantôme called his two sets of *discours* on women simply *Des Dames*. Later editors separated them into two volumes: *Les Dames illustres* and *Les Dames galantes*. My citations are taken from the 1991 Pléiade edition edited by Vaucheret.

2. I will refer to women writers by their family name. See DeJean 1991, 2–3 for a justification of this practice. In his review of her *Tender Geographies,* Ranum concurs: "[T]he persistent reference to women writers with their marks of respect (not onomastics) such as 'Mlle' de Scudéry or 'Madame' [de] Villedieu is, as DeJean observes, clear evidence of the prevailing sexism of the academicians" (1992, 815).

3. I am using the word "autobiography" in its broadest sense: a written account of the author's life. I will not be using it in the sense defined by Lejeune in *Le Pacte autobiographique* and later rejected by him as inadequate. A more complete discussion of my position on the question of what constitutes "autobiography" follows.

4. The best-known example of the antiwoman position is found in Rabelais's *Tiers* and *Quart Livres*. For a summary of the "Quarrel," see McLeod 1991; also see Grieco 1991.

5. For a summary of this issue as it relates to women's self-representation, see S. Smith 1993, 1–23.

6. See Benveniste 1971, 218.

7. The word was first used in English in the nineteenth century and was subsequently translated into French. Although his early attempts at defining "autobiography" have been frequently contested, Lejeune reflects mainstream critical thinking about the genre when he writes that the word designated a new reality for which the existing word "memoirs" was no longer adequate. This new reality came into being, he asserts, in the middle of the eighteenth century, when people began to publish the story of their own "personalities" (1971, 10).

8. For discussions of this position, pro and con, see B. Martin 1988, Flax 1992, and Modleski 1991.

9. See Weed and Schor 1997.

10. See Claridge and Langland's analysis of how both men and women participate in patriarchy (1990, 3–21).

11. This is comparable to Spelman's analysis of gender as constructed by class in Aristotle. "Slaves are without gender," she writes, "because, for Aristotle's purposes, their

sex doesn't matter. In any world in which for some people sex is made to matter—positively for males, negatively for females—then it also matters a lot if your sex doesn't matter" (1988, 55).

12. See Hendricks and Parker 1994, 5–6 for a discussion of the instability of the term "race" in early modern Europe.

13. "In the sixteenth century, except for some glorification of the ancientness of some individual upper-class families, the only really strong emphasis on birth and blood had been for the families of the kings, in order to separate, for instance, the princes of the blood from the peers. From the early seventeenth century on, then, nobility as a collective social group had joined the monarchy in becoming a hereditary entity" (Schalk 1986, 145).

14. See Gouesse 1985, 9–15.

15. For an extensive discussion of women and work in seventeenth-century France, see Gibson 1989, 97–140. See also Collins 1989 and Davis 1975, 69–74.

16. See Traer 1980, 15–16, and Maclean 1977, 17.

17. See Boursier 1987, 265.

18. Gournay 1985, 20v°–21r°. See Bauschatz 1990.

19. Bussy 1858, 3:362 (21 January 1671). Cited in Duchêne 1982, 148.

20. See Viguerie 1985, 29–30.

21. See Duchêne 1982, 78.

22. For the names of others who supported learning for women as a means of combating immorality, see Maclean 1977, 54–57.

23. For critiques of the idea that seventeenth-century France was a monolithic society, see Apostolides (1988, 100) and Mettam (1988, 5).

24. Gournay later incorporated this passage into her "Grief des Dames." See Schiff 1978, 89–91.

25. Valois's letter to Loryot was published as *discours docte et subtile* in his *Fleurs des secrets moraux* (Paris, 1614). It was a reply to his essay, ironically entitled "Pourquoi le sexe feminin est fort honoré de l'homme." See Valois 1999, 252–86.

26. See plates in Maclean 1977 between pages 208 and 209.

27. Harth 1992 admits that there was, nonetheless, a gap between learned women and their masculine counterparts. Although they attended the feminocentric salons, they were excluded from the more learned academies and conferences. Furthermore, their erudition tended to be acquired and disseminated orally rather than in writing.

28. Supposedly Madame de Rambouillet suffered greatly from the cold and received in bed in order to keep warm. Backer sees symbolic significance in the *précieuses'* predilection for receiving in bed. "These ladies found a whole new environment of expressive artifice in the little intimate alcove, screened from the public, hard to get into unless you played the lady's game" (1974, 169). She also points out that much of a woman's life was associated with the bed and that it dramatized her womanly functions and her frailty, as well as proclaiming that one of these functions was being denied (170).

29. The roots of the feminocentric salon culture can be traced back still further. Roelker (1972) argues that Louis XI's daughter Anne de Beaujeu (1460–1522) supervised the education of younger women at a "court school," instilling in them good manners, refined tastes, and virtuous behavior. Marguerite de Navarre's mother, Louise de Savoie, was Anne's protégée.

30. Goldsmith shows that the subject of conversation dominated conduct books for men and women in this century. Du Bosc's *L'Honnête Femme* (1633–36), Grenaille's *L'Honnête Fille* (1639–40) and *L'Honnête Veuve* (1640) argued that women should be trained

in conversational rhetoric if for no other reason than to protect their virtue against the verbal onslaughts of would-be seducers! (Goldsmith 1988, 20–21). Madame de Maintenon likewise urged her pupils at Saint-Cyr to practice "economy, restraint, and a systematic suspicion of other speakers" (Goldsmith 1988, 71).

31. See Garapon 1993, 98. See also my introduction in Montpensier 1999, 18–22.

32. Published as *Divers Portraits* in 1659.

33. For a concurring view, see François 1987, 117–23.

34. Stanton contends that they were ridiculed as "ugly or frustrated, sexual fake or deviant" because they voiced hostility to love and marriage (1981, 134). In *Les Précieuses ridicules,* Molière attributes to his two silly heroines the idea that marriage is "quite shocking" and has one of them exclaim, "How can one bear the thought of sleeping with a man who is completely nude?" In a lesser-known play, *La Princesse d'Elide,* he likewise has a woman say that a husband and death are the same thing. Armande in *Les Femmes savantes* considers marriage a "vulgar design," the very thought of which nauseates her. Her "philosophy" has made her reject the idea of being enslaved to a man's laws. Accordingly, she has refused her suitor Clitandre's proposal of marriage but offered to retain him as a suffering admirer. Today Molière's mockery is better known than the lives and writings of historical seventeenth-century women. As Stanton argues, his virulence stands as proof of the fear generated by the threat of *préciosité* to the traditional structure of society.

35. See Gouesse 1985, 16.

36. Richmond maintains that de Pure was in fact attacking the effeminate gallantry and pedantry that replaced the old "virile and heroic values" after the Fronde, and satirizing the "ascendance of woman on the social and literary life of the 1650s" (1977, 83). François disagrees (1987, 105–6).

37. DeJean writes, "[T]he fictional forms devised by seventeenth-century women writers were both feminocentric and the product of an ideology that sought to promote equality between the sexes." Moreover, "feminist ideas played a crucial role in . . . the evolution of political activity undertaken by seventeenth-century women and the intellectual bond repeatedly forged in this activity between the making of history and the making of literature" (1991, 5–6).

38. I shall have more to say about spiritual autobiography, which traced its origins back to Augustine of Hippo, in the chapter on Jeanne Guyon.

39. Fumaroli situates the birth of the genre between 1555 and 1570 (1979, 26). According to Bertière, no French text was designated as *Mémoires* prior to the fifteenth century (1977, 14). At the beginning of the Renaissance, the term was used to distinguish between unpolished accounts of plain facts and the *grande histoire* of the humanists. Early examples include Guillaume du Bellay's memoirs, which recount military history under François I, Pierre Matthieu's *Histoire des derniers troubles de France,* Jean de Serres's *Mémoires des guerres civiles et des derniers troubles de France,* Du Haillon's *De l'estat et succes des affaires de France,* and Monluc's *Commentaires.* See Knecht 1989 for a discussion of memoirs as military record in the texts of Florange, du Bellay, Monluc, Jean de Tavannes, de la Noue, and d'Aubigné. See Davies 1991, 8–15 for a discussion of historical biography included in the category of memoirs.

40. This criticism inspired Gournay's passionate defense of his practices in her 1595 preface to the *Essais.*

41. Bertière writes that memoirs narrating the Wars of Religion depict the confrontation between feudal and royal power, whereas those composed after the Fronde betray the knowledge that the battle was over and the feudal aristocracy had lost (1977, 31).

42. Lesne-Jaffro 1993 discusses this aspect of the memoirs of Bussy, Campion, and Arnauld.

43. See Karro 1993 for an analysis of memoirists' efforts to attach their texts to medieval/feudal traditions.

44. Watts concurs: "[O]ne of the main objects of the exercise was to *give account*, to set the record straight, to defend the individual's and the family's name in the eyes of posterity" (1975, 267). According to Ariès, memoirs were an "educational message" bequeathed from father to son (1979, 13). Fumaroli cites the duc de Bouillon, who desired "to perpetuate the honor and virtue of our race" (1971, 23). He also quotes Jean de Tavannes: "I write out of duty to our father and [his] precepts to you, my family" (24). See also Fumaroli's introduction to Henri de Campion's memoirs.

45. For the complete text, see Marin 1988, 39–41. He quotes Paul Pellisson-Fontanier, *Œuvres diverses* (Paris, 1735), 2:323–28.

46. See Davies 1991 on the role of propaganda in early biographical memoirs.

47. According to Georges May, the word *mémoires* may refer to three types of text: the narrative of external events in which the author was an active participant; the narrative of external events in which the author was a passive observer; and the narrative of the author's life in its most personal aspects. Modern usage, he observes, tends to define the first two as *mémoires* and the third as *autobiographie*. The difference between the two genres lies, therefore, in the extent to which the author/narrator reveals the private and intimate side of his or her character. Interestingly, May illustrates these classifications with two triads—one consisting of men authors (Joinville, Retz, and Rousseau) and the other of women authors (Motteville, Montpensier, and George Sand) (May 1979, 123).

48. See Dezon-Jones 1988, 137–39. This brief third-person account of Gournay's life was probably composed in 1616 for James I of England in the mistaken belief that he had requested it. It was published for the first time in *L'Ombre de la Demoiselle de Gournay,* 1626.

49. The *Apologie* appeared in *L'Ombre de la demoiselle de Gournay* (1626) and, with minor revisions, in *Les Advis et presens de la demoiselle de Gournay* (1634; 1641).

50. Of the women studied here, only Guyon is listed in Lejeune's repertory of early autobiographical texts (1971, 112). See also Huntington Williams: "The emphasis on the individual self is one aspect of a wide-ranging secularization that emerges in the eighteenth century. . . . If God underwrites individual existence for the Christian autobiographer, personal identity in modern autobiography is thought to be 'natural.' This is a major change, and one of its effects, broadly defined, is that personal value and moral sense no longer have their source in a transcendent 'outside,' in God or in Scripture. . . . I take Rousseau as exemplary for modern, Romantic autobiography, not just because he occupies a pivotal position historically, but also because he attempts to construct his personal identity primarily in his own writings" (1983, 3).

51. For a general survey of feminist work on seventeenth-century French literature, see Jensen 1991.

52. See, for example, Trinh T. Minh-ha 1989, S. Smith 1987, Gilmore 1994, and Lionnet 1989.

53. Georges May refuses to offer a definition of the genre, stating, "Experience seems to indicate that the moment has not yet come to formulate a precise, complete, and universally accepted definition of autobiography; and it is somewhat for that reason that this book disobeys the rule that insists one should begin by defining what one is talking about" (1979, 11). For mainstream attempts at such a definition, see Gusdorf 1980, Lejeune (1971, 1975),

Pascal 1960, Olney 1980, Spengemann 1980, Bruss 1976, Weintraub 1978, Fleishman 1983, Eakin 1985. For a summary of the history of autobiographical theory, see Folkenflik 1993, 1–17.

54. Such attempts were often based on Chodorow's theories of feminine development. Jelinek, one of the first to study the subject, writes that women's autobiographies are characterized by "Personal subject matter and disjunctive style" (1986, 17). Jelinek hypothesizes that the "disjunctive forms" she sees as typical of women's life-writing serve "a protective function, a way of obscuring the lack of a retrospective, coherent, and holistic sense of self; just as the linear, unidimensional life studies by men may—also unconsciously—protect them from their vulnerable inner selves as they delineate what society expects of them, a life centered around a career" (188). Many theoreticians also see the autobiographical act as invested with a different signification for women, because of their problematic status as "a 'subject' of/in discourse" (Hewitt 1990, 4). Sidonie Smith argues in her *Poetics* that because autobiography has signified men's "embeddedness in the phallic order" (1987, 39), women do not have an "autobiographical self" in the sense that men do: "That situating of the autobiographer in two universes of discourse accounts for the poetics of women's autobiography and grounds its difference" (50). For a rigorous critique of theories of feminine difference in autobiography, see the introduction to Stanton 1987.

55. The only exception to this was when the king's mother was named regent during his minority, a circumstance that occurred three times between 1550 and 1660, and that served to destabilize the rule that women should not participate in politics.

CHAPTER 2. MARGUERITE DE VALOIS

1. See Viennot 1992. Viennot bases her argument that Valois was not the author of this text on its stylistic dissimilarities to her other writings, and on the fact that it was never attributed to her during her own lifetime. Others continue, however, to ascribe the *Ruelle* to her. See, for instance, Tetel 1994. Cazaux's edition includes the *Ruelle,* which he describes as "a charming satire of herself by Marguerite" (Valois 1971, 27).

2. In any case, d'Aubigné, a Protestant, vilified her in his *Histoire universelle.*

3. See Viennot 1993, 243–47. See also Dubois 1994.

4. See Viennot 1993, 263–70.

5. She cites Marguerite's letters to Champvallon as proof (Viennot, 1992, 86).

6. The colloquium on Valois was held in Agen in 1991. See Lazard and Beynac 1994.

7. See Viennot 1993, 186.

8. See Viennot 1993, 185, 429 nn. 9 and 10.

9. Castarède seems to concur (1994, 51).

10. A reedition had appeared in 1649, only four years before Montpensier began her memoirs. See Garapon 1993, 101.

11. Pellisson 1653, 481. See Viennot 1993, 263.

12. See Mariéjol 1970, 318.

13. Viennot comes to the same conclusion in Viennot 1995.

14. Schrenck divides Brantôme's *discours* on Valois into three parts: the panegyric to her beauty, the reflections on the Salic law, and a summary of her generosity and artistic tastes (1991, 185).

15. For a study of Brantôme's panegyric, see also Vaucheret 1994 and Supple 1994.

16. For a study of Valois's role as poetic muse, see Magnien-Simonin 1994.

17. Schrenck writes, "[T]he *Dames galantes* exhibits on the other hand, the reverse side of [court women's] glorious appearances" (1991, 187). Significantly, Garnier made available in 1960 a modern edition of this part of Brantôme's writings about women, whereas the *Dames illustres* was not reedited until the Pléiade edition of 1991.

18. For Plutarch's influence on life-writing, see May 1979, 156–57. Amyot's French translation, which appeared in 1559, made the *Lives* available to a wide reading public and was largely responsible for its popularity in France.

19. See Valois 1999, 73 n. 21.

20. Following the Journée des Barricades (12 May 1588), an uprising instigated by the Guises, Henri III lured the duke to Blois and had him assassinated along with his brother, the cardinal de Lorraine.

21. See Fleishman 1983, 65.

22. "Above all, what has been forbidden to women is anger" (Heilbrun 1988, 13).

23. Many commentators have not believed Valois's protestations. Guessard writes that both the pamphleteers of her time and the chroniclers of the next generation—de Thou, Matthieu, Dupleix, and Mézeray—attest to her involvement with Guise (1842, 19). These are the very historians, however, who, according to Viennot, were convinced by Richelieu to defame Valois because she had sided with Marie de Médicis. Mariéjol believes a match with Guise was considered but that Valois was not necessarily involved in the negotiations (1970, 18). Viennot points out that Valois denies she and Guise had talked of marriage, not that she was friendly with him. She believes that she did carry on a "mild flirtation" with Guise, but at a later date (1993, 37).

24. Marguerite's lack of consent would eventually be used as one of the grounds for annulling the marriage.

25. "Mémoire justificatif pour Henri de Bourbon, roi de Navarre." See Valois 1999, 239–50.

26. Concluded 6 May 1576. See Cazaux's note in Valois 1971, 301.

27. Catherine hoped that the Flemish struggle against Spanish rule would provide an outlet for her youngest son's seditious energies.

28. It is interesting that Mariéjol seems to equate *préciosité* with a prudish attitude toward sex.

29. For an analysis of the topos of sisterhood here, see Viennot 1995.

30. See Ratel (1924, 1925) and Tachouzin (1994).

31. Boucher 1994 argues that Marguerite held conflicting opinions regarding her marital duties.

32. It is ironic that Henri's sexual exploits, which produced a host of illegitimate offspring, caused him to be admired for his virility, while his wife was vilified as a debauched woman. Viennot credits Voltaire with glorifying Henri IV because he saw him as a precursor of the Enlightenment. She writes, "[H]e [Voltaire] disassociates himself from his precursors by going farther than they in his praise, washing away even the 'sin' that had until then remained attached to his [Henri's] memory: his lust. He was accused, says he, of having made love too much, he was even supposed to have been castrated (Bayle); that is absurd: his multiple love affairs are mere peccadillos, and virility is inseparable from the appetite for victory" (1993, 302).

33. In a letter written to Brantôme about 1589, Marguerite again expressed this philosophical resignation: "I have learned that like me, you have chosen the quiet life, for I consider anyone who can lead it to be fortunate." Quoted by Guessard 1842, 299.

CHAPTER 3. MADEMOISELLE DE MONTPENSIER

1. See Cholakian 1986a, appendix.

2. See Cholakian 1986b.

3. The lacunae in this copy correspond to those found in the earliest editions of the *Mémoires,* suggesting that it served as the basis for the editions published immediately after Louis XIV's death. Only in 1735 did the edition of J. Wetstein and G. Smith (Amsterdam, 1735) fill them in from the Harlay manuscript.

4. A librarian's note (undated and unsigned) states that the eighty or so pages of the beginning were not with the manuscript when it came into the Bibliothèque Nationale. The unbound sheets were in two boxes, both of which were so full that there would have been no room in them for more pages. The note also states that the sheets were collected into ninety-five notebooks. Several pages of irregular size have been bound at the front of the ms. in no discernible sequence. The pages numbered 1 to 5 are all in Mademoiselle's hand except folio 2. The second volume contains parts 2 and 3 (292 sheets). The pages in part 3 are slightly smaller than those in part 2. Mademoiselle wrote on both front and back of sheets approximately 335×230 millimeters, leaving no margins at the top, bottom, or sides and using no punctuation or capitalization, although from time to time, she would quite arbitrarily begin a new paragraph. She seems to have written quickly, as events occurred to her. There are almost no corrections. She set down afterthoughts on scraps of paper, indicating where they belonged in the manuscript with crosses and pinning them to the proper pages. The Harlay version was acquired from the Harlay family during the French Revolution.

5. Although most scholars have preferred the autograph version, Hipp and Beasley base their analyses on the Harlay.

6. Garapon underlines the oral nature of Mademoiselle's education. Her father, Gaston, was a "brilliant conversationalist" who loved to talk of his heroic adventures and was always surrounded by an "erudite circle" engaged in moral or political debate. Later, of course, there were the salons of Rambouillet and Scudéry, where she was frequently a guest. In addition, as her memoirs attest, she was a great lover of the theater. She was also very fond of being read aloud to while she embroidered, and spent many hours thus engaged at Saint-Fargeau. It is evident that the spoken word was much more familiar and natural to Mademoiselle, a fact that explains in large measure her style (Garapon 1989c, 22–29).

7. Page numbers refer to the Fontaine reprinting of the Chéruel edition. Garapon (1989, 279–83) has included a table giving the corresponding page numbers in Chéruel.

8. The Réserve of the B.N. owns a copy of this edition with the following handwritten notation: "L'on a arresté et supprimé l'ed. de ces Mémoires; il ni [*sic*] a eu d'imprimé que ce seul volume qui ne fait au plus que le quart de l'ouvrage, il est fort rare" (Rés.Lb 37.191).

9. Evans takes Chéruel to task for not providing variant spellings, but an examination of the autograph ms. reveals that such an enterprise would only have underlined the author's illiteracy. In an age when the rules of orthography were not generally understood and spelling had not been standardized, she still made far more mistakes than the average writer. Here are a few examples: "avet" for *avoit* or *avoient,* "doner" for *donner,* "calite" for *qualité,* "otre" for *autre,* "can" for *quand,* "osi" for *aussi,* "sete" for *cette.* In addition she regularly uses "se" and "ce" interchangeably. Another of Evans's objections is better

founded: Chéruel's failure to indicate where passages had been crossed out or where Mademoiselle had put X's for the insertion of flyleaves.

10. See chapter 1.

11. In 1655, the duc de Richelieu agreed to return Champigny and pay for having torn down what she always referred to as "ma maison." When she finally came into legal possession of the property, she was overjoyed. She recounts in some detail a visit she made there after her exile (1985, 2:15–20). See also DeJean's comments on the significance of this affair and its relationship to Lafayette's *La Princesse de Montpensier* (1991, 108–9).

12. For summaries of the matrimonial negotiations carried out in her behalf, see Steegmuller 1957 and duc de La Force 1952.

13. Such activities would have seemed not only unfeminine but unaristocratic at this period, for unlike the British gentry, the French generally regarded life on a country estate with horror, equating it with vice, ignorance, and failure.

14. Supposedly Lauzun was not sent to prison for attempting to marry Montpensier, but at the insistence of the king's mistress, Madame de Montespan, whom he had insulted.

15. Segrais testifies that the original candidate was Longueville, but that she rejected him because she knew the king would never agree to the match. (1721, 1:32, 128).

16. See Cholakian 1986a.

17. Hipp sees the Corneille quotation as proof that Mademoiselle overdramatized her situation, representing herself as a theatrical heroine in a real-life drama (1976, 304).

18. See the discussion of Lougee 1976 in chapter 1.

19. According to DeJean, the topos of "retreat" signified passive feminine resistance, a demand for a "separate space" divorced from the historico/political realm ruled by the king (1991, 63–64). This is also true in Choisy's transvestite memoirs, where the desire to live in the provinces or suburbs in order to dress as a woman comes into conflict with his court duties. Both Verdier and Henein emphasize Mademoiselle's increasing taste for solitude. Watts and Beugnot find retreat from the court a characteristic of the genre. For another analysis of solitude as a topos during this period, see Stanton 1975, 79–104.

20. There were also good political reasons for her to protest her devotion to Louis. *Lèse-majesté* was a crime, as Apostolidès 1980, 5–14 shows.

21. The property seems to have had no connection with the abbé de Choisy's family.

22. See Montpensier 1985, 2:93–97.

23. For a discussion of Montpensier's lifelong interest in architecture, see Bourgoin 1954 and Mayer 1978.

24. She had undoubtedly acquired many of these while at Saint-Fargeau, where she first became interested in her genealogy.

25. The picture she refers to is undoubtedly the portrait of Mademoiselle and Gaston painted by Pierre Bourguignon in 1671, now in the collection at Versailles. See Beasley 1990, 74. Maclean 1977 discusses the vogue for such portraits.

26. Henein calls attention to this "phenomenon of compensation and this game of substitution," which she sees as one of the motivating forces behind the composition of Montpensier's memoirs (1976–77, 47).

Chapter 4. Hortense Mancini

1. Although I adhere to the belief that women writers should be referred to by their last names, I shall call the Mancini sisters "Hortense" and "Marie" to distinguish them from

each other. I think this is preferable to calling them by their husbands' last names: "Mazarin" and "Colonna."

2. It was rumored that she was pregnant by Courbeville.

3. See Mongrédien 1952, 182.

4. See G. Dulong 1921 for a study of the life and works of Saint-Réal (1642?–92). Saint-Réal's best-known work is his historical novel *Dom Carlos* (1672), which served as the basis for plays by Racine, Schiller, and Verhaeren, as well as Verdi's opera. He also wrote *De l'Usage de l'histoire* (1671), *La Conjuration des Espagnols contre La République de Venise* (1674), and *Césarion* (1684).

5. He cites the manuscript collections of Feuillet de Conches, Chambry, Boutron, and Renée in the Bibliothèque Impériale.

6. See Foucault 1978a, 1:61–62.

7. See also Pascal 1960. He writes, "Are we then to conclude that truth does not matter overmuch in autobiography? We cannot believe this. Not only does the reader expect truth from autobiography, but autobiographers themselves all make more or less successful efforts to get at the truth, to stick to it, or at least try to persuade us they are doing so" (83). Similarly, Lejeune (1975) sees the genre in terms of a "pact" between reader and writer, in which the signature of the latter offers a guarantee of a historically truthful self-representation. For more on the question of whether or not autobiography must be based on the true facts of the writer's life, see Adams 1990, Eakin 1985, as well as the classic definition of the genre in Gusdorf 1980.

8. This maxim appears to have been widely applied to women's conduct. Madame de Maintenon's *Conversation* entitled "Sur la bonne conduite" [On good conduct] begins with the question, "When one praises a person of good conduct, what does one mean?" To which the respondent answers, "That a woman is virtuous and that she has never gotten herself talked about." A third speaker agrees that this is certainly "an essential point," but goes on to assert that there is more to good conduct than this (Gréard 1912, 73).

9. The letter, written in 1672 to Mlle. de Scudéry, appears in Bussy-Rabutin 1858, 3:454.

10. See chapter 2.

11. For a sampling of such works see Boiteau and Livet 1972.

12. For a much more balanced discussion of this question, see Goldsmith 1995b, 33–34.

13. Marie is much more circumspect and respectful regarding Mazarin's death.

14. Démoris's position confirms what Leigh Gilmore says about the production of gender as a truth effect: "One tells the truth insofar as one also produces gendered identity appropriately. In this sense, the confession hypostatizes gender, condenses the differences among women into an institutional whole, and enforces that construction" (1994, 112).

15. Strictly speaking, Démoris's chronology is incorrect. Although not published until later, Mademoiselle de Montpensier's memoirs were begun in the mid-1650s. Madame de Mornay du Plessis wrote hers (first published in 1824) prior to 1605. Both of these women had impeccable reputations.

16. I use the masculine pronoun in my translation because it seems pretty clear to me that the "pleasure" Démoris is describing is that of a male reader.

17. Her cousin Anne-Marie Martinozzi was married to the prince de Conti. Like her spouse, she was a rigorously pietistic Jansenist, which would have made living with her very unpleasant for the fun-loving Hortense.

18. Aristocratic women who left their husbands were banned from respectable society.

Montpensier's half-sister, Mademoiselle d'Orléans, married against her wishes to the grand-duc de Toscane in 1661 and formally separated from him in 1670, was ordered by the king to live in the convent of Montmartre. He refused to give her an apartment at Versailles, and when Mademoiselle took pity on her and invited her to court from time to time, Louis ordered her to be back in the convent before the nuns' bedtime. (See Mayer 1978, 179.) His attitude appears doubly reprehensible in light of the fact that he openly committed double adultery and fathered illegitimate children, first with Louise de laVallière and then with Madame de Montespan.

Claude Dulong sums up the disenfranchisement and vulnerability of a woman like Hortense (1974, 63–72). A woman mistreated by her husband had almost no recourse. Legally she was a minor, and her husband had the same right to punish her as he had to punish his children. Spousal abuse did not justify abandoning the conjugal domicile. Only if the wife was wounded could a tribunal intervene, and then only if the case was judged sufficiently grave. Even if a husband killed his wife, he was usually not prosecuted. The sequestration of an unfaithful wife in a religious institution or even in a prison was not only legal but mandatory; and women condemned for this crime forfeited their dowries to their husbands, although judges were often skeptical of the husband's motives in such cases and plaintiffs were also discouraged by the necessity of paying high fees for room and board. Adulterous husbands were subject only to material damages (loss of the dowry and nuptial advantages). Divorce did not exist except if the marriage was bigamous, the wife had been abducted, or the union had never been consummated. Women had difficulty obtaining legal separations, even in cases of adultery, and they were expected to retire subsequently to a convent, even if they were the injured party.

19. Saint-Réal used this text to defend her in the suit her husband brought to deny her access to her dowry in 1689.

20. In Cixous 1976 she declares that even today the story of women's sexuality has not been told.

Chapter 5. Marie Mancini

1. Somaize wrote that she was extremely well-read. In "Maximiliane," the article on her, he called her "la perle des précieuses" (1861, 1:168).

2. There seems to be some evidence that Colonna was capable of murder. Perey cites an article in the *Mercure hollandais* (February 1676) stating that the constable, wearing a mask and carrying a sword disguised as a stick, went abroad during carnival season to assassinate his enemies (1896, 376). She also cites a letter to Louis XIV from the French ambassador, the duc d'Estrées, dated Rome, 18 April 1689, three days after Colonna's death, in which he writes that the pope was grieved by the constable's death "in spite of his disorders and even several assassinations, at which the pope expressed his horror at the beginning of his pontificate" (470).

3. Marie's brother-in-law, Dorio Spinola, marquis de los Balbasès, is believed to have been responsible for their publication. See C. Dulong 1993, 271. These pseudomemoirs have been republished as *Cendre et Poussière,* edited by Maurice Lever (= Lever 1997b).

4. Caldarini calls the "apparent candor" of the pseudomemoirs "particularly piquante and compromising" (1990, 15).

5. A misleading promotional band on Lever's edition reads, "Les Mémoires 'non autorisés' du premier amour de Louis XIV."

6. Brémond's oeuvre includes novels with titles like *Hattigé, ou les Amours du roi de Tamaran* (1676), *Le Double Cocu* (1678), *Le Galand Escroc ou Le faux comte de Brion* (1676), and *L'Heureux Esclave* (1677). For more on Brémond, see Grobe 1954.

7. Démoris asserts that in addition to correcting Marie's Italianisms and clearing up some ambiguities, Brémond conferred on her text "the unity and nobility of tone it lacked." He even claims that when modern editors wax eloquent about the style that came "naturally" to a "grande dame of Louis XIV's era" they are attributing to Marie what was in fact Brémond's (1975, 119–20). Neither Goldsmith nor Perey concurs. Perey argues that Brémond "denatured" Marie's text, which had "a savor, an originality, and a turn of mind, impossible to mistake and impossible to imitate" (1894, iv). Goldsmith writes, "The vivid and precise style of the original edition is largely lost; the editor having reworked it by omitting many proper names, lengthening the sentences, multiplying the negations, and regularly blurring precise references to the physical" (1992, 242). For a comparison of the two versions, see Cholakian and Goldsmith 1998.

8. See the analysis in Goldsmith 1992.

9. The idea that Marie's memoirs were the work of Saint-Réal can be traced to the 1676 preface to the pseudomemoirs, which implies that they are the work of the same person who prepared Hortense's text for publication. The false attribution to Saint-Réal was further strengthened by the fact that in 1678 "Marteau" had published the pseudomemoirs alongside Hortense's memoirs.

10. See Cholakian and Goldsmith 1998, 10–11.

11. Chanteleuze does not refer to *La Vérité*. Doscot alludes to it, but says only that her manuscript was revised by "a professional man of letters named Saint-Brémond" (1965, 28).

12. The pseudomemoirs reiterate this claim (Lever 1997b, 128–29) and refute the "false" reasons that were circulated concerning the *séparation de lit*, including the reason Marie would give in *La Vérité*.

13. Commentators have often assumed that there was some truth in these stories, even when they admitted that the pseudomemoirs were apocryphal.

14. See Cholakian and Goldsmith 1998, 10 for information about these letters.

15. *La Vérité* is more reticent on this point than either the pseudomemoirs or Brémond's *Apologie*. The pseudomemoirs have her say, like Racine's Bérénice: "Sire, vous êtes Roy et vous m'aimez; et pourtant vous souffrez que je parte?" adding that she exclaimed bitterly, "Ha je suis abbandonnée," and tore his sleeve as she left the room (Lever 1997b, 14). Brémond not only amplifies her references to her suffering after the king's return to France, but insists on mentioning what Marie pointedly omits—Louis's parting tears. Goldsmith has argued that Brémond's version tries to make the protagonist conform more closely to the romantic legend that had taken hold of the public imagination: "Her very concrete and specific style [in the *Vérité*] confirms the author's declared desire to state the facts of her life in opposition to what she considers the mystifications and defamations already published" (1992, 242). Goldsmith believes that Brémond may have been trying to enhance the apologetic aspects of the text by making Marie appear more sympathetic to the reader.

16. Colonna had reacted with fury when she hinted at the real reasons for her departure after she arrived in France. See C. Dulong 1993, 196 et seq.

17. Dulong believes that Marie's fears were sincere but that it was unlikely Colonna actually tried to kill her, since he would have had no real motive for doing so (C. Dulong 1993, 289).

18. See Démoris 1975 for an analysis of the similarities between Marie's memoirs and the novel.

19. *Le Grand Cyrus* was published between 1649 and 1653; *Clélie* between 1654 and 1660.

20. Marie's mother had married into the petty Roman nobility.

21. Although Mazarin settled a dowry on Marie, she was never his favorite and most of his estate went to Hortense (or rather her husband).

22. Brémond's revision completely obscures the practicality and honesty that Marie's text portrays. He makes her say, "I was still not disposed to accept a new passion. The fall I had just taken was too great, and I needed time and not tears to console me" (Mancini 1965, 114). The sentiment Brémond attributes to her is the exact opposite of what she describes.

23. According to C. Dulong, Mazarin rejected the match because he suspected that Lorraine hoped to gain his political support (1993, 87–88).

24. Commentators have tended to side with Colonna. Renée characterizes her decision as an "inflexible law," to which she forced the constable to submit "at the expense of their tranquillity" (1856, 277–78). Chanteleuze remarks sarcastically that she must have feared producing a progeny "as numerous as Priam's," thereby causing Colonna "who loved his wife tenderly," to become "an eternal widower," reduced "to the torments of Tantalus" by a wife who transformed herself into "an unassailable citadel"; meanwhile, he pictures Marie, "strange woman" *(sic!)*, as "more and more piqued and angered because he besieged other places, which offered him only minimal resistance" (1880, 241–43).

25. See chapter 1.

26. In *L'Amour au XVIIe siècle* Dulong writes that aside from coitus interruptus, continence was the only available form of contraception (1969, 90–100). The condom was not invented until the following century. The use of tampons is generally considered to have been limited to prostitutes. "Astringents" may have been known, but were vociferously condemned by both the Church and the medical profession. Furthermore, they were far from reliable and often had dangerous side effects. Even if courtisans and prostitutes did use some form of birth control, they were not able to avoid becoming pregnant. The celebrated Ninon de Lenclos is known to have had at least one child, and her colleague Marion de Lorme died of an abortion. Dulong concludes her survey in that book by writing, "One understands why, rather than have recourse to such extreme methods, certain women made the cruel choice of a relative or total abstinence" (100). However, in *Marie Mancini,* Dulong seems to contradict herself, arguing that contraceptives were available and that Marie was concealing the real reason behind her edict.

27. Perey offered this novel explanation for Marie's restlessness:

We are sure that the brain fever, accompanied by convulsions, that attacked her during her honeymoon caused a shock to the brain whose traces remained throughout her life; we do not want to say that she was mad, in the full sense of the word, but certainly her mind was deranged on some points; one noticed in her, when one observed her closely, a constant anxiety and agitation. Hardly had she stayed two months in the same place when she was seized by a nervous agitation that nothing could calm, and she would insist on leaving without considering the consequences of the unforeseen moves. In spite of the necessity for her husband to reside in Rome, she would always want to travel, be it to his Neapolitan estates, to Venice, or to Milan, and in spite of her pregnancies, which these continual movements endangered, nothing would keep her from pursuing her fantasy. Her desire once accomplished, and the most costly installations arranged to receive her—for the constable's wife always demanded a dwelling worthy of her rank—the princess, already bored, would depart again, and it would be thus as long as she remained on earth. It is impossible not to find a physical cause for this unhealthy state, which astonished all those who knew her. (1896, 42–43)

Perey gives no proof of this theory other than the highly suspect statement of Saint-Simon (who did not know her): "She is the best and the craziest of the Mazarines" and Madame de Villars's remark: "She is the best of women, she has never done harm to anyone but herself with the bizarre fantasies that pass through her head."

28. *Discorso astrofisico della mutazzioni de tempi e d'altri accidenti mondani dell'anno 1671.* See C. Dulong 1993, 391.

29. See Démoris 1975 and Goldsmith 1995b.

30. Calderini 1990 argues that Marie's preoccupation with the theme of liberty lends a modern and feminist note to her text that is perhaps unintentional on her part.

CHAPTER 6. JEANNE GUYON

1. See the bibliography in Gondal 1989b, 286–90 for a complete listing.

2. Bruno contends that these cuts are repetitions or digressions, devout remarks, and biblical citations, and that he has omitted nothing having to do with family relationships (Guyon 1962, 6).

3. See Bruneau 1998.

4. See Gondal 1989a. See also Goldsmith 1997 for a discussion of Guyon's concept of a dual readership, "one a limited circle of readers . . . , the other a larger, more anonymous public" (136).

5. Although Fénelon displayed considerable interest in Guyon's mystical insights, he doesn't seem to have been overly eager to read her life story, ostensibly because he had neither time nor taste for reading. In subsequent letters he does not refer to it, and it is not certain that he ever read it. In his *Réponse à la Relation sur le quiétisme,* he swore that he had read nothing of Guyon's but the *Moyen court* and the *Explication sur la cantique.*

6. Bruneau calls Guyon's position on the profeminist debates of her time "especially reactionary . . . a non-challenge to the status quo" (1998, 164).

7. Bruneau declares that Guyon holds "a unique place in the history of the representation of the self" (1998, 201). Hers is the only text discussed here that Philippe Lejeune lists in his *Autobiographie en France.*

8. "She is holy, her voices preach renunciation rather than confrontation. She is a woman: she thus knows the art of speaking without speaking, of suavely attenuating her resistance, of getting her way without seeming to do so" (Brémond 1916, 2:37).

9. See especially chapter 2, "The *Book of Her Life* and the Rhetoric of Humility," 42–76.

10. This episode shows that the la Mothe family had lofty connections. The queen of England, Henriette de France, was the daughter of Henri IV. She returned to France after Cromwell deposed and executed her husband, Charles I. Her daughter, Henriette d'Angleterre, was married to "Monsieur," Louis XIV's brother.

11. Again, Guyon may be following the lead of Teresa of Avila, who also confessed to her adolescent vanity: "I began to dress in finery and to desire to please and look pretty, taking great care of my hands and hair and perfumes and all the empty things in which one can indulge, and which were many, for I was very vain" (1976, 57).

12. Jeanne de Chantal, who was Madame de Sévigné's grandmother, had been inspired by François de Sales to leave her family and found the order of the Visitation.

13. See Guyon 1962, 15–16 n. 14. The Poiret edition says only that a young relative wanted to marry her, but her father opposed the match, "because he had vowed not to marry me to any of my relations because of the difficulty in obtaining a dispensation without putting forth false or frivolous reasons" (Guyon 1686, 44).

14. Traer's study of the family in the ancien régime shows that although both church and state forbade nonconsensual marriages, religious and social pressure forced women into them: "[The father] was the ruler of his own small realm, similar to the monarch in his kingdom. As his children matured, he decided whether or not they might marry and, if so, how to arrange their marriages so as to help them and the family to realize economic and social goals. . . . A variety of institutions and groups buttressed the traditional family, supporting its goals and helping to maintain the power of its chief" (1980, 15–16).

15. Jacques Guyon's father had made his fortune building the Briare canal.

16. An obvious exception is Margery Kempe (c. 1373–c. 1440), an English mystic who was married and had fourteen children. In 1413 she and her husband took a vow of chastity. She dictated her autobiography, *The Life of Margery Kempe,* to two clerics around 1434. The manuscript was not discovered until 1934, however, so it is very unlikely that Guyon was familiar with it.

17. Two memoirists not discussed here, Madame de Mornay and Madame de la Guette, represent themselves as happily married, but do not discuss sexual relations.

18. Weintraub finds in Guyon's narrative "a missionary didactic intent," whose theme is "being the maltreated martyr for God." He accuses her of making "an elaborate cult out of suffering every conceivable indignity," presenting her married life "as a grand schooling" for learning its central tenet: "to ask nothing for herself but to turn to God with selfless love." However, Weintraub finds that in her "extreme willingness to suffer, mysticism is here tipping toward its most dangerous side." He criticizes her overexuberant style and the way her "continuous reports of her willing suffering are meant to justify everything she does." Indeed, he characterizes her state as an "orgy of selfless love," "the purest subjectivism," against which it is difficult to apply any check." See Weintraub 1978, 223–26. Sidonie Smith takes Weintraub to task for applying an "androcentric paradigm" to Guyon: "Weintraub misses an opportunity to consider the impact of her experience as a married, rather than virginal, woman on the kind of mysticism she so emphatically pursued and defended" (1987, 10).

19. Mallet-Joris sees Guyon's intelligence as one of her essential traits. She characterizes her as a woman "with the kind of intellectual strength that needed the challenge of a goal and a project." She argues that she was far from being blinded by her enthusiasm: "She is not bedazzled, and if she acts at times with disconcerting candor, it is a deliberate decision to pursue to the limit an experience that is *also* intellectual" (1978, 118).

20. Freud, of course, identified narcissism as the primary characteristic of femininity. Beautiful women, he wrote, "develop a certain self-contentment which compensates them for the social restrictions that are imposed upon them in their choice of object." Such women love themselves "with an intensity comparable to that of the man's love for them" (Freud 1957, 88–89).

21. For a discussion of the importance of chastity in the lives of women saints, see Cazelles 1991, 43–61.

22. Marjory Kempe was so troubled on this point that she consulted Julian of Norwich as to whether she and her husband should take a vow of chastity. They eventually did so.

23. See also Kristeva 1979. Such diagnoses may have psychological validity, but they tend to ignore the fact that Guyon says she used such practices only as a means to an end. Mallet-Joris underlines this point in her discussion of Guyon's asceticism and points out that Teresa of Avila upheld the same general principle (1978, 118–19). Guyon writes that her purpose was to train herself to do God's will and to render her senses so supple that she could do anything without repugnance. She eventually ceased inflicting such tortures on herself.

24. Sidonie Smith writes in this regard, "[H]er projection of herself as proud and powerful in the willing victimization she suffers . . . reveals much about the complex attraction of mysticism for women of the period. For Madame Guyon, ruthlessly tyrannized in a patriarchally enforced and loveless marriage, mysticism offered the promise of unique empowerment in its exaggeration of the quintessential model of the feminine" (1987, 10).

25. Bruneau 1998 argues that female mysticism was always characterized by the somatization of the body.

CHAPTER 7. L'ABBÉ DE CHOISY

1. All citations are from the Mercure de France edition, edited by Georges Mongrédien.

2. D'Argenson, Choisy's literary executor, was his great-nephew. The abbé lived with him in his final years.

3. See Parish's analysis (1976) of the form and content of the *Mémoires pour servir à l'histoire de Louis XIV*.

4. See Van der Cruysse 1995, 102 et seq., for an analysis of the chronology of the two episodes. He argues that the discrepancies are probably due to the fact that Choisy was writing about events that had taken place forty years previously.

5. Parish maintains that the work is faithful to the facts, but he also characterizes it as rambling and digressive, strewn with portraits and reminiscences, the product of a born raconteur who "refuses to be constrained by formal composition" (1976, 224). See also Van der Cruysse 1976a and 1976b.

6. See chapter 1.

7. Butler writes that transvestism "destabilizes the very distinctions between the natural and the artificial, depth and surface, inner and outer through which discourse about genders almost always operates. . . . Does being female constitute a 'natural fact' or a cultural performance, or is 'naturalness' constituted through discursively constrained performative acts that produce the body through and within the categories of sex?" (1990, x). See also Fradenburg and Freccero, who write, "[T]he historiography of sexuality could, we believe, go further in its project of dislodging and indeed queering the truth-effects of certain historicist practices. Especially in question are those historicist practices that repudiate the roles of fantasy and pleasure in the production of historiography" (1995, xvii).

8. Madame de Choisy, like Mademoiselle de Montpensier, undoubtedly needed someone to correct her spelling and make a legible copy. Choisy, a future cleric, would have been more literate than she, in spite of his youth.

9. Van der Cruysse (1995, 51) points out that Choisy's executor, the marquis d'Argenson, also subscribed to this theory; he cites the latter's *Mémoires et journal inédits* (Paris: Paulmy and Jannet, 1857–58), 1:73–74.

10. Foucault argues (1978a, 1:137–39) that with the diminution of the sovereign's right to execute those who threatened his survival, control was vested increasingly in the

management of sexuality and reproduction. The power to manage life replaced the power to put to death, and the body came more and more to be treated as a machine. It was trained, educated, and integrated into control systems by the power procedures that characterize the "anatomo-political disciplines of the human body."

11.   Much of this story may have been eliminated by the marquis d'Argenson when he reduced the manuscript to what was "good or passable."

12.   This view was probably not held consistently or universally, however. Choisy also implies that gendered behavior was sometimes viewed as inborn. After unveiling Mazarin's plot to regender Philippe, he goes on to say that despite his effeminate appearance, the younger brother was quite capable of manly acts. Choisy also states that even when he himself was dressed as a girl, the queen's ladies smothered him with kisses (1966, 219).

13.   See Barker 1989, 49–56. Mademoiselle refers to this affair in Montpensier 1985, 2:52–59, 101. She writes that she did not share the sentiments of those who hoped to see Philippe replace Louis, because in her opinion he was too immature to govern, and she had no reason to believe he would change (53).

14.   Barker (1989) believes that Philippe may have been intellectually superior to Louis.

15.   Barker writes, "Lest he pose a threat to the sovereign, his person and style of life were bound and confined within the limits of the royal pleasure. Thus told, the case of Monsieur serves as merely another, if perhaps the most famous and tragic, example of the success of Louis XIV's policy of subordinating the greater nobility to his royal will" (1989, 239).

16.   Reynes mentions another example of Choisy's penchant for subverting established institutions (1983, 279). In 1687, he was elected to the Académie, and subsequently made secretary of the subcommittee charged with resolving grammatical disputes. Instead of merely noting the conclusions reached by his colleagues, he livened up his minutes with vivid accounts of all the tiny incidents and quarrels of the sessions. When his fellow academicians saw what was certainly the most lively and authentic summary of their proceedings ever produced, they immediately had it suppressed. This *Journal de l'Académie française* was eventually published in the *Opuscules sur la langue française* in 1754 (Reynes 1983, 335 n. 4).

17.   The preamble seems to be destined for the marquise de Saint-Lambert, whose salon was the center of literary life in the early part of the eighteenth century. She was the author of *Réflexions sur les femmes,* a copy of which she sent him along with the following note:

> Here, my dear abbé, is the little work you urged me to write. I have not had the time to perfect it: more serious thoughts occupy my mind, and more important affairs my leisure. Moreover, I have had difficulty recalling agreeable ideas, long forgotten. For you who always have them present, and who have never been able to exhaust the depths of joy within you, no matter how much you have spent it; you, on whom old age sits so well, since it does not put away either games or loves; you, who have been able to establish intelligence between passions and reason, for fear of being worried by it; you, who by wise economy, always have pleasures in reserve, and who make them follow each other; you, who have known how to manage nature in pleasures, so that pleasures sustain nature; you, finally, who like Saint-Evremond, in your prime lived for love, and who now love to live: you are right, my dear abbé, let us steal these last moments from the fatality that pursues us. (*Œuvres* [1748], 241–43; quoted by Reynes 1983, 289)

18. See, for instance, Marguerite de Valois's promise to tell the truth "naked and without ornament" (1966, 36).

19. Although there is good reason to believe that the "comtesse des Barres" episode preceded that of the "Madame de Sancy," I will discuss them in the order in which they appear in the Mongrédien edition.

20. Rowan sees many similarities between Choisy's transvestite memoirs and his fictional novella *L'Histoire de la Marquise-Marquis de Banneville,* which, she claims, "transmutes into fiction several of the Abbé's real life adventures" (1991, 225–26). She goes on to point out (226) that Choisy had other ties to fiction, having sometimes been identified as Perrault's collaborator on the *Contes de fées* and as the author of three fairy tales: "Histoire de la princesse Aimonette," reprinted in Jean Mélia, *Inédits et belles pages de l'abbé de Choisy* (Paris: Emile Paul, 1922); "Le Prince Kouchimen, histoire tartare"; and "Dom Alvar del Sol, histoire napolitaine" (Paris: J. Estienne, 1710)."

21. The faubourg Saint-Marceau (or Saint-Marcel) is now the neighborhood bordering Paris's Jardin des Plantes. In the eighteenth century, Mercier (1783–89, 1:157–59) described it as filled with ruined men, misanthropes, alchemists, and other marginal types who wanted to live in complete isolation and have no contact with the city. Such a neighborhood would have been an ideal location for someone like Choisy.

22. Reynes believes that the origin of his obsession with ear pendants was his desire to identify with his mother, the ear being a substitute for the female genitals, according to Freud (Reynes 1983, 121, 326 n. 11).

23. Van der Cruysse claims that regular applications of yellow arsenic were probably used to make his beard fall out (1995, 50).

24. "A woman's head-dress, often cone-shaped . . . worn by women from the 14th to the 18th centuries." *Random House Dictionary,* 1967 ed., s.v. "cornette."

25. Reynes explains his sudden panic by the political climate of the times: "Montausier's invective took place precisely in the royal box, in the Dauphin's presence, and before a large public. How would the king react when he heard of this scandal? Should Louis XIV decide that his son's dignity had been offended, Choisy knows that he risks the Bastille, or at the very least exile. The example of Monsieur, for once, far from protecting him, can become yet another reason for displaying severity" (1983, 76–77).

26. Garber writes, "One of the most important aspects of cross-dressing is the way in which it offers a challenge to easy notions of binarity, putting into question the categories of 'female' and 'male,' whether they are considered essential or constructed, biological or cultural" (1992, 10). Ackroyd concurs: "Transvestites abrogate . . . pervasive but unacknowledged codes, and by denying the symbolism invested in the clothing of their sex they break some of the most deeply-held beliefs about the male role and the constraints of a male-dominated society" (1979, 34).

27. According to Reynes 1983, Choisy invented this episode. No trace of it can be found in the *Mercure,* which published Choisy's *La Marquise-Marquis de Banneville* in February 1695.

28. Reynes implies a political dimension for Choisy's cross-dressing to the extent that she sees in it his desire to do as he pleased. Unlike many transvestites, she argues, his main preoccupation was not private sexual gratification, but public display. He was allowed to exercise his propensities so long as they did not infringe upon the king's power: "Choisy's talent (or luck) was to have always evolved within that narrow margin where his acts affected no one but himself: a faux pas, an error of judgment, and the fragile equilibrium

would have been broken" (1983, 55). But, she points out, he was also protected to a great extent by his privileged status.

29. In Reynes's view, if Choisy was reinforcing his tie to the phallic mother by cross-dressing, he was reinstating the father's law by gambling (1983, 182–87) She bases her argument on Freud's *Dostoevsky and Parricide*. She adds that Madame de Choisy, herself a fanatic gambler, was so concerned about her son's vice that she asked Segrais to admonish him (see Reynes 1983, 183–84). For a Freudian interpretation of Choisy's need to gamble when not dressed as a woman, see Tostain 1967.

30. Apostolidès writes, "Enclosed in the brilliant circle of the court, the aristocrats of the seventeenth century come to know an ersatz form of play, a turning aside of their playful dispositions, by playing for money. (1981, 57).

Bibliography

Ackroyd, Peter. 1979. *Dressing Up Transvestism and Drag: The History of an Obsession.* New York: Simon and Schuster.

Adams, Timothy Dow. 1990. *Telling Lies in Modern American Autobiography.* Chapel Hill: University of North Carolina Press.

Akermann, Simone. 1982–83. "La Grande Mademoiselle: Histoire et histoires baroques." *Bulletin, Société des professeurs de français en Amérique,* 3–16.

Alacoque, Marguerite-Marie. 1920. *Vie de Sainte Marguerite-Marie Alacoque écrite par elle-même.* In *Vie et Oeuvres de Sainte Marguerite-Marie Alacoque,* edited by François-Léon Gauthey, 2:29–119. Paris: Poussielgue.

Amiguet, Philippe. 1957. *La Grande Mademoiselle et son siècle d'après ses Mémoires.* Paris: Albin-Michel.

Apostolidès, Jean-Marie. 1980. "Image du père et peur du tyran au XVIIe siècle." *Revue française du Psychanalyse* 44, no. 1 (January–February): 5–14.

———. 1981. *Le Roi-machine: Spectacle et politique au temps de Louis XIV.* Paris: Minuit.

———. 1988. "Molière and the Sociology of Exchange." Translated by Alice Musick McLean. In *Literature and Social Practice,* edited by Philippe Desan, Priscilla Parkhurst Ferguson, and Wendy Griswold, 98–113. Chicago: University of Chicago Press.

Ariès, Philippe. 1979. "Pourquoi écrit-on des Mémoires?" In *Les Valeurs chez les mémorialistes français du XVIIe siècle avant la Fronde,* edited by Naomi Hepp and Jacques Hennequin. Actes et Colloques 22. Paris: Klincksieck.

Arnould, Jean-Claude. 1994. "La Mémoire dans les *Mémoires* de Marguerite de Valois." In *Marguerite de France, Reine de Navarre, et son temps,* edited by Madeleine Lazard and J. Cubelier de Beynac, 217–37. Actes du Colloque d'Agen (12–13 October 1991). Agen: Centre Matteo Bandello d'Agen.

Babelon, Jean. 1965. *La Reine Margot.* Paris: Berger-Levrault.

Backer, Dorothy Anne Liot. 1974. *Precious Women.* New York: Basic Books.

Balsamo, Jean. 1994. "Marguerite de Valois et la philosophie de son temps." In *Marguerite de France, Reine de Navarre, et son temps,* edited by Madeleine Lazard and J. Cubelier de Beynac, 269–81. Actes du Colloque d'Agen (12–13 October 1991). Agen: Centre Matteo Bandello d'Agen.

Barine, Arvède. 1901. *La Jeunesse de la Grande Mademoiselle, 1627–1652.* Paris: Hachette.

———. 1905. *Louis XIV et la Grande Mademoiselle, 1652–1693.* Paris: Hachette.

Barker, Nancy Nichols. 1989. *Brother to the Sun King: Philippe, Duke of Orléans.* Baltimore and London: Johns Hopkins University Press.

Bauschatz, Cathleen. 1988. "'Plaisir et proffict' in the Reading and Writing of Marguerite de Valois." *Tulsa Studies in Women's Literature* 7, no. 1 (Spring): 27–48.

———. 1990. "'L'Horreur de mon exemple' in Marie de Gournay's *Proumenoir de Monsieur de Montaigne* (1594)." *L'Esprit Créateur* 30, no. 4:97–105.

Bayle, Pierre. 1627. *Œuvres diverses.*4 vols. The Hague: P. Husson.

Beasley, Faith E. 1990. *Revising Memory: Women's Fiction and Memoirs in Seventeenth-Century France.* New Brunswick, N.J.: Rutgers University Press.

Beaujour, Michel. 1980. *Miroirs d'encre: Rhétorique de l'autoportrait.* Paris: Seuil.

Beauvoir, Simone de. 1949. *Le Deuxième sexe.* Paris: Gallimard.

Bell, Susan Groag, and Marilyn Yalom. 1990. *Revealing Lives: Autobiography, Biography, and Gender.* Albany: State University of New York Press.

Benstock, Shari, ed. 1988. *The Private Self: Theory and Practice of Women's Autobiographical Writings.* Chapel Hill: University of North Carolina Press.

Benveniste, Emile. 1971. *Problems in General Linguistics.* Translated by Elizabeth Meek. Coral Gables, Fla.: University of Miami Press.

Bernos, Marcel, and Sonia Branca-Rosoff. 1992. "Parole de femme, discours d'homme: A propos des *Confessions* de Louise de La Vallière." In *Correspondance: Mélanges offerts à Roger Duchêne,* edited by Wolfgang Leiner and Pierre Ronzeaud, 183–89. Tübingen: Narr.

Berriot-Salvadore, Evelyne. 1994. "Le Temps des malheurs, le temps de la philosophie: Marguerite et la vulgarisation des sciences." In *Marguerite de France, Reine de Navarre, et son temps,* edited by Madeleine Lazard and J. Cubelier de Beynac, 255–67. Actes du Colloque d'Agen (12–13 October 1991). Agen: Centre Matteo Bandello d'Agen.

Bertaud, Madeleine. 1990. "En marge de leurs *Mémoires,* une correspondance entre Mlle. de Montpensier et Mme de Motteville." *Travaux de Littérature.* (Boulogne, France) 3:277–95.

Bertaud, Madeleine, and François-Xavier Cuche, eds. 1995. *Le Genre des Mémoires, essai de définition.* Paris: Klincksieck.

Bertaud, Madeleine, and André Labertit, eds. 1993. *De L'Estoile à Saint-Simon, recherche sur la culture des mémorialistes au temps des trois premiers rois Bourbons.* Paris: Klincksieck.

Bertière, André. 1977. *Le Cardinal de Retz mémorialiste.* Paris: Klincksieck, 1977.

Beugnot, Bernard. 1976. "Morale du repos et conscience du temps." *Australian Journal of French Studies* (Clayton, Victoria) 13:183–96.

———. 1979. "Livre de raison, livre de retraite: Interférences des points de vue chez les mémorialistes." In *Les Valeurs chez les mémorialistes français du XVIIe siècle avant la Fronde,* edited by Naomi Hepp and Jacques Hennequin, 47–64. Actes et Colloques 22. Paris: Klincksieck.

Bitton, Davis. 1969. *The French Nobility in Crisis: 1560–1640.* Stanford, Calif.: Stanford University Press.

Boiteau, Paul, and C.-L. Livet, eds. 1972. *Histoire amoureuse des Gaules, suivies de romans historico-satiriques du XVIIe siècle.* Nedeln, Lichtenstein: Kraus Reprints.

Boucher, Jacqueline. 1994. "Le Double Concept du mariage de Marguerite de France, propos et comportement." In *Marguerite de France, Reine de Navarre, et son temps,* edited by Madeleine Lazard and J. Cubelier de Beynac, 81–98. Actes du Colloque d'Agen (12–13 October 1991). Agen: Centre Matteo Bandello d'Agen.

Boucher, Jacqueline. 1986. *La Cour de Henri III.* Rennes: Ouest-France.

Bourgoin, Marguerite. 1954. *En Puisaye: Saint-Fargeau, Mademoiselle, et son château.* Paris: Raphaël Maillot.

Bourrachot, Lucile. 1994. "Agen et Marguerite de Valois, Reine de Navarre." In *Marguerite de France, Reine de Navarre, et son temps,* edited by Madeleine Lazard and J. Cubelier de Beynac, 61–79. Actes du Colloque d'Agen (12–13 October 1991). Agen: Centre Matteo Bandello d'Agen.

Boursier, Nicole. 1987. "Avatars de l'héroïne chez Madeleine de Scudéry." In *Présence féminine: Actes de London* (Canada), edited by Richmond and Venesoen, 261–87. Biblio 17, no. 36. London, Canada: Papers on Seventeenth-Century French Literature.

Bowman, Frank Paul. 1976. "Suffering, Madness, and Literary Creation in Seventeenth-Century Spiritual Autobiography." *French Forum* 1, no. 1 (January): 24–48.

Brantôme, Pierre de Bourdeilles, seigneur de. 1991. *Recueil des dames.* Edited by Etienne Vaucheret. Paris: Gallimard (Pléiade).

Bray, René. 1948. *La Préciosité et les précieux.* Paris: Nizet.

Brémond, Henri. 1916. *Histoire du sentiment religieux en France depuis la fin des guerres de religion jusqu'à nos jours.* Paris: Bloud et Gay.

Brockliss, Laurence W. 1987. *French Higher Education in the Seventeenth and Eighteenth Centuries: A Cultural History.* New York: Oxford University Press.

Brodski, Bella, and Celeste Schenck, eds. 1988. *Life/Lines: Theorizing Women's Autobiography.* Ithaca: Cornell University Press.

Bruneau, Marie-Florine. 1982. "Mysticisme et folie ou l'expérience de Jeanne Guyon." *Papers on French Seventeenth-Century Literature* 9:37–55.

———. 1983a. "La *Vie* de Madame Guyon: Frigidité et masochisme en tant que dispositifs politiques." *French Forum* 8, no. 2 (May):101–8.

———. 1983b. "Le Projet autobiographique: Guyon à l'orée de la modernité." *Papers on French Seventeenth-Century Literature* 10:59–68.

———. 1985. "The Writing of History as Fiction and Ideology: The Case of Madame Guyon." *Feminist Issues* 5 (Spring): 27–38.

———. 1998. *Women Mystics Confront the Modern World: Marie de l'Incarnation (1599–1672); Mme Guyon (1648–1717).* Albany: State University of New York Press.

Bruss, Elizabeth W. 1976. *Autobiographical Acts: The Changing Situation of a Literary Genre.* Baltimore: Johns Hopkins University Press.

Burke, Peter. 1992. *The Fabrication of Louis XIV.* New Haven: Yale University Press.

Bussy, Roger de Rabutin, comte de. 1857. *Mémoires.* Edited by Ludovic Lalanne. Paris: Charpentier.

———. 1858. *Correspondance.* Edited by Ludovic Lalenne. Vol. 3. Paris: Charpentier.

———. 1930. *Histoire amoureuse des Gaules suivie de La France galante: Romans satiriques du XVIIe siècle attribués au comte de Bussy.* Edited by Georges Mongrédien. Paris: Garnier.

Butler, Judith. 1990. *Gender Trouble: Feminism and the Subversion of Identity.* New York and London: Routledge.

Bynum, Caroline Walker. 1987. *Holy Feast and Holy Fast: The Religious Significance of Food to Medieval Women.* Berkeley: University of California Press.

Caldarini, Ernesta. 1990. "Maria Mancini: 'On m'écrivit de France qu'il courait une Histoire de ma vie.'" In *L'Effetto autobiografico: Scritture e letture del soggetto nella letteratura europea,* edited by Edda Melon, 11–26. Varieté 3. Torino: Tirrenia Stampatori.

Capasso, Ruth Carver. 1993. "Sun, Veil and Maze: Mlle. de Scudéry's Parthenie." *PFSCL* 20, no. 38:97–111.

Castarède, Jean. 1992. *La Triple Vie de la reine Margot: Amoureuse, Comploteuse, Ecrivain.* Paris: France-Empire.

———. 1994. "Quelques énigmes de la reine Margot ou ses conduites d'échec." In *Marguerite de France, Reine de Navarre, et son temps,* edited by Madeleine Lazard and J. Cubelier de Beynac, 43–53. Actes du Colloque d'Agen (12–13 October 1991). Agen: Centre Matteo Bandello d'Agen.

Cazaux, Yves. 1971. Introduction to *Mémoires de Marguerite de Valois La Reine Margot, suivis de Lettres et autres écrits.* Edited by Yves Cazaux. Paris: Mercure de France.

Cazelles, Brigitte. 1991. *The Lady as Saint: A Collection of French Hagiographic Romances of the Thirteenth Century.* Philadephia: University of Pennsylvania Press.

Chanteleuze, François Régis. 1880. *Louis XIV et Marie Mancini d'après de nouveaux documents.* Paris: Didier.

Chéruel, A., ed. 1858–59. *Mémoires de Mlle. de Montpensier. Collationnés sur le manuscrit autographe avec notes biographiques et historiques.* 4 vols. Paris: Charpentier.

Chodorow, Nancy. 1974. "Family Structure and Feminine Personality." In *Women, Culture, and Society,* edited by Michelle Zimbalist Rosaldo and Louise Lamphere. Stanford, Calif.: Stanford University Press.

Choisy, l'abbé de. 1966. *Mémoires de l'Abbé de Choisy: Mémoires pour servir à l'histoire de Louis XIV; Mémoires de l'Abbé de Choisy habillé en femme.* Edited by Georges Mongrédien. Paris: Mercure de France.

Cholakian, Patricia Francis. 1986a. "A House of Her Own: Marginality and Dissidence in the Mémoires of La Grande Mademoiselle." *Prose Studies* 9, no. 3 (December): 3–20.

———. 1986b. "A Re-Examination of the Manuscript Versions of the *Mémoires* of Mlle. de Montpensier." *Romance Notes* 27, no. 2 (Winter): 175–84.

———. 1989. "The Identity of the Reader in Marie de Gournay's *Le Proumenoir de Monsieur de Montaigne* (1594)." In *Reading Women: Feminist Contextual Criticism of Medieval and Renaissance Texts,* edited by Janet Halley and Sheila Fisher. Nashville: University of Tennessee Press.

———. 1991. *Rape and Writing in the Heptameron of Marguerite de Navarre.* Carbondale: Southern Illinois University Press.

Cholakian, Patricia Francis, and Elizabeth C. Goldsmith. Introduction to *La Vérité dans son jour, ou les véritables mémoires de M. Manchini, Connétable Colonne.* Edited by Patricia Francis Cholakian and Elizabeth C. Goldsmith. Delmar, N.Y.: Scholars Facsimiles and Reprints.

Cixous, Hélène. 1976. "The Laugh of the Medusa." Translated by Keith Cohen and Paula Cohen. *Signs* 1:873–93.

Claridge, Laura, and Elizabeth Langland. 1990. Introduction to *Out of Bounds: Male Writers and Gender[ed] Criticism*, 3–21. Amherst: University of Massachusetts Press.

Clough, Patricia Ticineto. 1994. *Feminist Thought: Desire, Power, and Academic Discourse.* Oxford: Blackwell.

Cocula, Anne-Marie. 1994. "Marguerite de Valois, de France et de Navarre: L'impossible identité de la reine Margot." In *Marguerite de France, Reine de Navarre, et son temps,* edited by Madeleine Lazard and J. Cubelier de Beynac, 17–27. Actes du Colloque d'Agen (12–13 October 1991). Agen: Centre Matteo Bandello d'Agen.

Collins, James B. 1989. "The Economic Role of Women in Seventeenth-Century France." *French Historical Studies* 16, no. 2 (Fall): 436–70.

Cooper, Richard. 1994. "Marguerite de Valois en Gascogne: lettres inédites." In *Marguerite de France, Reine de Navarre, et son temps,* edited by Madeleine Lazard and J. Cubelier de Beynac, 107–32. Actes du Colloque d'Agen (12–13 October 1991). Agen: Centre Matteo Bandello d'Agen.

Courtois, Alfred de, ed. 1878. *Lettres de Madame de Villars à Madame de Coulanges.* Paris: Plon.

Crosby, Christina. 1992. "Dealing with Differences." In *Feminists Theorize the Political,* edited by Judith Butler and Joan Scott, 130–43. New York and London: Routledge.

Cuénin, Micheline. 1995. "Mademoiselle, une Amazone impure?" *Papers on French Seventeenth-Century Literature* 22, no. 42:25–36

Davies, Joan. 1991. "History, Biography, Propaganda, and Patronage in Early-Seventeenth-Century France." *Seventeenth-Century French Studies* 13:5–17.

Davis, Natalie Zemon. 1975. *Society and Culture in Early Modern France.* Stanford, Calif.: Stanford University Press.

———. 1995. *Women on the Margin: Three Seventeenth-Century Lives* Cambridge: Harvard University Press.

———. 1998. "Displacing and Displeasing: Writing about Women in the Early Modern Period." In *Attending to Early Modern Women,* edited by Susan D. Amussen and Adele Seeff. Newark: University of Delaware Press.

DeJean, Joan. 1991. *Tender Geographies: Women and the Origins of the Novel in France.* New York: Columbia University Press.

De Lauretis, Teresa. 1987. *Technologies of Gender: Essays on Theory, Film, and Fiction.* Bloomington and Indianapolis: Indiana University Press.

Démoris, René. 1975. *Le Roman à la première personne: Du Classicisme aux Lumières.* Paris: Armand Colin.

Dewald, Jonathan. 1993. *Aristocratic Experience and the Origins of Modern Culture: France, 1570–1715.* Berkeley: University of California Press.

Dezon-Jones, Elyane. 1988. *Marie de Gournay: Fragments d'un discours féminin.* Paris: Corti.

Dieckmann, Liselotte, trans. and ed. 1984. *Memoirs of Marguerite de Valois.* Paris: Papers on French Seventeenth-Century Literature.

Doolittle, James. 1971. "A Royal Diversion: Mademoiselle and Lauzun." *L'Esprit Créateur* 11, no. 2 (Summer): 123–40.

Doscot, Gérard. 1965. Introduction and notes to *Mémoires d'Hortense et de Marie Mancini*. Paris: Mercure de France.

Dubois, Claude-Gilbert. 1994. "La Divorce Satyrique de la Reyne Marguerite." In *Marguerite de France, Reine de Navarre, et son temps,* edited by Madeleine Lazard and J. Cubelier de Beynac, 99–106. Actes du Colloque d'Agen (12–13 October 1991). Agen: Centre Matteo Bandello d'Agen.

Ducasse, André. 1937. *La Grande Mademoiselle: La plus riche héritière d'Europe.* Paris: Hachette.

Duchêne, Roger. 1982. "L'Ecole des femmes au XVIIe siècle." In *Ecrire au temps de Mme de Sévigné: Lettres et texte littéraire.* 2d ed. Paris: Vrin.

Dulong, Claude. 1969. *L'Amour au XVIIe siècle.* Paris: Hachette.

———. 1974. *La Vie quotidienne des femmes au Grand Siècle.* Paris: Hachette.

———. 1993. *Marie Mancini: La première passion de Louis XIV.* Paris: Perrin.

Dulong, Gustave. 1921. *L'Abbé de Saint-Réal: étude sur les rapports de l'histoire et du roman au XVIIe siècle.* 2 vols. Paris: Champion.

Dumas, Alexandre. 1887. *La Reine Margot.* Paris: Calmann Lévy.

Eakin, John Paul. 1985. *Fictions in Autobiography: Studies in the Art of Self-Invention.* Princeton: Princeton University Press.

Evans, Joseph C. 1965–66. "Versions of the Mémoires of Mademoiselle de Montpensier." *Romance Notes* 7:161–64.

Faguet, Emile. 1927. *Histoire de la poésie française.* Vol. 3: *Précieux et Burlesques.* Paris: Boivin.

Fanlo, Jean-Raymond. 1994. "'Meurtrière Venus', Marguerite de Valois dans l'oeuvre d'Agrippa d'Aubigné." In *Marguerite de France, Reine de Navarre, et son temps,* edited by Madeleine Lazard and J. Cubelier de Beynac, 182–92. Actes du Colloque d'Agen (12–13 October 1991). Agen: Centre Matteo Bandello d'Agen.

Finke, Laurie. 1993. "Femina Academica: Medieval Studies in Feminism." *Medieval Feminist Newsletter* 15 (Spring): 1–3.

Flax, Jane. 1992. "The End of Innocence." In *Feminists Theorize the Political,* edited by Judith Butler and Joan Scott. New York and London: Routledge.

Fleishman, Avrom. 1983. *Figures of Autobiography.* Berkeley: University of California Press.

Folkenflik, Robert. 1993. "Introduction: The Institution of Autobiography." In *The Culture of Autobiography,* edited by Robert Folkenflik. Stanford, Calif.: Stanford University Press.

Foucault, Michel. 1972a. *The Archeology of Knowledge.* Translated by A. M. Sheridan Smith. New York: Harper. Originally published as *L'Archéologie du savoir* (Paris: Gallimard, 1969).

———. 1978a. *History of Sexuality.* Translated by Robert Hurley. 3 vols. New York: Pantheon. Originally published as *Histoire de la sexualité,* 3 vols. (Paris: Gallimard, 1976).

———. 1978b. *Power/Knowledge: Selected Interviews and Other Writings, 1972–1977.* Edited by Colin Gordon. Translated by Colin Gordon, Leo Marshall, John Mepham, and Kate Soper. New York: Pantheon.

———. 1988. "Technologies of the Self." In *Technologies of the Self,* edited by Luther H.

Martin, Huck Gurman, and Patrick H. Hutton, 16–49. Amherst: University of Massachusetts Press.

Fowler, Lois J., and David H. Fowler. 1990. *Revelations of Self: American Women in Autobiography.* Albany: State University of New York Press.

Fradenburg, Louise, and Carla Freccero, eds. 1995. *Premodern Sexualities.* With Kathy Lavezzo. New York: Routledge.

Fragonard, Marie-Madeleine. 1994. "La Reine Marguerite au rang des Illustres." In *Marguerite de France, Reine de Navarre, et son temps,* edited by Madeleine Lazard and J. Cubelier de Beynac, 194–202. Actes du Colloque d'Agen (12–13 October 1991). Agen: Centre Matteo Bandello d'Agen.

François, Carlo. 1987. *Précieuses et autres indociles: Aspects du féminisme dans la littérature française du XVIIe siècle.* Birmingham, Ala.: Summa.

Freud, Sigmund. 1957. "On Narcissism." In *1914–1916,* vol. 14 of *Standard Edition of the Complete Psychological Works of Sigmund Freud.* translated by James Strachey. London: Hogarth.

Fumaroli, Marc. 1971. "Les Mémoires du XVIIe siècle au carrefour des genres en prose." *XVIIe Siècle* 94–95:7–37.

———. 1979. "Mémoires et histoire: Le dilemme de l'historiographe humaniste au XVIIe siècle." In *Les Valeurs chez les mémorialistes français du XVIIe siècle avant la Fronde,* edited by Naomi Hepp and Jacques Hennequin. Actes et Colloques 22. Paris: Klincksieck.

Furetière. 1958. *Le Roman Bourgeois.* 1666. Reprinted in *Le Roman Français au XVIIe siècle,* edited by Antoine Adam, 900–1104. Editions de la Pléiade. Paris: Gallimard.

Fuss Diana. 1989. *Essentially Speaking: Feminism, Nature, and Difference.* New York and London: Routledge.

Garapon, Jean. 1988. "Mademoiselle de Montpensier: L'Autobiographie d'une princesse du sang." *Cahiers de l'Association Internationale des Etudes Françaises* 40 (May): 39–49.

———. 1989a. *La Grande Mademoiselle Mémorialiste.* Paris: Droz.

———. 1989b. "Les Mémorialistes et le réel: L'Exemple du Cardinal de Retz et de Mademoiselle de Montpensier." In *La Littérature et le réel,* edited by Georges Forestier. Paris: Aux Amateurs de Livres.

———. 1989. "Mademoiselle devant la Fronde d'après ses Mémoires." In *La Fronde en Question,* edited by Roger Duchêne and Pierre Ronzeaud, 63–71. Actes du dix-huitième colloque du centre méridional sur le XVIIe siècle, Marseilles, Cassis 1988. Aix-en-Provence: SODEB.

———. 1993. "Mademoiselle de Montpensier dans ses *Mémoires:* L'Exemple d'une culture princière." In *De L'Estoile à Saint-Simon, recherche sur la culture des mémorialistes au temps des trois premiers rois Bourbons,* edited by Madeleine Bertaut and André Labertit, 93–107. Paris: Klincksieck.

———. 1994a. "Mademoiselle et l'exil." *Papers on French Seventeenth-Century Literature* 21, no. 41:345–55.

———. 1994b. "Une Autobiographie dans les limbes, Les *Mémoires de la reine Marguerite.*" In *Marguerite de France, Reine de Navarre, et son temps,* edited by Madeleine Lazard and J. Cubelier de Beynac, 206–16. Actes du Colloque d'Agen (12–13 October 1991). Agen: Centre Matteo Bandello d'Agen.

————. 1995. "Mademoiselle à Saint-Fargeau: La Découverte de l'écriture." *Papers on French Seventeenth-Century Literature* 22, no. 42:37–47.

Garber, Marjorie. 1992. *Vested Interests: Crossing-Dressing and Cultural Anxiety*. New York: Routledge.

Garrisson, Janine. 1984. *Henry IV*. Paris: Seuil.

Gibson, Wendy. 1989. *Women in Seventeenth-Century France*. New York: St. Martin's Press.

Gilmore, Leigh. 1994. *Autobiographics: A Feminist Theory of Women's Self-Representation*. Ithaca: Cornell University Press.

Goldsmith, Elizabeth C. 1988. *Exclusive Conversations: The Art of Interaction in Seventeenth-Century France*. Philadelphia: University of Pennsylvania Press.

————1992. "Louis XIV, Marie Mancini et la politique de l'intimité royal." In *Ordre et Contestation*, edited by Roger Duchêne and Pierre Ronzeaud, 1:235–43. Biblio 17, no. 73. Paris and Seattle: Papers on French Seventeenth-Century Literature.

————. 1995a. "The Politics and Poetics of the Mancini Romance: Visions and Revisions of the Life of Louis XIV." In *The Rhetoric of Life Writing in Early Modern Europe*, edited by Thomas F. Mayer and D. R. Woolf, 341–72. Ann Arbor: University of Michigan Press.

————. 1995b. "Publishing the Lives of Hortense and Marie Mancini." In *Going Public: Women and Publishing in Early Modern France,* edited by Elizabeth C. Goldsmith and Dena Goodman, 31–45. Ithaca: Cornell University Press.

————. 1997. "Mothering Mysticism: Mme Guyon and her Public." In *Women Writers in Pre-Revolutionary France: Strategies of Emancipation,* edited by Colette H. Winn and Donna Kuizenga, 127–39. New York and London: Garland.

Gondal, Marie-Louise. 1989. "L'Autobiographie de Madame Guyon (1648–1717): La découverte et l'apport de deux neauveaux manuscrits." *Dix-Septième Siècle* 164, no. 3:308–23.

————. 1989. *Madame Guyon (1648–1717): Un nouveau visage*. Paris: Beauchesne.

Gosselin, Chris, and Glenn Wilson. 1980. *Sexual Variations: Fetishism, Sadomasochism, and Transvestism*. New York: Simon and Schuster.

Gouesse, Jean-Marie. 1985. "La femme et la formation du couple en France à l'époque moderne." In *La Femme à l'époque moderne (XVIe–XVIIIe siècle),* 5–27. Paris: Presses de l'Université de Paris Sorbonne.

Gournay, Marie de. 1985. *Le Proumenoir de M. de Montaigne par sa Fille d'Alliance*. Paris: Abel l'Angelier, 1594. Reprint, with an introduction by Patricia Francis Cholakian, Delmar, N.Y.: Scholars Facsimiles and Reprints.

————. 1989. "Préface à l'édition des Essais de Montaigne (Paris: Abel L'Angelier,1595)." Edited by François Rigolot. *Montaigne Studies I,* 1:7–60.

Greenberg, Mitchell. 1992. *Subjectivity and Subjugation in Seventeenth-Century Drama and Prose: The Family Romance of French Classicism*. Cambridge: Cambridge University Press.

Grieco, Sara F. 1991. *Ange ou diablesse: La représentation de la femme au XVIe siècle*. Paris: Flammarion.

Gréard, Octave. 1912. *Mme de Maintenon: Extraits de ses lettres, avis, entretiens, conversations et proverbes sur l'éducation*. Paris: Hachette.

Grobe, Edwin Paul. 1954. "Sébastien Bremond: His Life and His Works." Ph.D. diss., Indiana University.

Guessard, M. F. 1842. *Mémoires et lettres de Marguerite de Valois.* Nouvelle édition revue sur les manuscrits des Bibliothèques du Roi et de l'Arsénal. Paris: Jules Renouard.

Gusdorf, Georges. 1980. "Conditions and Limits of Autobiography." In *Autobiography: Essays Theoretical and Critical,* edited by James Olney, 28–48. Princeton: Princeton University Press.

Guyon, Jeanne-Marie Bouvier de la Mothe. 1686. *Moyen court de faire oraison.* Jacques Petit: Grenoble.

———. 1962. *La Vie de Madame Guyon, extraits, première partie: 1648–1681, selon le ms. d'Oxford.* Edited by Jean Bruno. *Cahiers de la Tour Saint-Jacques* 6:3–26.

———. 1983. *La Vie de Madame Guyon écrite par elle-même.* Edited by Benjamin Sahler. Paris: Dervy Livres.

———. 1992. *Récits de captivité [Relation de Madame Guyon].* Edited by Marie-Louise Gondal. Grenoble: Jérome Millon.

Haddad, Gabriel. 1990. "Héroïsme et valeurs aristocratiques dans les Mémoires du Cardinal de Retz." *Cahiers du dix-septième siècle* 4, no. 2:211–22.

Hanley Sarah. 1987. "Family and State in Early Modern France: The Marriage Pact." In *Connecting Spheres: Women in the Western World, 1500 to the Present,* edited by Marilyn J. Boxer and Jean H. Quataert, 53–63. Oxford: Oxford University Press.

Harth, Erica. 1983. *Ideology and Culture in Seventeenth-Century France.* Ithaca: Cornell University Press.

———. 1992. *Cartesian Women: Versions of Subversions of Rational Discourse in the Old Regime.* Ithaca: Cornell University Press.

Hartmann, Cyril Hughes. 1926. *The Vagabond Duchess: The Life of Hortense Mancini, duchesse Mazarin.* London: Routledge.

Heilbrun, Carolyn G. 1988. *Writing a Woman's Life.* New York: W. W. Norton.

Hendricks, Margo, and Patricia Parker. 1994. *Women, "Race," and Writing in the Early Modern Period.* London: Routledge.

Henein, Eglol. 1976–77. "Mademoiselle de Montpensier à la recherche du temps perdu." *Papers on Seventeenth-Century French Literature* 6:37–52.

Hennequin, Jacques. 1979. "La Paternité chez quelques mémorialistes." In *Les Valeurs chez les mémorialistes français du XVIIe siècle avant la Fronde,* edited by Naomi Hepp and Jacques Hennequin, 289–306. Actes et Colloques 22. Paris: Klincksieck.

Hewitt, Leah D. *Autobiographical Tightropes.* Lincoln: University of Nebraska Press, 1990.

Hipp, Marie-Thérèse. 1976. *Mythes et Réalités: Enquête sur le roman et les mémoires (1660–1700).* Paris: Klincksieck.

Howarth, William L. 1980. "Some Principles of Autobiography." In *Autobiography: Essays Theoretical and Critical,* edited by James Olney, 84–114. Princeton: Princeton University Press.

Howe, Irving. 1992. "The Self in Literature." In *Constructions of the Self,* edited by George Levine, 249–67. New Brunswick: Rutgers University Press.

Hutton, Patrick H. 1988. "Foucault, Freud, and the Technologies of the Self." In *Technologies of the Self,* edited by Luther H. Martin, Huck Gurman, and Patrick H. Hutton, 121–44. Amherst: University of Massachusetts Press.

Jelinek, Estelle C. 1986. *The Tradition of Women's Autobiography: From Antiquity to the Present.* Boston: Twayne.

Jensen, Katherine Ann. 1991. "La Nouvelle Querelle des Femmes: Feminist Criticism and Seventeenth-Century Literature." *Oeuvres et Critiques* 16:87–95.

Jones, Ann Rosalind. 1986. "Surprising Fame: Renaissance Gender Ideologies and Women's Lyric." In *Poetics of Gender,* edited by Nancy K. Miller. New York: Columbia University Press.

Jordan, Constance. 1987. "Boccaccio's In-Famous Women: Gender and Civic Virtue in the *De mulieribus claris.*" In *Ambiguous Realities: Women in the Middle Ages and Renaissance,* edited by Carole Levin and Jeanie Watson. Detroit: Wayne State University Press.

Karro, Françoise. 1993. "Le Moyen Age dans les Mémoires de Louis XIV." In *De L'Estoile à Saint-Simon, recherche sur la culture des mémorialistes au temps des trois premiers rois Bourbons,* edited by Madeleine Bertaut and André Labertit, 51–76. Paris: Klincksieck.

Kavanaugh, Thomas M. 1993. *Enlightenment and the Shadows of Chance: The Novel and the Culture of Gambling in Eighteenth-Century France.* Baltimore: Johns Hopkins University Press.

Kelly, Joan. 1984. *Women, History, and Theory.* Chicago: University of Chicago Press.

Knecht, Robert J. 1989. "Military Autobiographies in Sixteenth-Century France." In *War, Literature and the Arts in Sixteenth-Century Europe,* edited by J. R. Mulryne and Margaret Shewring. New York: St. Martin's Press.

Kolakowski, Leszek. 1969. *Chrétiens sans église: La Conscience religieuse et le lien confessionnel au XVIIe siècle.* Translated by Anna Posner. Paris: Gallimard.

Kristeva, Julia. 1979. "Un Pur Silence: La perfection de Jeanne Guyon." In *Histoires d'amour,* 53–90. Paris: Denoël.

Lafayette, Madame de. *Histoire de Madame Henriette d'Angleterre et mémoires de la cour de France pour les années 1688 et 1689.* Paris: Mercure de France.

La Force, duc de. 1952. *La Grande Mademoiselle.* Paris: Hachette.

Lathuillère, Roger. 1966. *La Préciosité: Étude historique et linguistique.* Geneva: Droz.

Laude, Patrick. 1990. "Perspectives on Subjectivity and the Ego in Seventeenth-Century French Thought." *Papers on French Seventeenth-Century Literature* 33:531–46.

Lazard, Madeleine, and J. Cubelier de Beynac. 1994. *Marguerite de France, Reine de Navarre, et son temps,* edited by Madeleine Lazard and J. Cubelier de Beynac. Actes du Colloque d'Agen (12–13 October 1991). Agen: Centre Matteo Bandello d'Agen.

Lejeune, Philippe. 1971. *L'Autobiographie en France.* Paris: Collin.

———. 1975. *Le Pacte autobiographique.* Paris: Le Seuil.

Le Moel, Michel. 1995. "Mademoiselle et Paris." *Papers on French Seventeenth-Century Literature* 22, no. 42:15–24.

Lesne-Jaffro, Emmanuelle. 1993. "Une culture de l'action, l'honnête homme et les grands honneurs de la guerre." In *De L'Estoile à Saint-Simon, recherche sur la culture des mémorialistes au temps des trois premiers rois Bourbons,* edited by Madeleine Bertaut and André Labertit, 109–28. Paris: Klincksieck.

Lever, Maurice. 1997a. Preface to *Marie Mancini, princesse Colonne: Cendre et Poussière Mémoires.* Paris: Le Comptoir.

——, ed. 1997b. *Marie Mancini, princesse Colonne: Cendre et poussiére Mémoires*. Paris: Le Comptoir. Originally published as *Mémoires de M.L.P.M.M* (Cologne: Pierre Marteau, 1676).

Lévi-Strauss, Claude. 1969. *The Elementary Structures of Kinship*. Translated by James Harle Bell and John Richard von Sturmer. Edited by Rodney Needham. Boston: Beacon.

Lionnet, Françoise. 1989. *Autobiographical Voices: Race, Gender, Self-Portraiture*. Ithaca: Cornell University Press.

Livet, Charles. 1870. *Précieux et précieuses*. Paris: Didier.

Lougee, Carolyn. 1976. *Le Paradis des femmes: Women, Salons, and Social Stratification in Seventeenth-Century France*. Princeton: Princeton University Press.

Louis XIV. 1978. *Mémoires*. Edited by J. Longnon. Paris: Tallandier.

Maclean, Ian. 1977. *Woman Triumphant: Feminism in French Literature (1610–1642)*. Oxford: Clarendon.

——. 1980. *The Renaissance Notion of Woman: A Study in the Fortunes of Scholasticism and Medical Science in European Intellectual Life*. Cambridge: Cambridge University Press.

Magendie, Maurice. 1970. *La Politesse mondaine et les théories de l'honnêteté en France au XVIIe siècle, de 1600 à 1660*. 1925. Reprint, Geneva: Slatkine.

——. 1978. *Le Roman français au XVIIe siècle: De l'Astrée au Grand Cyrus*. 1932. Reprint, Geneva: Slatkine.

Magnien-Simonin, Catherine. 1994. "La Jeune Marguerite des poétes (1553–1578)." In *Marguerite de France, Reine de Navarre, et son temps*, edited by Madeleine Lazard and J. Cubelier de Beynac, 135–57. Actes du Colloque d'Agen (12–13 October 1991). Agen: Centre Matteo Bandello d'Agen.

Mallet-Joris, Françoise. 1966. *Marie Mancini, le premier amour de Louis XIV. Paris: Hachette*. Published in English as *The Uncompromising Heart: A Life of Marie Mancini, Louis XIV's First Love*, trans. Patrick O'Brian (London: W. H. Allen, 1966).

——. 1978. *Jeanne Guyon*. Paris: Flammarion.

Mancini, Hortense (Mazarin). 1965. *Mémoires d'Hortense et de Marie Mancini*. Edited by Gérard Doscot. Paris: Mercure de France.

Mancini, Marie (Colonna). 1998. *La Vérité dans son jour, ou les véritables mémoires de M. Manchini, Connétable Colonne*. Edited by Patricia Francis Cholakian and Elizabeth C. Goldsmith. Delmar, N.Y.: Scholars Facsimiles and Reprints.

Marie de l'Incarnation. 1929a. "La Relation de 1654." 1677. Reprinted in *Les Ecrits spirituels et historiques*, edited by Albert Jamet, 129–479. Paris: Desclée-de Brouwer.

——. 1929b. "Supplément à la relation de 1654." 1677. Reprinted in *Les Ecrits spirituels et historiques*, edited by Albert Jamet, 477–98. Paris: Desclée-de Brouwer.

——. 1964. *The Autobiography of Venerable Marie of the Incarnation, O.S.U.: Mystic and Missionary*. Translated by John J. Sullivan. Introduction by James Brodrick. Chicago: Loyola University Press.

Mariéjol, Jean H. 1970. *La Vie de Marguerite de Valois, Reine de Navarre et de France (1553–1615)*. Paris, 1928. Reprint, Geneva: Slatkine Reprints.

Marin, Louis. 1988. *The Portrait of the King*. Translated by Martha M. Houle. Foreword by Tom Conley. Minneapolis: University of Minnesota Press. Originally published as *Le Portrait du roi* (Paris: Minuit, 1981).

Martin, Biddy. 1988. "Feminism, Criticism, and Foucault." In *Feminism and Foucault: Reflections on Resistance,* edited by Irene Diamond and Lee Quinby, 3–19. Boston: Northeastern University Press.

Martin, Henri-Jean. 1969. *Livre, pouvoirs, et société à Paris au XVIIe siècle, 1598–1701.* 2 vols. Geneva: Centre de Recherches d'Histoire et de la Philologie.

Martin, Luther H., Huck Gutman, and Patrick H. Hutton, eds. 1988. *Technologies of the Self: A Seminar with Michel Foucault.* Amherst: University of Massachusetts Press.

Marwick, Arthur. 1991. *Beauty in History: Society, Politics, and Personal Appearance c. 1500 to the Present.* London: Thames and Hudson.

Mason, Mary G. 1988. "The Other Voice: Autobiographies of Women Writers." In *The Private Self: Theory and Practice of Women's Autobiographical Writings,* edited by Shari Benstock. Chapel Hill: University of North Carolina Press.

Masson, Maurice. 1907. *Fénelon et Mme Guyon: Documents nouveaux et inédits.* Paris: Hachette.

May, Georges. 1979. *L'Autobiographie.* Paris: Presses Universitaires de France.

Mayer, Denise. 1978. "Mademoiselle de Montpensier et l'architecture d'après ses *Mémoires.*" *XVIIe siècle* 118, no. 118–19 (1978): 57–71.

McLeod, Glenda. 1991. *Virtue and Venom: Catalogs of Women from Antiquity to the Renaissance.* Ann Arbor: University of Michigan Press.

Melchior-Bonnet, Bernardine. 1985. *La Grande Mademoiselle.* Paris: Perrin.

Mercier, Louis-Sébastien. 1783–89. *Le Tableau de Paris.* 12 vols. Amsterdam.

Mettam, Roger. 1988. *Power and Faction in Louis XIV's France.* Oxford: Basil Blackwell.

Miller, Nancy K. 1980. "Women's Autobiography in France: For a Dialectics of Identification." In *Women and Language in Literature and Society,* edited by Sally McConnell-Ginet, Ruth Borker, and Nelly Furman, 258–73. New York: Praeger.

———. 1988. "Writing Fictions: Women's Autobiography In France." In *Subject to Change: Reading Feminist Writing,* 47–64. New York: Columbia University Press.

Millett, Kate. 1970. *Sexual Politics.* New York: Ballantine Books.

Modleski, Tania. 1991. *Feminism Without Women: Culture and Criticism in a "Postfeminist" Age.* New York and London: Routledge.

Mongrédien, Georges. 1939. *Les Précieux et les précieuses.* Paris: Mercure de France.

———. 1952. *Une Aventurière au grand siècle la duchesse Mazarin.* Paris: Amiot-Dumont.

———. 1966. Introduction to *Mémoires de l'Abbé de Choisy: Mémoires pour servir à l'histoire de Louis XIV; Mémoires de l'Abbé de Choisy habillé en femme.* Edited by Georges Mongrédien. Paris: Mercure de France.

Montpensier, Anne-Marie Louise d'Orléans. 1806. *Lettres de Mlle de Montpensier.* Paris: Collin.

———. 1985. *Mémoires.* 2 vols. Paris: Fontaine. Reprinted from the edition of A. Chéruel.

———. 1999. *Histoire de Jeanne Lambert d'Herbigny, marquise de Fouquesolles.* 1653. Facsimile reproduction with an introduction by Patricia Francis Cholakian, Delmar, N.Y.: Scholars Facsimiles and Reprints.

Moriarty, Michael. 1988. *Taste and Ideology in Seventeenth-Century France.* Cambridge: Cambridge University Press.

Nussbaum, Felicity A. 1988. "Eighteenth-Century Women's Autobiographical Common-places." In *The Private Self: Theory and Practice of Women's Autobiographical Writings,* edited by Shari Benstock. Chapel Hill: University of North Carolina Press.

Olivet, abbé de. 1742. *La Vie de Monsieur l'abbé de Choisy.* Lausanne and Geneva: Bousquet.

Olney, James. 1980. "Autobiography and the Cultural Moment: A Thematic, Historical, and Bibliographical Introduction." In *Autobiography: Essays Theoretical and Critical,* edited by James Olney, 3–27. Princeton: Princeton University Press.

Parish, R. J. 1976. "An Introduction to the *Mémoires* of the abbé de Choisy (1644–1724)." *Australian Journal of French Studies* 13:213–24.

Pascal, Roy. 1960. *Design and Truth in Autobiography.* London: Routledge.

Pellisson, Paul. 1653. *Relations contenant l'Histoire de l'Académie Françoise.* Paris: Pierre Le Petit.

———. 1735. *Œuvres diverses.* Paris.

Pensa, Henri. 1935. *Hortense Mancini, duchesse de Mazarin: Ses démêlés conjugaux, Sa vie aventureuse (1646–1699).* Paris: Félix Alcan.

Perey, Lucien. (pseudonym for Clara Adèle Luce Herpin). 1896. *Une Princesse romaine au XVIIe siècle: Marie Mancini Colonna d'après des documents inédits.* Paris: Calmann Lévy.

———. 1894. *Le Roman du grand roi: Louis XIV et Marie Mancini d'après des lettres et documents inédits.* Paris: Calmann Lévy.

Peterson, Linda H. 1993. "Institutionalizing Women's Autobiography: Nineteenth-Century Editors and the Shaping of an Autobiographical Tradition." In *The Culture of Autobiography: Constructions of Self-Representation,* edited by Robert Folkenflik, 80–103. Stanford, Calif.: Stanford University Press.

Petitot, Claude Bernard, ed. 1819–29. *Collection des mémoires relatifs à l'histoire de France.* [Sér. 1] vols. 1–52, 1819–26; [sér. 2] vols. 1–78, 1820–29. Paris: Foucault.

Picard, Roger. 1943. *Les Salons littéraires et la société française (1610–1789).* New York: Brentano.

Piettre, Monique A. 1974. *La Condition féminine à travers les âges.* Paris: France-Empire.

Pure, Abbé Michel de. 1938. *La Prétieuse.* Edited by Emile Magne. Paris: Droz.

Ranum, Oreste. 1979. *Artisans of Glory: Writers and Historical Thought in Seventeenth-Century France.* Baltimore: Johns Hopkins University Press.

———. 1992. Review of *Revising Memory,* by Beasley, and *Tender Geographies,* by DeJean. *MLN* 107, no. 4 (September): 810–16.

Ratel, Simone. 1924. "La Cour de la Reine Marguerite." *Revue du seizième siècle* 11, nos. 1–29:193–207.

———. 1925. "La Cour de la Reine Marguerite." *Revue du seizième siècle* 12, no.1:43.

Renée, Amédée. 1856. *Les Nièces de Mazarin: Études de moeurs et de caractères au XVIIe siècle.* 2d ed. Paris: Firmin Didot.

Reynes, Geneviève. 1983. *L'abbé de Choisy ou l'ingénu libertin.* Paris: Presses de la Renaissance.

Richmond, Ian M. 1977. *Héroïsme et galanterie: L'Abbé de Pure, Témoin d'une Crise (1653–1665).* Sherbrooke, Québec: Naaman.

Riley, Denise. 1988. *"Am I that Name?": Feminism and the Category of "Women" in History.* Minneapolis: University of Minnesota Press.

Rival, Paul. 1938. *Marie Mancini.* Paris: Gallimard.

Roelker, Nancy. 1972. "The Appeal of Calvinism to French Noblewomen in the Sixteenth Century." *Journal of Interdisciplinary History* 2:391–418.

Ronzeaud, Pierre. 1975. "La Femme au pouvoir ou le monde à l'envers." *Dix-septième siècle* 108:9–33.

———. 1988. *Peuple et représentation sous le règne de Louis XIV.* Aix-en-Provence: Publications de l'Université de Provence.

Rowan, Mary M. 1991. "Crossing Borders: Tales of the Abbé de Choisy." In *Actes de Las Vegas,* edited by Marie-France Hilgar. Actes du XXIIe colloque de la North American Society for Seventeenth-Century French Literature, University of Nevada, Las Vegas (1–3 March 1990). Biblio 17, no. 60. Paris, Seattle, Tübingen: Papers on French Seventeenth-Century Literature.

Rowbotham, Sheila. 1973. *Woman's Consciousness, Man's World.* London: Penguin.

Sainte-Beuve, Charles. 1851. *Causeries du Lundi.* Vol. 3. Paris: Garnier.

Saint-Evremond, Charles. 1927. *Oeuvres.* Edited by René de Planhol. Paris: Cité des Livres.

Saint-Simon. 1983–88. *Mémoires.* Edited by Yves Coirault. 8 vols. Paris: Gallimard.

Salazar, Philippe-Joseph. 1997. "Towards a Genealogy of Women's Rhetoric in Seventeeenth-Century France: The Eloquence of Ecstasy." In *Women Writers in Pre-Revolutionary France: Strategies of Emancipation,* edited by Colette H. Winn and Donna Kuizenga. New York and London: Garland.

Schalk, Ellery. 1986. *From Valor to Pedigree: Ideas of Nobility in France in the Sixteenth and Seventeenth Centuries.* Princeton: Princeton University Press.

Schibanoff, Susan. 1983. "Early Women Writers: In-scribing, or, Reading the Fine Print." *Women's Studies International Forum* 6, no. 5:475–89.

Schiff, Mario. 1978. *La Fille d'Alliance de Montaigne: Marie de Gournay.* Geneva: Slatkine.

Schrenck, Gilbert. 1991. "Brantôme et Marguerite de Valois: D'un genre l'autre ou les Mémoires incertains." In *La Cour au miroir des mémorialistes: 1530–1682,* edited by Noëmi Hepp, 13–92. Paris: Klincksieck.

Sedgwick, Eve Kosofsky. 1990. *Epistemology of the Closet.* Barkeley: University of California Press.

Segrais, Jean Regnauld de. 1721. *Segraisiana.* Paris: Compagnie des Libraires Associés.

Sévigné, Marie de Rabutin-Chantal, Mme de. 1972–78. *Correspondance.* Edited by Roger Duchêne. 3 vols. Paris: Gallimard (Pléiade).

Smith, Paul. 1988. *Discerning the Subject.* Theory and History of Literature, vol. 55. Minneapolis: University of Minnesota Press.

Smith, Sidonie. 1987. *A Poetics of Women's Autobiography: Marginality and the Fictions of Self-Representation.* Bloomington: Indiana University Press.

———. 1993. *Subjectivity, Identity, and the Body: Women's Autobiographical Practices in the Twentieth Century.* Bloomington: Indiana University Press.

Smith, Sidonie, and Julia Watson, eds. 1992. *De/Colonizing the Subject: The Politics of Gender in Women's Autobiography.* Minneapolis: University of Minnesota Press.

Solnon, J.-F. 1987. *La cour de France.* Part 1. Paris: Fayard.

Somaize, Sieur Badaud de. 1861. *Le Grand Dictionnaire des prétieuses*. Edited by Charles Livet. 2 vols. Paris: Jannet.

Spack, Patricia Meyer. 1980. "Selves in Hiding." In *Women's Autobiography: Essays in Criticism,* edited by Estelle C. Jelinek. Bloomington: Indiana University Press.

Spelman, Elizabeth V. 1988. *Inessential Woman: Problems of Exclusion in Feminist Thought.* Boston: Beacon Press.

Spengemann, William. 1980. *The Forms of Autobiography: Episodes in the History of a Literary Genre.* New Haven: Yale University Press.

Stanton, Domna C. 1975. "The Ideal of Repos in Seventeenth Century French Literature." *L'Esprit Créateur* 15:79–104.

———. 1981. "Préciosité and the Fear of Women." *Yale French Studies* 62.

———, ed. 1987. *The Female Autograph.* 1984. Reprint, Chicago: University of Chicago Press.

Starobinski, Jean. 1980. "The Style of Autobiography." In *Autobiography: Essays Theoretical and Critical,* edited by James Olney, 73–83. Princeton: Princeton University Press.

Steegmuller, Francis. 1957. *La Grande Mademoiselle*. Paris: Del Duca.

Supple, James. 1994. "Brantôme: chevalier humaniste?" In *Marguerite de France, Reine de Navarre, et son temps,* edited by Madeleine Lazard and J. Cubelier de Beynac, 171–80. Actes du Colloque d'Agen (12–13 October 1991). Agen: Centre Matteo Bandello d'Agen.

Tachouzin, Patrick. 1994. "Marguerite de Valois et Nérac: Un mariage d'amour." In *Marguerite de France, Reine de Navarre, et son temps,* edited by Madeleine Lazard and J. Cubelier de Beynac, 57–60. Actes du Colloque d'Agen (12–13 October 1991). Agen: Centre Matteo Bandello d'Agen.

Tallemant des Réaux, Gédéon. 1960. *Historiettes.* Edited by Antoine Adam. Paris: Gallimard (Pléiade).

Teresa of Avila. 1976. *The Book of Her Life.* Vol. 2 in *The Collected Works of St. Teresa of Avila,* translated by Kieran Kavanaugh and Otilio Rodríguez. Washington, D.C.: Institute of Carmelite Studies.

Tetel, Marcel. 1994. "Les Visages de Marguerite de France." In *Marguerite de France, Reine de Navarre, et son temps,* edited by Madeleine Lazard and J. Cubelier de Beynac, 31–41. Actes du Colloque d'Agen (12–13 October 1991). Agen: Centre Matteo Bandello d'Agen.

Timmermans, Linda. 1992. "Une Hérésie féministe? Jansénisme et préciosité." In *Ordre et contestation au temps des classiques,* edited by Roger Duchêne and Pierre Ronzeaud, 1:159–72. Paris, Seattle, Tübingen: Papers on French Seventeenth Century Literature.

Tostain, R. 1967. "Le Joueur, essai psychanalytique." *L'Inconscient* 2 (May–June).

Traer, James F. 1980. *Marriage and the Family in Eighteenth-Century France.* Ithaca: Cornell University Press.

Trinh T. Minh-ha. 1989. *Woman, Native, Other: Writing Postcoloniality and Feminism.* Bloomington: Indiana University Press.

Valois, Marguerite de. 1971. *Mémoires.* Edited by Yves Cazaux. Paris: Mercure de France.

———. 1999. *Mémoires et autres écrits, 1574–1614.* Edited by Eliane Viennot. Paris: Champion.

Van der Cruysse, Dirk. 1995. *L'Abbé de Choisy: Androgyne et mandarin.* Paris: Fayard.

———. 1996a. "Choisy historien de Louis XIV, du Moyen Age, de l'Eglise et de lui-même." In *Proceedings of the Western Society for French History* 23. Boulder: University Press of Colorado.

———. 1996b. "'Peser son mérite dans la balance de la vérité': L'Abbé de Choisy et le mythe louis-quatorzien." In *Vingt Etudes pour Maurice Delcroix: Retours du mythe,* edited by Christian Berg, Walter Geers, Paul Pelckmans, and Bruno Tristmans. Amsterdam: Rodopi.

Van Slyke, Gretchen. 1994. "Ad-Dressing the Self: Costume, Gender, and Autobiographical Discourse in l'abbé de Choisy and Rosa Bonheur." In *Autobiography, Historiography, Rhetoric,* edited by Mary Donaldson-Evans, Lucienne Frappier-Mazur, and Gerald Prince. Amsterdam: Rodopi.

Vaucheret, Etienne. 1994. "Brantôme, Sigisbée de Marguerite de Valois." In *Marguerite de France, Reine de Navarre, et son temps,* edited by Madeleine Lazard and J. Cubelier de Beynac, 160–70. Actes du Colloque d'Agen (12–13 October 1991). Agen: Centre Matteo Bandello d'Agen.

Verdier, Gabrielle. 1983. "Mademoiselle de Montpensier et le plaisir du texte." *Papers on French Seventeenth-Century Literature* 10, no. 18:11–33.

Viennot, Eliane. 1992. "Marguerite de Valois et *La Ruelle mal assortie:* Une attribution erronée." *Nouvelle Revue du Seizième Siècle* 10:81–98.

———. 1993. *Marguerite de Valois: Histoire d'une femme, histoire d'un mythe.* Paris: Payot.

———. 1994. "La Légende de la Reine Marguerite, ou le pouvoir des femmes en question." In *Marguerite de France, Reine de Navarre, et son temps,* edited by Madeleine Lazard and J. Cubelier de Beynac, 311–28. Actes du Colloque d'Agen (12–13 October 1991). Agen: Centre Matteo Bandello d'Agen.

———. 1995. "Les ambiguïtés identitaires du *Je* dans les *Mémoires* de Marguerite de Valois." In *Le Genre des Mémoires: Essai de définition,* edited by Madeleine Bertaud and François-Xavier Cuche, 69–79. Paris: Klincksieck.

Viguerie, Jean de. 1985. "La Femme et la religion en France, en milieu Catholique, au XVIIe siècle." In *La Femme à l'èpoque moderne (XVIe–XVIIIe siècle).* Paris: Presses Universitaires de Paris Sorbonne.

Voltaire. 1957. *Le Siècle de Louis XIV.* In *Oeuvres historiques,* edited by René Pomeau. Paris: Gallimard.

Watson, Julia. 1993. "Towards an Anti-Metaphysics of Autobiography." In *The Culture of Autobiography: Constructions of Self-Representation,* edited by Robert Folkenflik. Stanford, Calif.: Stanford University Press.

Watts, Derek A. 1975. "Self-Portrayal in Seventeenth-Century French Memoirs." *Australian Journal of French Studies* 12, no. 3:264–85.

Weaver, F. Ellen. 1989. "Erudition, Spirituality, and Women: The Jansenist Contribution." In *Women in Reformation and Counter-Reformation Europe: Public and Private Worlds,* edited by Sherrin Marshall, 189–206. Bloomington and Indianapolis: Indiana University Press.

Weber, Alison. 1990. *Teresa of Avila and the Rhetoric of Femininity.* Princeton: Princeton University Press.

Weed, Elizabeth, and Naomi Schor. 1994. *The Essential Difference*. Bloomington: Indiana University Press.

———. 1997. *Feminism Meets Queer Theory*. Bloomington: Indiana University Press.

Weintraub, Karl. 1978. *The Value of the Individual: Self and Circumstance in Autobiography*. Chicago: University of Chicago Press.

White, Hayden. 1987. *The Content of the Form: Narrative Discourse and Historical Representation*. Baltimore: Johns Hopkins University Press.

Williams, Hugh Noel. 1906. *Five Fair Sisters: An Italian Episode at the Court of Louis XIV*. New York: Putnam.

Williams, Huntington. 1983. *Rousseau and Romantic Autobiography*. Oxford: Oxford University Press.

Winn, Colette. 1993. "'De Mères en filles': Les manuels d'éducation sous l'Ancien Régime." *Atlantis* 19, no. 1 (Winter): 23–30.

Wright, Wendy M., and Joseph F. Power. 1988. Introduction to *Francis de Sales, Jane de Chantal: Letters of Spiritual Direction*. New York: Paulist Press, 9–33.

Yon, Bernard. 1994. "L'Astrée et le salon de Marguerite." In *Marguerite de France, Reine de Navarre, et son temps,* edited by Madeleine Lazard and J. Cubelier de Beynac, 297–307. Actes du Colloque d'Agen (12–13 October 1991). Agen: Centre Matteo Bandello d'Agen.

Zilli, Luigia. 1994. "L'Italianisme à la cour parisienne de Marguerite de Valois." In *Marguerite de France, Reine de Navarre, et son temps*, edited by Madeleine Lazard and J. Cubelier de Beynac, 240–54. Actes du Colloque d'Agen (12–13 October 1991). Agen: Centre Matteo Bandello d'Agen.

Zimmerman, T. C. Price. 1971. "Confession and Autobiography in the Early Renaissance." In *Renaissance Studies in Honor of Hans Baron,* edited by Anthony Molho and John A. Tedeschi, 119–40. Dekalb, Ill.: Northern Illinois University Press.

Index

Académie Française, 29, 149, 190n. 16
Acarie, Madame, 130
Ackroyd, Peter, 191n. 26
Adams, Timothy Dow, 183n. 7
*Advis et presens de la Demoiselle de
    Gournay, Les,* 148n. 49
Alacoque, Marguerite-Marie, 128, 130, 143
Alcôves. See salon movement
Alençon, François de Valois, duc de (later
    duc d'Anjou), 58, 59
Amyot, Jacques, 180n. 18
Anne d'Autriche, 30–31, 70, 71, 85, 154–
    55, 173
Anne de Beaujeu (Anne de France), 39,
    176n. 29; *Les Enseignements d'Anne
    de France à sa fille Suzanne de
    Bourbon,* 39
Apostolides, Jean, 176n. 23, 182n. 20,
    192n. 30
Argenson, René Louis, marquis d', 149–
    50, 189nn. 2 and 9, 190n. 11
Ariès, Philippe, 178n. 44
Aristotle, 175–76n. 11; *Poetics, 52*
Arnauld, Antoine, 178n. 42
Arquien, Henri de La Grange, marquis d', 149
Astrée, L', (d'Urfé), 32, 46, 115
Aubigné, Agrippa d', 47, 177n. 39, 179
    n. 2; *Histoire universelle*
Augustine of Hippo: *Confessions,* 125,
    126–27, 128, 140, 177n. 38
Autobiography: authenticity in, 13, 88,
    103; autobiographical act in, 19, 42,
    76, 106, 119, 171; autobiographical
    pact in, 113, 157–58, 183n. 7;

beginnings of 36–37, 40; biography
    and, 10, 119–20; confessional
    practices and, 88–89; conversion
    experience in, 55, 127; definition of,
    40–41, 51–52, 175nn. 3 and 7, 178
    nn. 47 and 53; early women and, 37,
    39–41, 43–44, 62, 79, 130, 178n. 50;
    poetics of women's, 41–42, 179n. 54;
    temporal distancing in, 51. *See also*
    childhood narrative; coming-of-age
    narrative; memoirs; origins, narrative
    of; spiritual autobiography; truth-
    telling in autobiography
Autonomy: of speaking subject, 131;
    women's lack of, 127, 128

Babelon, Jean, 47
Backer, Dorothy Anne Liot, 176n. 28
Banishment. *See* exile; imprisonment
Barker, Nancy Nichols, 154, 190nn. 14
    and 15
Bassompierre, François de, 47
Bauschatz, Cathleen, 60, 62
Bayle, Pierre, 87
Beasley, Faith, 40, 181n. 5
Beauvoir, Simone de, 22
Bellay, Guillaume du, 41, 177n. 39
Bentley, Richard, 105
Bertière, André, 38, 40, 177n. 39
Beugnot, Bernard, 182n. 19
Bienséance, 100, 105
Blood: marriage and, 36, 173; class and,
    69, 167–68, 176n. 13; gender and, 82;
    race and, 24

210